CRONE RISING

Edited by
TIFFANY CURRY, & SEAMUS KING

Foreword by
DR. K.P. KING

Copyright © 2021 by Jazz House Publications

All rights reserved. This book or any portion thereof may not be reproduced or used in any manner whatsoever without the express written permission of the publisher except for the use of brief quotations in a book review.

Printed in the United States of America

First Printing, 2021

ISBN 978-1-955373-00-5

Jazz House Publications
300 Lenora Street # 1119
Seattle, WA 98121
www.JazzHousePublications.com

Supervising Editor: Tiffany Curry
Cover art: Fay Lane
Formatting: Nicole Scarano

CONTENTS

Foreword Dr. K.P. King	v
TASTING SILT A.J. Van Belle	1
MY LIFE WITH HANNAH COLSON Cathy Warner	5
Too Late	33
INADVERTENT LIFE LESSONS Patti Lee	39
REKINDLED WANDERER Michelle Teems	63
OPHELIA'S SONG Rene Urbanovich	95
LESSONS IN BEAR HUNTING Rhoda Weber Mack	129
A JOURNEY THROUGH ETHIOPIA D. Magada	163
ALCHEMY OF THE SOUL Lucy James	187
WEEDS JoAnne Potter	211
PRELUDE: WEIGHT Carmela McIntire	239
MAIDEN TO CRONE: A LIGHT BEARER'S JOURNEY Lisa Lucca	263

THE GODDESS DREAMS   299
Susan R. Brown

NO ONE ELSE DOES   333
L.T. Ward

Author Biographies   359

FOREWORD

DR. K.P. KING

Welcome to a splendid collection of stories illuminating the insight and wisdom women cultivate in their midlife to later years. Individually, these moving revelations have value in documenting and communicating the reflective perspective of women in their 40's and beyond. However, as a collection, they become even more powerful because they provide a variety of vantage points and experiences that are seldom heard.

As you read this book, we invite you to join in the celebration of personal growth, insight, and victory experienced among women as they mature. You will enjoy the discoveries they experience as well as the darker places of self-doubt, conflict, and grief they sometimes travel through on their journeys.

These women have chosen to do something very unusual in our society. In their commitment to honest reflection and contribution to community, they reveal their difficulties, missteps, and, sometimes, failures in the course of sharing their accomplishments and earned wisdom.

What will you find between these pages? A wide spectrum of experiences with brilliant threads woven throughout. Those threads are honesty, hope, resilience, transparency, power, humor, self-examination and retrospective insights. You will discover women who overcome the tyranny of the urgent in motherhood, to rediscover their self-worth and embrace new careers. Some articulate battles to prioritize self-expression and trust their instincts more. In many chapters, there is a turning point, a crisis, death or precipitating event which catalyzes a new way to think about their life and call to action. The stories are real; the capacity for transformation remains unexpected and encouraging.

As a result of medical science and better living conditions, people in many parts of our world will live longer than prior generations. Previously, human development stages were simply defined as childhood, teenage years, adulthood, and later adulthood. The additional years of life, by virtue of physical development, lengthen the span of adulthood. Therefore, scholars now recognize adulthood as having many phases including, but not limited to, early-, middle-, late middle-, later-, and wisdom/elder-adulthood.

The increased time of adulthood has had many ramifications across societies worldwide. Not least among these changes are the ways that adults struggle with the eternal questions of making meaning of their lives, existence and purpose. Even in popular culture we are acutely aware that at different stages in one's adulthood, people tend to focus on different issues. Compounding this fact, with the multiplicity of factors which continue to change in modern life, the stages of adulthood become a rich space for literary exploration.

Western societies highly value youth, career advancement, and materialism; as a result, women in midlife often may be treated as invisible and/or absent. In these cultures, individuals' value is often assessed according to their perceived financial, professional and social standing. Customarily, public meritorious achievements and contributions vastly outrank personal growth.

Life is often a powerful time of growth for individuals because they are beyond the identity development strife of the teenage and younger adult years. However, this period can also be a crucible amidst balancing the multitude of responsibilities, pressures and expectations for midlife adults. This volume provides a window into how some women not only navigated this pivotal stage of life but also made meaning and sometimes radical life changes.

As you turn the page and begin to share in these personal accounts, we invite you to join us in celebrating women's creative energy, resilience, dedication and power.

TASTING SILT

A.J. VAN BELLE

We changed clothes for P.E class. Bruises studded her back like railroad ties, salmon-shaded welts at regular intervals up her spine. She said she tripped over the cat and fell backward into the couch.

We went from there to lunch, the dark-haired new girls in a duo. She was leggy, short-haired, nails chewed blunt and bloody. Freckled, bare face more beautiful than any magazine photo. I was smaller, frizzy-haired, plainer. "We need to find you a guy," she said on the way, as passing classmates sneered at us, the new students, the untouchables. "I can't believe you're still a virgin." We were thirteen. I answered with a thin thread of laughter, caught between her world-weariness and the dregs of my childhood.

Months went by. She wrote a short story, showed it to me and no one else. A haunting tale about a seven-year-old girl walking down a dusty road. The child's mother had cut off the girl's hip-length magnificent black curls. Relieved of the weight, the child traveled alone, free from the past, carrying only the memory that once she belonged at the circus. A place of gritty sand and elephants, dimness under the big top, crowd's roars dulled by a dusky veil over the inner ear. A place where strange and twisted human forms were commonplace. A place where the little girl belonged. She walked in silence, tasting silt on the air, seeing no end to the dirt road. She was going back to the circus.

She arrived late to school one day, holding ice to her face. Said she walked into a door. I'd have trusted her words better if she said she fell from a tightrope, stood in the way of a swinging gray trunk, antagonized a bitter clown.

The lateness, the bruises, were only a brief laugh for the boys, who were more intrigued by the myths they built for us than by the reality we all ignored. "Lesbian lovers," they taunted in the hall. I didn't understand why love was their insult. "You two use the same vibrator," said one. At home, I asked my mom what a vibrator was.

When she vanished, her mother called me, thought I was the one person who would know where she'd gone. I knew nothing. Later, we learned she went to New York, lived in a halfway house for troubled teens. Later still, not yet seventeen, she lived with an architect in his studio apartment. More months down the line, a graduate student from Columbia University called me. Said my friend was part of a study, and they had my number as someone who might know where she was if they lost touch. Again, I knew nothing.

Until one day, at age seventeen, I confronted what my circus-self understood all along, cleared the dust and saw what I already knew about her cheerful, youthful mother with her own raven hair cascading to her waist. It came to me unbidden, while I washed my face one day: I knew where the bruises came from. And why she ran away.

Some shade of myself stands with her in a shared inner landscape, squinting down the long tan road into beige clouds that obscure the horizon. We've always known there's no circus at the end of this road. No end to the road at all. But we keep walking.

MY LIFE WITH HANNAH COLSON

CATHY WARNER

Lady Macbeth

Hannah at ten, five-foot-two—like my mother, wearing sensible heels—like her mother, and a black velvet pantsuit with a ruffled white blouse and cameo pin at her throat, as if she were thirty—like my mother, and at a cocktail party—like her mother. Hannah center stage in the auditorium, Lady Macbeth's soliloquy her selection for the fifth grade speech contest. She tucks her long gleaming hair behind her ears, cranes her neck, and looks toward us. Her audience shoddy peers, our elastic-exhausted knee-socks drooping around our ankles. We scuff the holey toes of our Keds along the linoleum outlining the tiles with playground dust and grass clippings. We are unworthy of Shakespeare, uninterested in this odd girl in velvet who reminds us of perfumed grandmothers on Christmas Eve. We are bored even though her voice is strong, reaching our newly pierced ears, peace signs dangling.

We hear but don't listen. We listen but don't hear, acting, as we do for all school assemblies, as if we're paying attention. Our thoughts meander, our stomachs murmur and we wonder if back in our classrooms, underneath the jumble of books and paper inside our desks, if with luck, we might scrounge up fifteen cents to buy an ice cream sandwich during recess. We pretend to listen as Hannah recites, our feet jiggling, our arms crossed over grumbling bellies, and ask ourselves: *Is she speaking English? It sounds like English. It must be English.* We stare at her mouth as if we can read lips, and watch her pacing purposefully—two steps left, one step right, a turn of hip, dip of shoulder, as if embodying Morse code. She leans toward us, utters a secret we fail to understand. And then she wrings her hands, staring at her pink fingers and pale palms jutting from the cuffs of her black jacket as if they belong to someone else.

"Out damn spot. Out I say."

Her voice reverberates in the auditorium, and we bite our lips and sit up straighter marveling at the abruptness of recognition. *This is definitely English.*

With a single damn, precocious and ridiculous Hannah has been transfigured. She is radiant and we are pleased. If it had it been anyone of us outside this auditorium, away from the musty velvet curtains and spotlight, perhaps on the sticky blacktop, or in our classrooms smelling of sour milk, if it had been us, a curse escaping our lips, someone would have sent us to the principal or issued detention. Instead Mr. Weaver claps, smiles, shakes hands and presents Hannah with a slippery blue ribbon. She takes a bow, shiny hair falling around her face. We, the converted, clap and clap for our new hero. I applaud longer than the others, not by much but just enough I hope that when we file outside for recess and Hannah borrows a utility ball from the playground monitor and searches the crowd for a two-square partner, that she will choose me.

Piano Lessons

Fingers poised over chipped ivory keys. Hannah's over mine, as she teaches me the proper fingering for the treble clef. Our thumbs rest on middle C. We plunk the scale with our twinned fingers, a dissonant progression on the out-of-tune player piano my father found at a garage sale two streets away and pushed down the alley to our garage two years before he sailed out of our home to rent an apartment in Long Beach. A parachute hangs from the garage rafters, a false billowy ceiling as if raw wood can become cloud as if my father were never a solid, but always cumulus, his drift inevitable. Hannah's father evaporated before mine and we do not talk about disappearances too recent for long-term implications. We are ten and still resilient. She teaches me to read music from acronyms. The ladder of lines gives us the sentence *Every Good Boy Does Fine.* And the spaces create a *FACE*. Hannah charges me twenty-five cents for each half-hour of her wisdom. I take what is given and learn to play it, coaxing a feeble tune from my worn out piano.

Slap

Voice cracking with age, wrinkled and bony Mrs. Kelsey recites Shakespeare as if exposing fifth graders to classic literature will inspire us to think deeply, or at least to think quietly. Proffering imaginary eye of newt and toe of frog, stirring an invisible cauldron, she will select three of us to act out this witchy dialogue. I crave performance and think costume—pointed hat, pointy-hemmed black dress, a dirty broom and stuffed black cat. I think rubber frogs and cat-eyed marbles, a huge black kettle borrowed from the high school cafeteria, with boiling water and real steam, giant wooden spoons to stir our brew and an audience of wide-eyed third and fourth graders, feet tucked up under the auditorium seats, frightened by our ferocity, believing in our capacity for evil. I don't care about Shakespeare, or his plays, or the context of our reading. I want to flirt with danger, or appear to, anyway. I am ten years old, double digits, tired of being good, bored with the Sullivan reading program and the wimpy adventures of Sam and Ann. I want to play a witch, distinguishing myself from the unfortunate students chosen to play Ferne and Charlotte, dressed in overalls and construction paper strips stapled to their shirts in order to mimic a spider. They will sit on or next to a three-legged stool, chewing on a piece of straw and exclaiming over messages in a web.

Hannah is Mrs. Kelsey's favorite student and lingered in her classroom after school as our teacher coached her through Lady Macbeth's monologue, and now she has chosen Hannah to play a witch, entrusting her with Shakespeare again. This is the first year I've been in a class with Hannah, and she has toppled me from my reign as teacher's pet. Mrs. Kelsey is enamored with Hannah, and my homeroom teacher has chosen Lori, the fat shy girl with greasy hair for the honor. My homeroom teacher is also fat, but her hair is fluffy, and maybe she will inspire Lori in the art of personal hygiene. But skeletal Mrs. Kelsey dislikes me and I don't understand why. I am cooperative, or at least I have been until recently. I am smart, almost as smart as Hannah, and even though I am short and skinny, I can project my voice to the back of any room. I came in second in the speech contest Hannah won earlier this year. And maybe that is why Mrs. Kelsey selects me to play the second of the three witches.

We three witches shove our chairs together and read for weeks from our mimeographed sheets, "Double, double toil and trouble; fire burn, and cauldron bubble," until we have memorized our scene and consign our papers to the obscurity of our desks. As our performance nears, my theatrical fantasies meet reality—we construct a one-dimensional cauldron from black poster board and secure it with masking tape to the back of a folding chair. We are issued choir robes. They are red. *We are not playing devils*, we grumble to each other, *everyone knows that witches wear black*. Surely three of our classmates have the necessary costumes stored in closets or under beds, saved from previous Halloweens to be worn by younger siblings in future years. But, no, dull Mrs. Kelsey, intent on thwarting our stardom, will not allow us to pester our classmates for costumes. Or props. There are no newts, no eyes, no bubbles. But there are troubles.

Waiting off-offstage, beyond the wings and out the door, standing on the bottom stair waiting for our cackling performance, Hannah and I are joking and laughing, making fun of Mrs. Kelsey's ancient voice and directorial gestures. We are much too gleeful about her loose skin, flapping from her upper arm like curtains. Why is she wearing short sleeves? And why are we snorting with laughter? And why don't we realize that her hearing is still quite keen, and that she has been listening from the stage door, if not to our content, to our volume? And why is that when she appears between Hannah and me, taller than both of us, sneering disapproval, that I have no interest in her reprimand? She has already failed me with her lack of props and wrong-colored robes. I am a witch and I refuse to repent. "Shut up," I tell her. And she slaps me. My cheek stings and I glare at her. She calls me insolent, and I don't know what that means. But I know that if I didn't hate her before, I do now. And now that I hate Mrs. Kelsey I will punish her. I will leave her class and refuse to return.

I will renounce Shakespeare and make my homeroom teacher transfer me into a different language arts class, where, without a teacher who hates me, and without Hannah to overshadow me, I will shine. Hannah will say I did the right thing and start to mouth off in class herself. Mrs. Kelsey will retire at the end of the school year, and Hannah and I will delude ourselves into thinking we had something to do with her decision.

But before I stomp away, indignant, I will wipe my cheek, as if to rid it of shame. I will climb the stairs behind Hannah and Witch Number Three, walk through the wings, past the velvet curtain onto the stage, take my place behind the paper cauldron, and act the part I have been assigned.

Classroom

Morning thick with mist, shivering in too short shorts while Mr. Schoemer unlocks the classroom then shuffles off to the teachers' lounge. Chalk in Hannah's hand rasping across the board drawing a symbol for me, her only pupil, to replicate. I stand next to her, chalk in my left hand, smearing white powder across the green board as I try to follow the lines and angles she has assembled. Backward Z's, one-dimensional pinwheels. She sits at a desk in the first row coaching as I fill the board, from left to right with wobbly and ill-angled lines. Imagine you're working inside the face of a clock, she says. Hold the chalk at noon, draw a short line down toward ten, turn, chalk a longer line toward four, turn, make a short line toward six. Lift the chalk, wipe the dust from the pad of my hand, place the chalk at three, draw a line up toward one, turn, draw a long line toward seven intersecting the other long line, turn, and draw a short line up toward nine. Push hard on the chalk until it is a stub. Pick up a new piece from the tray. Ignore the squealing scratch over the board, teeth on edge, hair on forearms prickling. Don't bother erasing simply try again, over and over until I get it right. The swastika. If I have seen a swastika before, it must have been on *Hogan's Heroes*, a flag perhaps, or a red armband worn by an S.S. officer come to check on the incompetent Sergeant Shultz, who likes to say *I know nothing*.

I know nothing. Nothing about the millions killed because of the intersecting sticks I've drawn on the board. Nothing about the power of symbols and how this one has Mr. Schoemer trembling with anger spraying from his mouth, spittle lands on my blouse as he says *pure evil*, which is why the chalk falls from my hand and snaps in two at my feet when he enters the classroom, slams the door, barks my name, breaks my concentration.

Mr. Schoemer is ancient and unkempt, his white shirts stained green under the arms, his crepe soles sticky on the classroom floor, and we, the followers of Hannah, are merciless in his math class, rhythmically tapping the metal rings of our pencils against the edges of our desks until he turns, confused, from the chalkboard and the algebra equation to locate the source of the sound that has become intolerable, like a dripping faucet at midnight. His first name is Stanley, his pants are belted far above his waist, and outside at recess when Hannah chants *Stanley Steamer*, we her subjects respond with *Toot-toot*, shuffling backward and hiking our hip-huggers up to our ribs. For all this, he is endlessly patient, never reprimanding or frustrated with our inability to grasp algebra. He calls us to the board, hands us a piece of chalk, stands back as we work, stepping in to tap his own chalk on a factor or a sign we might want to look at again, more closely, leaning toward us with his breath of stale coffee and old man so that we hold our breath and when, upon solving correctly we turn away from him and toward our desks, our inhale is not simply triumph, but necessity.

Mr. Schoemer sends Hannah outside asking her not to let anyone in the classroom even though the bell has rung. My teacher and I stand before one another quivering. I am expecting him to raise his voice, the way teachers do when they lose control, or like my father, to shake his head and say how disappointed he is in my behavior. Instead, he gazes at me his blood-shot eyes glistening as if he might cry and asks in a choked barely audible voice, "Do you have any idea what this means?" I will answer no and ask Hannah at lunch, and she will tell me about Jews and camps and ovens, but here now, Mr. Schoemer wants me to understand something else, something beyond explanation. He places an eraser in my hand and I wipe back and forth removing everything I've drawn until the blank board is white with powder as the students file in and our instruction begins.

Camp Out

Fog clings to the coast, to our hair, to the lawn where we've pitched our pup tents. We smell of briquettes, roasted hot dogs and marshmallows, our breath of graham crackers and chocolate squares. Tonight, we are liberated from the prison of seventh grade. Tonight, starless and white with mist, we are official eighth graders and the long days of summer stretch before us. Late mornings rising from sleep as the fog burns off. Cheerios and *All My Children*. Long afternoons slathered in baby oil, crisping in the sun, coated in sand like breaded shrimp, and bodysurfing the small break in Seal Beach. This summer we are no longer children, and we must leave our childish ways behind. We are teenagers. It is time to see clearly what until now we have viewed through a glass darkly—Sex.

Our troop leaders and the younger Girl Scouts are fast asleep in their tiny tents pitched near the scout house under the halo of the moth-flocked porch light. We gather on the far side of the yard near a geranium border and a picket fence, ringed like disciples around the tent of our teacher, Hannah, who sits in her doorway, looking out at us, and with a sweep of her arm, invites us closer. We wear our sleeping bags like coats, knees drawn to our chests, shivering in the damp night. Even in this dark, Hannah's eyes shine, her face glows and we scoot toward her, knocking each other with our trembling elbows. Her knowledge shocks and astounds us. These things she knows about boys and girls. The kingdom of sex is like baseball, she tells us. These are the things we will do, or rather, that boys will do to us, in this particular order. In this moment, we don't know enough to ask if it is a single boy who will do all this. Will he round each base in succession, in the course of one inning, one game, or one season? Or will it be a series of boys, each batting one base further than the last, until some player—the lucky one—scores a home run?

It is too much for us, this glimpse into our future. We squirm in our sleeping bags. We have not touched our own bodies in the places Hannah says boys will, and we cannot imagine wanting to ourselves, or wanting to allow a boy, no matter how much we might like him, to know us in this way. And when our lesson is finished, we return to our pup tents two by two, curl tightly in our sleeping bags, stare at one another and ask—*Who is this girl? Isn't she the daughter of gray-haired single mother, a realtor? And haven't we been in math class and Girl Scouts and choir with her day after day? And where did she acquire such knowledge?*

But it will come to pass. And as always, Hannah will

have been accurate, if not entirely truthful. She will have failed to tell us that someday, fueled by love or passion or an elixir of both, that we girls will want to touch the boys whose hands are warm under our blouses, whom we imagine marrying, and that these boys will rise to our caresses, that we will possess a certain power over them, if not ourselves. And when that time comes, we will forget our teacher and her baseball game and embrace the mystery.

Beach

The breeze and the surf and Hannah on the beach one Saturday in Indian summer. Hot sand and beach towels, baby oil and transistor radios tuned to KKDJ. Hannah's hair in two braids, thick dripping ropes, water beading on her bare belly. Salt on her lips and the taste of salt on her tongue, Willy Mueller's mouth fused to hers. They lean against the pillar of a lifeguard tower, its rectangular deck casting a shadow, cooling the burning sand. Feet burrowed into the grains like sand crabs, they take hold of each other's waists and lean into one another into this thing they are becoming—girlfriend, boyfriend. Hannah at thirteen, trying on passion as if it were bell-shaped sleeves or striped hip-hugger pants, something to wear because it's in fashion, whether or not the style is flattering, whether or not Willy suits her. It looks easy, maybe too easy, for her to step out from under the tower, to sneeze in the glare and brush the gritty sand from her back.

Hannah squeezing the last wet drops from the tips of her braids as if they are watercolor brushes. She won't tell us what it's like and she doesn't hop gingerly across the sand to join us on our patch of beach. Her friends slathered in baby oil, basting in a row, prickles of sweat dotting our newly budding breasts, listening to Barry Manilow on the radio, wishing we could be *Mandy*, who came and gave without taking. The sun flames through our closed eyes, searing purple azaleas that float just out of reach, disappearing as we sit up and watch. Hannah running through the sand, braids slapping at her back, her long coyote yip escaping into September as she plunges under the surf.

Suffrage

In the voting booth the morning of student council elections, the foyer of the auditorium dark, the heavy curtain brushing against Willy Mueller's back, he closes his eyes, brown lashes fringing against his cheeks and tilts his head, purses his lips, leans forward, not to cast a vote, but to French kiss me. I can't even begin to feign calm, both my stomach and eyelids fluttering, my toes clenched against the wooden knobs of my Dr. Scholl's sandals. This is serious business, kissing Hannah's boyfriend, not because I've stolen him from her, but because she is waiting outside the auditorium on this chilly morning with two of our friends, Sheri and Nikki, who along with me, one at a time, will allow Willy's tongue inside our mouths, despite our reluctance, despite our nervous laughter.

Hannah has offered the services of her boyfriend, a seventh grader, a Southern California fantasy boy—white smile, surfer's tan, and blond hair feathered across his forehead. She plucked him from the trumpet section of the marching band as if he were a pair of Levi's, and has French kissed him into perfection, a perfection she, and therefore he, must share with her nearest and dearest.

So here we are, as if we had any choice, the teacher and his pupil. This is my first kiss and I can say this is not the way I imagined it, an activity inspired not by my own desire, but by Hannah's passion, scheduled and completed like a homework assignment. Willy, who smells like Irish Spring soap and Downey fabric softener, is nothing if not persistent, brushing aside my giggling fits, urging me to compose myself, neither one of us willing to disappoint Hannah, and when our tongues meet, I am a wind-up toy shocked into hyper-speed by the intruder in my mouth, flailing like a hooked fish in mid-air, unable to breathe until he's released me. "How was I?" I ask since this is a lesson and I am an A student. "A little fast," he answers, kind with truth and suggests we try it again. We do and now that I know what to expect I commit myself to his tutelage, mimicking the slow movements of his tongue in my mouth, in this moist cavern we've built with our lips, our tongues tasting of toothpaste and toaster waffles. I feel his breath on my upper lip and I breathe through my nostrils, and remembering to breathe it is possible to kiss and kiss, longer than I've ever seen in person, or in the movies. Before last summer when Hannah told me about French kissing, I thought that people simply pressed their lips together and turned their heads a bit and sort of smooched around, and what would be the point in dragging that out for more than a few seconds?

The French are onto something, and I am determined to figure out just what that is. I will experiment this school year, French kissing half-a-dozen boys from marching band and the student body president we elect today, unable to find the elusive quality that will arrive in my future. When I fall in love I will climb inside that boy through his mouth, and kiss us down a tunnel into a single eternal moment, trying to possess him. But right here, right now, Willy and I, Hannah's protégés, are satisfied in simply carrying out her orders.

Pacific Coast Highway

Seven and eight and nine years old, dashing across Pacific Coast Highway, barefoot, scabby-kneed, we crouch just off the shoulder in gravel and dirt, plunging our grubby hands in the drainage ditch thick with waterweeds and oily runoff, grabbing for tadpoles we scoop into an empty jar of imitation mayonnaise along with the murky ditchwater. In front of us, on the far side of the trench, a sound attenuation wall, no passage left between the concrete bricks, no way for the children, like Hannah, who live on those streets with names like Marlin and Sandpiper to slip from their subdivision to the highway, to race across to our side where they could watch a snake devour a mouse at Norm's Bait shop, or beg a giant pickle from Dave, who owns the bar where the lifeguards drink. They are trapped, but we are free. We screw the nail punctured lids onto the mouths of our turbid jars, climb out of the trench, pause at the shoulder, look both ways like our parents taught us, and fly over the asphalt across the highway that partitions our town in two, back to our side with numbered streets and abandoned railroad tracks. Our block, full of auto mechanics, cocktail waitresses, shift workers at the Bernstein's plant, housewives like my mother, and one deputy, my father.

First Home

Too young to remember living anywhere but the beach, I am three, and my sister eighteen months, when my parents move from an apartment in the San Fernando Valley to our rented house on Fifteenth Street. They buy that same small home four blocks from the ocean when I am six for twenty-six thousand dollars, and my father backyard to celebrate. I dust bricks red powder the color of my father's ms, making me sneeze. I arrange the les at his feet. He trowels, bricks and om our back steps into our yard, ending the laundry room meets the side fence, and in that ro... ver patch he presses first my sister's palm, and then mine into wet cement that oozes like cold oatmeal between our fingers, then hands us each a twig snapped from the bottle brush tree and we sign our names. *For posterity,* he says.

For posterity he leaves the house to my mother when he leaves us, and by the time she sells it for ninety thousand dollars, she, like my father, has married someone else. My mother's new husband, a truck driver, wants to live across the highway in a house behind the wall, like Hannah and her mother, in the subdivision we call Bullet Hill. I have friends, like Hannah, who live on Catalina and Crestview Avenues. No ocean in sight. Their fathers, if they haven't disappeared like Hannah's, are firefighters, architects and businessmen and their mothers, except for Hannah's, gather at the Main Street bakery weekday mornings to drink coffee and gossip. There are no alleys, and only Balboa Drive connects the residents to the highway, and the streets forsake the grid of Old Town, curving into each other at strange angles. My father, who is now a lieutenant, owns a house on Bullet Hill, a pie-shaped lot on Harbor Way with a built-in swimming pool. He keeps my sister, and his neighbors keep boats and recreational vehicles in long driveways abutting their attached garages.

Mena Colson, Realtor

Mena Colson, Realtor, her ad familiar from the bus stop

bench at the corner of Pacific Coast Highway and Seal Beach Boulevard. *Mena Colson, Realtor*, the neat type on her business card fastened by a magnet to our refrigerator door. It is Hannah's mother who sells our old house and guides my mother and stepfather into their purchase on South Shore Drive with three large bedrooms opening onto an enclosed patio called an atrium. The whole affair is on Bullet Hill less than a half-mile from my father. *Mena Colson, Realtor* walks through our Fifteenth Street house in her three-piece-suit and sensible heels, running her tape measure across our floors, tapping on our cabinets, opening our closet doors, scribbling notes on her yellow pad, while my mother and I trail behind like puppies, waiting to find out our worth.

Mena Colson, Realtor has a German accent and something like a lisp that makes my shoulders shirk toward my ears when she speaks. I am in eighth grade and her daughter, Hannah, is rapidly becoming my best friend. I can't call this fifty-year-old mother Mrs., like I do the other younger mothers, and I can't call her Mena, even though Hannah does, because Mena sounds like a nickname, too chummy for this authoritative woman. *Mena Colson, Realtor* has become a single name in my mind, a proper noun, and one I certainly can't use aloud. I will say *hello* and *how are you* and *fine, thank you* and *thank you* when I am a guest in her home, looking her straight in the face. Even though I will never address her properly, she will think me polite, Hannah's most pleasing friend.

Drill Team

Gathering at the picnic benches outside the band room before we board the bus, Mrs. Dressler yanks and teases our hair, pulling it into buns so tight our brows slant skyward. Eyes watering, we are sprayed like rioters with aerosol, coughing into the sticky cloud of VO-5 that clings to our bare arms, as well as our updos, each strand plastered in place, bobby pins strategically plunged to prevent straggling. Our dresses, rich red velveteen in micro-mini length that Mrs. Dressler charged thirty-five dollars to construct from a Butterick pattern. I paid for the fabric and sewed my own, adjusting the darts at the bust twice, and still the dress hangs where there should be form. Our throats and hems ringed with a white ruffle topped by a strip of sequins two inches wide. White patent boots up to our knees, white gloves on our hands. We march through the streets of Southern California, in straight sharp rows behind the band in their black uniforms and faux fur helmets, holding their instruments at precise angles until cadence ends and their Sousa march begins. Other girls carry banners in front of the band and flags behind. We bring up the rear, our hands crossing over our chests, snap against our shoulders, a pattern we repeat in rhythm to the drums.

Before a bandstand we stop, right leg bent at the knee, left hand sharp at the waist, right hand angled against our foreheads and salute the judges. Hannah, our leader, distinguished from us in white velveteen with long transparent sleeves, and a bust that fills out her darts, lifts her whistle to her lips, blows three sharp tweets as the band begins to play and we launch our routine, the heels of our boots clacking the asphalt in time as we perform a series of hitch-kicks, skip-aheads, sidesteps and pivots, our arms swinging up and down, forward and back, precise and controlled. Hannah and I choreographed this routine together, even though I am not the leader, or even her assistant. One early-September afternoon before parade season began, we slipped out of our sandals and toed our way up and down the grassy patch between the band room and library, working out something complicated, technical and elegant, a routine that would show off the velveteen panties we wore under our mini-dresses, a routine that would call attention to our long thighs, perfectly tanned after a summer of sunning.

Mrs. Dressler didn't bank on fog when she chose our sleeveless uniforms, hadn't realized she would send a troop of blue and goose-pimpled girls in front of the judges on misty mornings and evenings. She pictured two p.m., seventy-two degrees and sunny. Somehow, even in late November, trudging four miles in the Santa Claus Lane Parade from twilight into streetlight, my exposed thighs seem yards long, planks that are bumpy with cold, but remain tan, single toned as I kick up my legs. Ahead of me, marching alone, Hannah's legs have burst into a riot of color. Her thighs not straight but shaped, like my mother's, are mottled pale pink and flesh and even a hint of yellow, and under the skin a network of blue and purple diffused and strange. Leading us through our routine and one final salute after the trumpets' last blast, she doesn't simply appear cold like the rest of us. Hannah, five-foot seven without her boots, perfect bun refusing to budge, sleeves shimmering as she resumes cadence, is thirteen like me. But here, on Hollywood Boulevard she is unquestionably grownup, the woman in her surfacing, leading the rest of us who parade obediently behind her into the future.

Trust Fund

Eighth grade after school, Hannah and I, legs folded Indian-style on her double bed, plaid coverlet worn and yielding against our skin. Hannah spilling the bills and coins from her secret fund in our laps like pirate treasure.

Sifting through the riches we rain presidents' faces into random configurations on the geometric print. Our fingers like brooms, we sweep the pennies, nickels, dimes and quarters into separate piles, each denomination resting in its own plaid square. A quarter for each piano lesson she taught me in fifth grade. Fifty cents an hour to babysit children she doesn't like—all of them whiny, demanding, lacking in some essential quality she requires—and the occasional dollar or two left from the child support checks her mother receives from a father she never sees. Hannah has earned every cent.

My personal fortune consists of two dollars and seventy-four cents inside a mesh coin-purse in my underwear drawer. The little purse a souvenir my mother brought back from a trip to Greece with a boyfriend too fond of scotch to marry. My cash, carefully portioned, might buy me a week's worth of soft-serve chocolate dipped cones from Tastee Freeze, the crisp coat carefully bitten off, my tongue running busily around the melting ice cream, catching drips, my forehead zinging from the cold.

In three years of saving Hannah has become wealthy—One hundred thirty-eight dollars and 67 cents. *Nouveau Riche*. We return her fortune to the jar—dull coins, shiny coins, the crumpled bills green and white, and stare at the money, as if it were a specimen worthy of a shelf in Mr. Christensen's science room. As if we had pulled it down and set it between us, together identifying its class and phylum.

How to spend such riches? I imagine an endless supply of Tastee Freeze cones, platform sandals and a pair of real Levi's, not the imitator jeans my mother buys at J.C. Penney with her employee discount. Hannah, sitting cross-legged on her bed, knees bumping against mine, holds the jar in both hands, shakes it, and we listen to the metal clatter. It does not ring or sound beautiful, like I thought a fortune should. Hannah leans toward me, her long hair falls in front of her face and I smell her Herbal Essence shampoo. "My mother doesn't know I have this money. No one knows I have this money." She pulls back the curtain of hair, cradles the jar in the crook of her arm, gazes at the money and at me to make sure I'm ready for the gravity of her secret. Dramatically, as if she is Lady Macbeth, she says, "This is my abortion fund."

Hannah straightens her legs, picks up the jar, and slides it back into its hiding place under the bed. She stands and holds up three fingers as if she's going to recite the Girl Scout Promise we say at each Cadet meeting. "Be prepared," she says, stating the motto. We are both thirteen and I have kissed a boy once, and only because she wanted me to. What am I supposed to think of Hannah's preparations for sex? Is she contriving to be wantonly careless, planning to be overcome by sensation and impulse? Or does she understand something I don't about losing yourself in the moment and surrendering to desire? It is easy to believe at our age that sex is simply about exploration of the body, that passion is clinical, and that one hundred and thirty eight dollars can insure against consequences or conscience.

But before I can believe her, I must ask, as though I am in fifth grade and she is speaking Shakespearean English I don't comprehend, "Hannah, what is an abortion?"

Bridge

Toe to heel, heel to toe, Hannah and I walk our way across the bridge, counting our steps, converting to feet. Two hundred of them move us from the Condo complex at Marina Pacifica, where she lives with *Mena Colson, Realtor* and her new stepfather, Bud. Bud is retired and we are compelled to spend as little time in his presence as possible, hence our impossibly slow trek over the pedestrian walkway that bridges Alamitos Bay from the condos on one end to the shopping center on the other. Tonight, we will cross over again, browse the bath shop and race each other through the center, stairs to the elevator. Tonight we will wander into Lucky's Supermarket, buy a frozen pizza and two cans of Coke, and as we return across the bridge, Hannah will produce two Snickers bars from the pocket of her jeans, hand me one, and when I take my first bite, she will tell me, without remorse, that my candy is stolen.

Likewise, this afternoon will not be dull. We stand at the midpoint of the bridge, and Hannah dares me to jump. I look over the rail. If it is low tide, the cool salt water ripples twenty-five feet below my feet. If it is high tide, my descent will be a mere fifteen. But I do not know the tide. I have never consulted a chart, using the ocean as I have at my convenience and on impulse. I first swam in Alamitos Bay when I was six, secured in a Donald Duck floating ring by my father who waded out with me. Terrified even though there was no surf, doubting even then, that I could trust my father with my life. I have no such qualms about Hannah. It is late May, our eighth grade year nearly over, but her power over me has not waned. I don't know if I have pledged allegiance to adrenaline, or to her, but I never refuse her dares—anyone's for that matter—as if being reckless means that I am brave.

She promises to jump with me. We climb over the guardrail and cram our feet onto the narrow ledge. We are not strangers to the high dive, both of us taking springboard lessons at the school pool last summer. Standing on that board, ten feet high, we looked down and the lane lines wavered at the bottom of the swimming pool twenty-two feet below. It is difficult to dive without going long and slapping your back hard, stinging your skin, knocking the breath from your lungs as you hit the unforgiving water. It is best to jump, kick your feet and circle your arms as you drop, to ensure you remain upright, but upon entry tuck your arms alongside your torso, pull your legs together, point your toes, slip into the water, one fluid slice of body. Even though the marina is choppy and opaque, giving no clue to its depth, the same principles must apply as we prepare to step off the bridge.

The network of my nerves buzzes with industry, my body on high alert, shaking, imperceptibly, I hope. We must coordinate our jump. We each keep one hand on the guardrail, and with our free inside hands, she reaches for my arm, and I for hers. We wrap our fingers around one another's wrists, the unbreakable grip we learned years ago in P.E. when Mrs. Peterson taught us to Indian wrestle. Hannah will count to three and we will simultaneously release our grip on the bridge and step straight down. One, two, three, and I am propelled into the marina, shrieking in terror and triumph, plummeting as the water rises to meet me, taking one long breath and squeezing my eyes shut as I splash down. My arms are too far from my sides at impact. Underwater, the slap jolts through them and the pain zings as I stroke my way back toward the surface, eyes still closed, kicking up through the water, ten feet, maybe more, until finally, my head emerges and I gasp for air. Water drips down my face, salt stings my eyes and startles my mouth. I wipe my eyes, making them burn more, tread water, and look around for Hannah. There is a ripple emanating from me, but only one and I'm dimly aware that I felt light, not tethered, hurtling from the bridge. I hear her laugh drifting down toward me, and she is atop the bridge, on the proper side of the guardrail, pointing first at my gullibility and next at the harbor patrol boat motoring toward me. The officer will lift a megaphone to his lips, informing me of my criminal activity and his gracious nature, my punishment his lurking presence and motor exhaust as I make my slow crawl from the clear open water, toward the boats bobbing in oily slips, hoist myself onto a dock, and walk dripping to find the place where Hannah is hiding, waiting for me, laughing.

Boarding School

Back East in states as small as our California counties, things are old and infused with capital C culture and capital H history. Boston and New York are two hours by train, not distant ideas on the opposite edge of our continent. Beaches there aren't thronged by school kids licking popsicles and blaring transistor radios, their parents hanging laundry in the backyards of modest homes on the other side of abandoned railroad tracks. And they don't say *the beach*, they say *the coast*, and it belongs to the elite and their ilk, accessed through the French doors of mansions owned by families whose ancestors founded the very towns in which they live. Their casual doesn't mean cut-offs and surfboards; it means polo shirts with tiny embroidered alligators, Sperry topsiders sans socks, and sailboat races. These are the things Hannah wants, the secret dream she has been nursing. She is ready to leave us all, her mother the realtor, her stepfather Bud, their new condo at Marina Pacifica, which is supposed to be exclusive, but isn't really, if you have money.

Hannah has exhausted Seal Beach and McGaugh School, and all her old endeavors—her boyfriend Willy, the gymnastics club, the French club, the art club, the cheerleading squad, the orchestra, and all the sopranos who sang her part in choir, and all the girls in drill team who marched behind her, and me, the girl who did everything she said. She is easily the smartest person in our school, boy or girl. Her mother selling beachfront condos may be the wealthiest of all our parents, but it's all too easy. Where's the challenge when the smartest boy is one of eight children wearing faded hand-me-downs, and glasses taped at the bridge, his hands always trembling, and when the second smartest girl is me, her minion, her underling, her groupie? Hannah wants intellectual rigor and kids with money who aren't afraid of anything or anyone, classmates who exude confidence and privilege, and are as fascinated with each other as I am with her. She wants friends who can persuade her to jump from a bridge, a dormitory and a headmaster and a boarding school, as if she lives in England, but will settle for New England. A school built in 1891—older than any structure in our city—to prepare young men for Yale and their futures as captains of industry. She persuaded her mother to spend thousands on tuition, room and board, and convinced all of us that she, a west coast new money transplant, will thrive in the snowy grounds of tradition, flourishing with preppies at a school that only began admitting girls last year.

It is the end of eighth grade, a season of awards and banquets, of speeches and graduation. The smartest boy wears new glasses and addresses us with gravity. This, he says, marks the zenith of our educational careers, and I don't want him to be right. We plan for the future, Hannah for boarding school and Columbia University, and a career as a famous novelist, and me with aspirations for law school and the U.S. Senate. We wonder if we are too young for nostalgia. Sewing machines and Simplicity patterns, dresses worn much too short, longhair with split-ends, Herbal Essence shampoo, straight A's, English muffin pizzas, inward dives from the one-meter board, Love's Baby Soft perfume, Robert Redford's smile, kissing trumpet and trombone players, platform sandals, precision arm movements, sleepovers, an aversion to parents. I am supposed to miss these things I shared with Hannah. Instead, I think about *not* having her around, about all the kids I've grown up with and ignored, perhaps slighted, in Hannah's presence, hopeful they will forgive me and excited for September when all of us are bussed to the giant high school in the neighboring town where we can start over without anyone telling us what to do, our adventure small compared to Hannah's.

But that fall, I don't wait in the fog the first day of school for an eight-mile bus ride down Pacific Coast Highway. Instead I sweat in the Sacramento Valley heat, a misfit in an inland town where ninth grade is still junior high, living with strangers, wearing last year's faded dresses, hems let down as far as they will go, embarrassed by how much thigh I expose. Hannah might be happy living without her parents. She might fit in because everyone in her ninth grade class is a new kid. Back East, they might like the novelty of her California tan and super short skirts, but not here. My parents are coming, but not yet, and if anyone else here is new, how am I to know? Hannah won't be lonely because she wanted to leave. I will be lonely because I wanted to stay. I will write her once, pretending that we can be pen pals sharing confidences across three thousand miles. But I don't write that I am miserable, that the people I live with don't like me. I poke fun at them and their ugly house, their bad taste in furniture and cereal, just like I would've with Hannah. She doesn't send me a reply, not that I expected her to, but I'd hoped that like me, she might try to pretend our friendship was based on something deeper than proximity.

Proximity

Queued for the buffet, plates in hand, my long-ago lost friends from Seal Beach greet each other amidst trays of cold meats and sliced fruit. We make our way along the banquet table brimming with breadsticks, cocktail shrimp, and meatballs skewered by plastic swords. Twenty-five years ago, these are the people I should have sat next to in chemistry and government, in concert choir and Key club, at beach bonfires and Christmas concerts, wearing black and orange to football games, tossing our caps in triumph as we received diplomas from Huntington Beach High School. I thought about them so often during my high school and college years four hundred miles north and inland, air scented with tomato crops and burn days, Tule fog that lingered for weeks each winter. My life peppered with the growing number of my parents' divorces, the girl from Seal Beach dressed in miniskirts and confidence, evaporating like beach fog.

I never moved back. My father moved away, and I had no old home to return to. Tonight at our elementary reunion, I flit among tables at the Hyatt Edgewater, married, not a lawyer or senator, a part-time worker who left local government for full-time motherhood. I arrive curious about my old friends and their trajectories as if I can extrapolate from their lives to mine and draw a figure of the woman I might have become had I stayed. Hannah finds me in the ladies' restroom after dinner at the sink washing my hands, watching my old friends reapply their lipstick. They look beautiful and grown up, but Hannah doesn't. She looks like a worn-out version of the girl who was my best friend. Her skin still pale and splotchy, her face makeup free, her long straight hair almost stringy. "P.B. is it you?" she asks using my childhood nickname and sliding her sunglasses atop her head. "It's really you. I can't believe it," she says hugging me as if she'd lost me in a crowd and had been searching for days. Her bare arms are bony against my back. Her jeans are tight but there is not enough of her inside the fabric. The generous thighs I remember winnowed to wisps. Hannah is hyper and twitchy, holding my hand and asking, "So, tell me who do we know here? Is Willy here? Do you think he remembers me? Is Nikki here? Sheri? Who else? Take me around. C'mon." I was never the leader of our activities, but I answer that I haven't seen her old boyfriend and allow Hannah to cling to my arm. She stands so close, I almost trip on her feet as I escort her from table to table introducing her to everyone that I have already introduced myself to this night. She doesn't let go and tightens her grasp as she answers questions. She is not a novelist. She is not famous. She is not married. She has no children. She did live in New York, but not anymore. Now she lives in Los Angeles and if she has a job, she doesn't say what it is. We don't know quite what to make of this woman who so clearly outshone us, who so clearly left us to burn brighter.

Hannah tugs at my sleeve as if she were my daughter. "Let's get out of here. I can't stand these people. Let's go somewhere else, just you and me like old times," as if we might walk across Pacific Coast Highway and stroll the pedestrian bridge to her mother's condo. As if we could make English Muffin pizzas and eat them on her bed, rating the boys in the band according to their kissing ability. "I don't think so," I say. That I am here with my husband, a stranger making small talk while I act as tour guide among our childhood friends, means nothing to Hannah. "Come on," she implores, "It'll be fun." "I'm sorry. I'm going to stay here," I answer. She stares at me a moment and I think I am supposed to notice something meaningful. But I only see her eyes, several shades of brown and bloodshot. When it's clear I won't follow her into the night, into our past, she squeezes me fiercely and then lets go. She slips her sunglasses over her eyes and I watch her walk toward the door, shoulders squared. The ballroom doors close behind her. I rub my arm, as if I had a muscle cramp, return to my table, sit next to my husband and reach for his hand. Half a dozen of my old friends are talking about Hannah. Anorexia, bulimia, drugs they speculate, she was acting so strangely she must've been on something. And I don't want to know these things, or even suspect Hannah of them, but I too wonder how she became so thin. Was it something she learned at boarding school after getting drunk and smoking pot and bingeing on junk food? Was it a freshman requirement demonstrated by her roommate, the daughter of a rich thin socialite? Just a finger down the throat until she gagged and puked, and in this manner ate with impunity. Insurance, like the abortion fund she once kept in a jar.

All these years while I cooked and cleaned for my family, concocted magical dogs and horses for bedtime stories, and vacation-binged on novels, I anticipated coming across Hannah's novel in a big display at the front of a bookstore. And I imagined that maybe, someday, if I was really lucky, the tour for her fifth or sixth book would stop in Santa Cruz or San Jose, and I would read about it in the newspaper, leave my girls home with their dad, drive an hour, and find her behind a stack of books. She would sign my copy with her eighth grade flourish, and we would laugh at her dramatic flair and I would hug the book to my chest thankful that I knew her, thankful that more than all of us, Hannah was the woman she intended to become.

TOO LATE

I'm in trouble. Again.

Was I too loud? Did I say something wrong? I can't recall. I try desperately to remember. Maybe, if I figure it out, I can say I'm sorry before it's too late.

Suddenly, my mother kicks me under the metal-rimmed restaurant table. A sharp, piercing stab that brings tears to my eyes. Then another. I wince as shooting pains ricochet through my leg.

Too late.

Her piercing glare seethes and writhes with that all too familiar 'you'd-better-smile-like-everything's okay'… look. I dare not react or it will happen again. And worse when we get home. Anger and hurt swell up in my throat as I quickly look away and stare at nothing.

A single teardrop teeters perilously on the edge of my eye lid, but I quickly wipe it away before she sees. I used to cry. I thought it would make her stop. But it didn't. I must not show emotion, or everyone will know. *That's* how the game is played. No one must *ever* know.

Nearly every table in the restaurant is occupied. I open my mouth to cry out, but no sound escapes. I am silently screaming, but no one hears. How could they? My face remains frozen. Not even a flinch.

I may only be ten… but I am an excellent actress.

'Sit up straight! Don't talk! Do as I say! Never interrupt! You'll eat what I order you!'
I gag on the liver and onions. I choke on my shame.

Lively chatter drones on at the table next to us. The burly, gentle-faced man cracks a joke. It must be funny because laughter erupts in my ears. A middle-aged couple, in the corner table, turn to see what the commotion is about, then smile as they watch the happy, carefree children giggle, wriggle and bounce in their chairs. I wish I could be at *that* table.

No one comes to my rescue, for I have played the game too well. I have everyone fooled. I am invisible.

I may only be ten… but I am an excellent actress.

I'm in trouble. Again.

We've just finished dinner when the phone rings. It's my friend Judy from up the road. She's upset and wants to talk. After a few minutes pass, a stabbing pain shoots through my ankle and up my leg. *What did I do?* I cringe as my eyes start to water. I stare wide-eyed at my assailant.

"Get off the phone!" Through clenched teeth, my mother hisses and spits at me under her scowling breath. "You have homework to do. *Move it!"*

"But it's all done Mom! I finished it at school. Honest!"

"I said, GET OFF THE PHONE NOW!!!"

My hand cups the mouthpiece in hopes my friend can't hear. "I'm trying," I insist. "But Judy is upset. I don't want to hurt her feelings. I won't be long. I promise!"

Her piercing glare seethes and writhes with that familiar 'you'd-better-sound-like-everything's-okay'… look. I have to get off the phone quickly or she will lash out at me again.

Too late.

"Get off the phone." (Kick) *"NOW!"* (Kick) *"Did you hear me?"* (Kick) (Kick) (Kick)

I try desperately to avoid the assaults; moving, shifting, shrinking, turning, contorting - all while trying to sound normal and nonchalant. My face is hot with shame and embarrassment. It's getting difficult to breathe. Or pretend.

"Please stop, Mom! I'm getting off!"

I can hear myself apologizing, "I'm sorry Judy. I have to go." My lip quivers as I try to keep my voice from shaking. I can't let on that I'm in pain. That *isn't* the way to play the game.

I may only be thirteen… but I am an excellent actress.

~

I'm in trouble. Again.

I am just getting home from a date with a nice boy from my church youth group. I look at the clock on the stove and realize I'm a few minutes late. The house is dark, so I don't see her at first. She is waiting for me behind the front door. She switches on the light and glares at me. A piercing glare that seethes and writhes with that familiar 'you'd-better-obey-me-if-you-know-what's-good-for-you' … look.

"I'm sorry Mom. I didn't realize. I won't be late again."

Nothing. Not a word. Just silence. A shudder runs down my spine.

Her eyes are daggers as she quietly and methodically removes her watch, and places it on the kitchen table. Next, her ring. She rolls up her sleeves, her eyes never leaving mine.

Too late.

The first punch lands in my stomach. *"I told you what would happen if you were late!"*

Another punch. *"How dare you disobey me!"*

Two more punches. *"Are you going to be late again?"*

My mind is exploding, screaming, '*I hate you! I hate you! Stop!*' But no words come out. I want to cry but
I won't give her the satisfaction.

I may only be fifteen… but I am an excellent actress.

Something inside me snaps. I watch in disbelief as my hand comes out of nowhere and slaps her on the face.

"Enough!" I shout.

She stumbles backward, confused. Is that a glimmer of fear I see in her eyes? Confusion turns to rage.

She hits me even harder, but I don't care. She's slapping and kicking and hitting, her arms flailing everywhere and anywhere on my body they can possibly reach. But I no longer feel anything. And I don't back down.

Suddenly, it's all over. She's staring at me as if she's seeing me for the very… first… time.

I am no longer invisible. I am no longer paralyzed. My mother never hits me again.

I may only be fifteen… but I have found my voice.

It's not too late.

INADVERTENT LIFE LESSONS

PATTI LEE

"I love you because I have to, you're my daughter," he said. I stood in his shadow, staring up at him as the stones from the driveway dug into my bare feet. He leaned closer and looked down on me with narrowed blue-green eyes. "But I don't like you." I blinked a few times, and I opened my mouth as if to say something, but nothing came out. My first thought was "Well, I don't like you either!" My mind raced with question after question. What kind of father would say something like that? What kind of father treated his teenage daughter that way? What kind of father didn't care who he hurt with his words or his actions? Why would he say such a thing? Why didn't he like me? He turned on his heel and left me frozen in place on that spring afternoon in 1982.

I realized then and there that words mattered. What people thought was one thing, but to say it out loud to the person on which it would inflict the most pain? That was something else. Words said in anger that come from a place of hurt, even if they aren't really meant, matter.

Maybe he *didn't* like me. I was a moody teenager after all. And it was true I looked on in judgement as he drank his beer and whiskey and laughed loudly with his friends. I protested the stench of that burning skunky smell as I waved my hand about, trying to dispel the clouds of smoke as I walked through the room, desperately hoping the reeking odor wouldn't cling to me. Sometimes I was impatient waiting in line to use our one and only bathroom. Groups of two and three people came out at once. They sniffed forcefully and wiped their noses with their fingers and then put said fingers in their mouth, rubbing their gums. On school nights, rock music blared outside well after midnight and the revving engines of his friends' motorcycles kept me awake. My need for sleep and my desire to do well in school taking precedence over my fear of his retaliation, I'd open my window and yell, "People are trying to sleep!"

I was afraid of my father; terrified, actually. We all were, my two siblings and I. My mother was too, but did her best to placate him. When he'd been drinking, it made her job harder. The marijuana helped keep him mellow, but it didn't always work. His angry outbursts were evidenced by the holes punched in the walls and a family full of PTSD. He earned his nickname: "Crazy Ronnie".

Although I was scared, that didn't stop me from standing up to him and doing what I thought was right or saying what I thought needed to be said. Even though I was the youngest, I confronted him where my brother rebelled and my sister remained quiet and obedient.

Fed up after a confrontation, exasperated, I'd demand, "Why can't we just be normal?!"

His bulging eyes, cold and steely, stared down at me as he offered a quick tilt of his head. "There's no such thing."

This was my dysfunctional family; an out of control

father and an enabling mother. This was the life I led growing up in a small town in Connecticut, one I swore I would never have for myself.

The first house I remember living in was referred to as a summer cottage, which, as an adult, brings visions of a cute, quaint get-away. This was anything but that. As I got older, I realized it was just a shack, probably nothing more than an old hunting camp. Set up high on a heavily wooded hill, it wasn't visible from the road. It was the early '70s, and there was no bathroom or running water. My mother's words, sometimes said seriously, and sometimes just a statement, have stayed with me my whole life because she never really got what she wanted: "I just want a house with a closet." I would have put indoor plumbing over a closet, but I understood her point.

I shared a room, a bed actually, with my sister. My brother had his own room, but it was more of a closet than an actual room. It was a tiny area off of the living room with no space for anything but a mattress on the floor. A sheet strung across the doorway provided privacy for my parents who slept on a pull-out couch in the living-room area. This house essentially only had the two rooms; the living/kitchen area and the room I shared with my sister. My father was a firm believer in corporal punishment, and my first memory of being spanked was in that house.

I was around four years old. Sometimes he would make us go get our own switch from outside; a small branch that made that distinctive swooshing sound when swung. But not this time. I had no idea why he had us all line up in the living room that night and hold our hands out in front of us. My four-year-old's memory is fuzzy on those details, but I guessed it had something to do with the hairbrush he held in his hand. He glared as he hovered over us, sneering, "You brought this on yourselves!"

He went down the line, first my sister who was three years older than me. Then my brother, who was one year older than me. I looked on as he struck each of my siblings on the back of their hands. I flinched as they cried out with each blow. I waited. My stomach twisted in knots. My legs could barely hold my own weight. My whole body shook. I waited for it to be my turn, hoping he'd find out whatever information he was looking for before he got to me.

He didn't.

He yanked me toward him, and like a ragdoll, flung me over his knee. He brought the hairbrush down on my bottom. The brush had spiky black bristles that bit into my tender flesh. I don't know how many times he struck me. When he was finished, and I was in my room getting my pajamas on, I struggled to contort myself in order to see the stinging marks. The bristles left small pink pin-prick dots on my backside, and my four-year-old brain wondered if that was what measles looked like.

That was the first time I remember being hit. And though it wasn't the last time, another traumatic memory burned in my brain happened when I was eleven.

I had been hanging around with two of my friends, exploring the property my parents owned where our old house, the shack, burned down a few years before, about a half a mile down the street. It was set on the top of the hill and hard to see unless you knew it was there. There was a long, steep driveway off to the side of the property; the area around it was overgrown, keeping the path almost hidden from the road. Cars couldn't manipulate the steep, bumpy path and only 4-wheel-drive trucks with brave drivers would venture up that hill. There was a space at the very bottom of the hill where my parents parked our car. The surrounding area was dense, and although no cars had been parked there for years, that spot was still just packed dirt.

We'd climbed the steep hillside to play in the wooded area behind where the house once stood and decided to go in search of "the Cliff House." We'd heard stories of the Cliff House, which was a house literally built on the side of a high cliff. It was supposed to have a deck with a view of the river and a deadly drop if you weren't careful. While we traipsed around in the woods in search of the house, we played games to pass the time.

'Freeze tag' and 'Sardines' were favorites. We soon grew tired of looking for the house and decided to go home. Though it wasn't really dark, it was chilly and seemed later than it was as the dense foliage of the branches and trees above blocked the daylight. The shorts I put on earlier were a good idea for playing in the sunshine, but now I longed for my jeans. We started running down the driveway, but the area was incredibly steep and overgrown. We ran faster and faster, almost tripping down the overrun path. As I neared the bottom of the hill, I couldn't stop myself and momentum carried me half-running half-stumbling right into the road.

I looked up just in time to see a car coming over the crest of the hill and around the corner. I caught a glimpse of a face behind the windshield, and my stomach dropped when I saw it was my mother driving home from work. Her eyes were wide, but her brows were narrowed. Her lips were pressed together and slightly puckered. I stood on the side of the road while my mother stopped the car next to me. She rolled down her window. "What the hell are you doing?" She shouted. "I almost ran you over! Do you know how lucky you are that I was able to stop in time?!" I said I was sorry and tried to explain, but it was no use. She told me to go home.

My stomach got that familiar sensation; like butterflies, but worse. My heart started to race and sweat trickled down my back. I felt like I was going to throw up. My friends knew a little about my father and figured I was in for it, so they both said they'd walk me home, reassuring me the whole time it was not as bad as I thought. I agreed to let them walk with me and not stop at their own homes that we'd pass on the way, selfishly and, it turns out, foolishly, thinking nothing would happen if they were around. We walked together up the hill and back toward my house. It was about a ten minute walk, and the burning in the pit of my stomach grew with each step. We could see the mailbox at the top of my driveway.

My parents bought this house after the 'cottage' burned down. It was an old, small, cape-style home with two rooms on the bottom floor and the second story was really just an attic that served as bedrooms for us kids. It was set back away from the road quite a bit, and the house could not really even be seen when the trees and shrubs in the wooded area in front of the house were in full bloom. We shared the driveway with a neighbor, and ours was the first house on the left and was about 50 yards from the top of the driveway where it met the road. The driveway was Y shaped where people often turned their vehicles around to change directions.

As we got closer, I saw my father in the center point of the Y of the driveway working on a car - he was always working on a car. Either one of ours or one of his friends. His friends who were always around, and today was no different. There were three there, leaning against the car, drinking beer.

My father looked up from under the hood of the car as I walked down the driveway with my friends. He was wearing his standard garb of a plain white t-shirt, soiled now with engine grease, blue jeans he called dungarees, a red bandana around his neck, and black motorcycle boots. He'd pulled the dipstick from the engine and held it in his hand as he stood up to his full height. Out from under the hood now, he bore a half-smile on his mustached face, really more of a sneer I realized as I got closer. His eyes glinted as he started walking toward me, gently tapping his open palm with the dipstick.

He continued to advance. I froze but kept my eyes on the dipstick. Tap-tap.

One step. Two steps closer. His movements were slow and deliberate. Tap-tap.

The sneer never left his face. "So you like to play in the road, huh?"

As quick as a snake, he struck. The dipstick connected with my lower left thigh. Even though I knew it was coming, I wasn't prepared for the stinging bite of metal on skin.

He swung again. I twisted away. The dipstick left a burning welt on the side of my leg. His face was flushed and his eyes were dark and hard. I held my hands up in front of my chest, palms facing him, as I stepped back. The house was about 40 yards away. I was stubborn and didn't want to cry in front of all those people. I planned to make a run for it. A glance toward the road and there were my friends. Eyes wide, mouths hanging open, slowly backing away. My father's friends were standing next to the car, but I didn't have time to figure out the looks on their faces as I felt another whack against my leg.

"It was an accident!" I cried. But he didn't care. I turned and tried to run. He kept striking out. Each swat that landed slowed me down. He chased me as I ran away from him - away from my friends, away from his friends and away from that dipstick. He kept hitting, swatting at my ass and yelling at me. I couldn't even tell what he was saying – all I heard was yelling and the sound of my own heartbeat as I felt the sting of each smack of the metal rod. I tried to block the blows with my hands as I ran, closer now to the house. So close.

And then as I tried to shield my raw, tender skin with the palm of my hands, the hook at the end of the dipstick tore into my pinky. It ripped open the fleshy part just above the bottom knuckle..

I gulped air. "Stop! Stop! I'm bleeding," I cried. I kept going, keeping my eyes on the black tar shingles of the porch roof and then as I got closer, the wooden porch steps.

I hoped my mother would hear his shouts, or my cries, and make him stop. The blood dripped from my hand and splattered against my leg as I tried to block the swats.

"It's your own fault!" he growled back at me. "If you didn't put your hand there, it wouldn't have happened."

All this transpired in front of several grown men and probably the next-door neighbor too. No one, not one of them, made any effort to stop him. I wasn't safe anywhere or with anyone. Usually if he had friends around, he was more easygoing. Not this time. Maybe he felt more pressure with the audience. Like he had to show everyone he was the boss. Was there ever any doubt?

I thought of my mother as a traitor and wondered why she'd said anything knowing his temper. Knowing what he was capable of. Maybe she thought because his friends were there, it wouldn't be so bad. But part of me still wondered why. Why did my mother tell him anything at all?

By the time I made it to the porch of the house, my father had retreated. Either too tired to continue or just eager to return to his friends and the car that needed work.

I was safe. As safe as I could be anyway. The wound on my finger probably needed stitches, but that wasn't going to happen.

My mother was there at the door, grimacing at me as I limped inside. Neither my tears nor the blood dripping from my gouged hand elicited an apology or an explanation of why she told my father what happened. She steered me toward the bathroom, which was just across from the front door.

We stood in the cramped bathroom as she turned on the water in the sink. She didn't speak as she wet the washcloth. "You should have known better than to be playing in the road," she murmured. Her eyebrows gathered, intent as she assessed the open wound, ignoring the bright pink welts on my arm and legs.

My whole body was trembling, but I fought the tears.I spoke each word carefully and with purpose. "I *wasn't* playing in the road. I *fell* into the road. It was an accident." A quick intake of breath and a wince as the cold water hit the half inch flap of skin the hook tore open.

She breathed a heavy sigh as she pulled a butterfly bandage out of the box in the medicine cabinet. "Well," she raised her brow, and her mouth was set in a frown as she stated, "now you'll be more careful, won't you."

It's these inadvertent life lessons that tend to stick and help shape who you not only *don't* want to be, but who you eventually *will* be.

I thought we were poor growing up, but as I got older, I realized my parents were just bad with money. They didn't put the family first when it came time to decide where the paychecks went. Dad always seemed to have the things he wanted. New guns, motorcycles, and other assorted toys. He always had marijuana, which I learned to appreciate as it helped improve his often sour mood, but there were times we went without.

I was a good student. I always completed my homework and did well in school. So when my 6th grade teacher, Mrs. Giuditta, had me stay after class one day, I got that uh-oh feeling. I always liked Mrs. Giuditta. Her huge, brown, square rimmed glasses accentuated her brown eyes. She had Farrah Fawcett hair, but it was brown with red highlights. She was young for a teacher, at least younger than the teachers I remembered. She was probably in her 30s and wore trendy skirts and heels.

Wondering what I had done, I walked up to her desk. She hesitated before she pulled a brown bag from under her desk, picked it up by the twine-like handles and set it on her desk. The words "Big Brown Bag" were boldly written in dark brown ink across both sides of the bag. She was fidgety, her hands flying to her hair before pushing up her glasses.

"I cleaned out my closet. There are some things I was going to get rid of – just some sweaters. And a couple of blouses. Do you think you want to take a look?" She frowned as she stood up and adjusted her glasses again. "You don't have to take anything. You might not like any of it..."

I stared at the bag and peeked inside. I swallowed in relief and was touched by her kindness; I didn't see it as charity at the time, though I realize now it was. I was also glad I wasn't in trouble. I thanked her and took the entire bag. I couldn't wait to go home and try them all on. And yes, some were new. I didn't find out until much later that the "Big Brown Bag" was the trademark of Bloomingdales, a store I had only ever heard people talk about but had never set foot in, let alone worn clothes from. I walked a little taller when I wore anything from that bag.

There were times we had no electricity, and sometimes we couldn't cook on the stove or have hot water because the gas bill hadn't been paid. We drove around in junk cars, and my father was continually working on one car or another. Sometimes he'd work into the wee hours of the morning, swearing and making noise the entire time, ensuring none of us got a good night's sleep.

My parents bought a new car when I was 13. That was the only brand-new car they ever owned. They had been renting a car by the week so my father could still work as a rural mail carrier; rural carriers had to use their own vehicle to deliver the mail. So when they drove down the driveway in that ugly white AMC Eagle with a brown stripe across the doors, I didn't pay it much attention.

We'd had the car a day or two and my mother and I were heading to the grocery store. As she buckled my little brother into his car seat, she asked, "What do you think of our new car?" I scoffed at her. "I know you didn't *really* buy this car. That would be stupid. It's not big enough for all of us." Her wince turned to a scowl as she lowered her head, busy with the buckle of the car seat. I didn't believe, *couldn't* believe that they actually bought that car.

It was a painfully inadequate 2-doored five-seater vehicle for a six-person family. She didn't say anything but I imagine between the credit needed and the monthly car payment, it was the best my parents could do. But even that car didn't last long. It wasn't cared for properly and after a year or so, it had a blown engine. It found a place next to the other broken cars next to the garage in the front yard. Along with a rusty old washing machine, car parts and assorted piles of junk.

Until I was 12, I was the youngest of three kids. My siblings and I often wondered aloud to each other, in hushed voices as we huddled on the floor of our bedroom, why our parents ever had children when it was obvious they didn't want them. My father especially. We were more like servants and scapegoats to him than cherished offspring. So we did our best to stay out of his crosshairs. But sometimes we had no choice and he put us there.

Our house was just another version of one of our cars; old and not very well taken care of. There was no central heating and we relied solely on a small wood stove for heat. There were times my father woke us up in the middle of the night to go outside and search for kindling because the fire had gone out. Or the pipes froze, and we had to take turns going down into the dark, wet, cobwebby basement to hold the hair dryer to the elbow of one pipe or another. Somehow, the fire going out and the pipes freezing not only became our fault, but our responsibility.

The fact that our mother was there was of little comfort; he took his frustrations out on her as much as he did us. More, actually. Worse. And my father had a rule: "what happens in this house, stays in this house."

Not to imply these examples were typical of every day of my life growing up. Unfortunately, any happy moments were overshadowed by the feeling of dread, waiting for that other shoe to drop. Even holidays were a stressful time, and I honestly can't remember one single happy holiday. Most kids looked forward to Christmas and Easter. Not me. There was always tension in the air. For one thing, a holiday meant Dad would be home at some point when we all knew he didn't want to be. He was easily annoyed and even though it was Christmas (or Thanksgiving, or Easter), his friends came first. He would spend his time with them, making it crystal clear he'd rather be with them than with us. He would leave and come back when he felt like it, or his friends would stop by for a cold beer and whatever my dad had in his bag of tricks.

I vowed my own holidays would look very different.

I vaguely remember my mother hosting one holiday dinner at our home growing up, but we usually traveled and visited with family for holiday festivities. In theory, it was a great idea, but in reality, there were a number of problems with that plan. My father was not a slave to time or tradition. He would go when he wanted and not until he was good and ready. If he had a friend over, everyone else just had to wait. If he wasn't home yet and it was time to leave, we had to wait for him. It never occurred to him that the rest of the extended family was waiting on all of us to arrive before their own holiday could begin. He didn't seem to care that dinner was ready and waiting 45 minutes away. He wasn't leaving. He still had to 'shit, shower and shave' before anyone could go anywhere.

Before the Eagle, and then again after it died in the driveway, we drove junk cars. There was always something wrong, which didn't help us to arrive on time to any family gatherings, either. We always had to stop and fix something during the long ride. Cruising along, hitting a frost heave or a pothole, the roar of the muffler immediately followed by the scraping sound as it was dragged along the road forced us to pull over. He would re-attach the muffler and adjust the coat hanger that held it in place.

When there was a leak in the radiator, we'd stop along the way and he'd fill the radiator with water from old milk jugs he filled and kept in the trunk. If it was a longer ride, he'd take the back road where there was a brook and he'd pull the now-empty milk jugs from the trunk for us to refill with water, hoping it would be enough until we got to our destination. We always seemed to be late, and in anticipation of getting there, the drive seemed to take forever.

I loved to go to my grandparents' house for the holidays, or any time really. That was the only place I ever felt happy, safe, and truly loved.

My father's parents were typical grandparents. Their faces lit up when we walked in the door, their eyes shining as they doled out hugs. My grandmother, my father's mother, adored me. She didn't play with me as a grandparent might, but we spent a lot of time together, and more importantly, she wanted to spend time with me. She'd let me spend school vacations there as often as my own parents allowed; my grandmother retired from her job at the rubber factory where my grandfather worked until he retired years later.

She taught me about gardening and how she left a little cup of beer near her vegetables so the slugs would leave her tomatoes alone. She showed me how to keep a clean house, not by making me clean her house, but by talking to me while she cleaned, unwittingly teaching me the value of cleanliness and order. We watched television into the wee hours of the morning, often falling asleep together on the couch while we watched Kojak or Carol Burnett. She bought me Fig Newton cookies and cooked eggs for me because she wanted to. And when she'd come and check on me in the middle of the night, I'd pretend to be asleep. Savoring the priceless feeling of being cared for as she pulled the covers up over me and tucked me in, I relished the feeling and was so glad I'd stayed awake.

I knew I wanted to be more like my grandmother – thoughtful and kind - and less like her son.

When I was 12 and my little brother was born, I was immediately taken with him and felt compelled to care for him. I'd been babysitting since I was eight years old, and the desire to nurture came naturally to me. But this was different. I needed to protect him. To keep him safe from

INADVERTENT LIFE LESSONS

my father, sheltered from the life we lived. And I wanted him to feel loved.

My sister and I both spent a lot of time babysitting while my mother worked as a city mail carrier. My father bounced from job to job. He worked at the post office for a few years but quit that job, saying he was afraid he himself would 'go postal'. He tried to make it on his own doing tree removal and later as a gunsmith, but he wasn't great at actually being employed. Not that he would have or *could* have taken on the responsibility of caring for an infant. I spent so much time with my little brother, he called me 'Mom.' It was cute until he did it at the pharmacy and people thought my 15-year-old self was actually that little boy's mother. My face hot, I would correct him and move quickly along.

The birth of my brother ended up being a significant catalyst in my parent's marriage, in all of our lives really. He was the apple of my father's eye and the light of my mother's life. He had new shoes, new clothes and healthy food. Though my teenage mind thought it somewhat u

nfair, I was glad my parents showed up for him. I knew I couldn't keep him safe from my father's angry outbursts and I happily doubted his rear-end would ever see the welts mine did. I was relatively certain his childhood would be nothing like mine, but I still had to make sure he wasn't exposed to things no child should have to look at or listen to – I had to be there in case something happened and he needed someone.

In early 1984, my mother finally found the strength to put her foot down when my father came home drunk and high on something one wintry night. The house was cloaked in a sense of foreboding as soon as he walked in, and we all scattered when we sensed it. This was nothing new. We'd usually just wait it out. His booming voice echoed off the walls of our small house. But the smashing of glass – first the thud as it hit the wall or the door – followed by the shattered tinkling sound as it rained down to the floor, couldn't be ignored.

My mother, through sobs and hiccups, placatingly murmured, "I'm sorry. I'm sorry…" Her screams soon followed, sometimes muffled as my father held her mouth closed and chided her, "You don't know when to shut up, do you?"

I stayed out of sight, playing with my brother, not quite four years old now, in his room. The burning sensation in the pit of my stomach grew worse with each thump I heard from the kitchen just a few feet away. Each wince made it harder to keep the tears from welling over. I distracted myself and my brother by playing pretend and reading books, hoping the cries and crashes would be over soon.

But when I heard him bellow, "Get your asses in here!" I knew I had to go.

My mother pleaded with him and begged him to stop. He spat out, "This is your fault!"

I apprehensively made my way into the kitchen, my little brother at my heels as my sister crept down the stairs and followed behind us. Pieces of broken ceramic littered the room. I took in the shattered plates, shards of glass and splatters of deep red. The sweet vinegary smell quickly confirmed it was splatters of ketchup on the floor and on the counter. He stood next to my mother at the back of the room, she was almost against the wall. Her eyes were squeezed shut. She hung her head. When she looked our way, she shook her head slowly. Her half-closed eyes carried the weight of the world and were tinged with sorrow, as if she'd failed us.

She wore her postal uniform, the light blue blouse now

stained with whatever food my father had thrown at her. And her long brown hair, usually in a bun or ponytail, was messy and strands hung about her face and clung to her cheeks, wet with tears. Her eyeglasses were gone, lost somewhere or broken along with the remnants of what seemed like every dish we owned scattered around her feet. His face was red, and his eyes were wide and wild. He breathed heavily, overexerting himself between the yelling and the tantrum. My mother stood hunched and stock still, her arms at her sides, pleading with him. Begging him to stop.

She took a shaky breath. "Let the kids go. They don't need to be here."

His lips contorted, finally settling into a smirk. He turned my way, but I couldn't look him in the eye. I couldn't think. I was frozen. He told us all to watch, his eyes on us to make sure we followed his command. As he stood next to her, he stepped back and lifted his arm. There was a gun in his hand, and he put that shiny black pistol right up to the side of my mother's head.

My mother flinched and pulled her head away as she closed her eyes, screaming, "No!"

She sobbed as she spoke. Her voice quiet but thick. "Please don't…"

Her whole body trembled as she shook her head. Tears streamed down her face. Her eyes were frantic as she looked up at us. She shouted, "Call the police!"

The gun still on my mother, he looked at us. His nostrils flared and his voice was steely. He uttered the words slowly and with intention. "Don't move."

What happens in this house, stays in this house – we were programmed not to talk about it, and none of us even thought to call for help or try to leave. We did what we were told.

My mother's voice rose to a scream. "Do it! Somebody call the police!"

It happened so fast, but it felt like slow motion. Her shriek pierced through me, and springing into action, I scooped up my little brother. But that was as far I got. I held him on my hip, and like a deer in the headlights, I was motionless. My eyes were on that gun.

Is he going to kill her? How many bullets does he have? Is he going to shoot all of us? I tried to convince myself that although he didn't love me, my father loved my little brother. And because he loved him, he would not shoot him. Relief mixed with guilt flooded me as I hoped that because I held my little brother, my father would not fire that gun at *me*.

"Call the police! Just do it!" My mother begged.

My sister lunged toward the phone on the wall, just a few feet away. I don't know if it was the threat of arrest, the look on our faces or the pleas from my mother – maybe all of it – but my father ran out the door. The rest of that night is a blur, but my mother finally decided she'd had enough.

After a few days of my father away – either in jail or at a friend's house – I don't know where he was – my mother told my father he had to leave. She gave him an ultimatum: get help or don't come back.

So he got out, and then he got help. What kind of help, I wasn't sure. But a few months later, much to my and my sister's dismay, he was back. He might have been leashed, but he would never be tamed.

I knew this was not the life I wanted for myself. I wanted to get out.

I quit high school and worked full-time so I could save money. In the meantime, I paid my mother rent and helped with the bills. I met my husband in 1986 but I didn't move away until 1991, after I had gotten married and had my three kids. My brother was 11 when I packed up and headed 100 miles north. I carried some guilt knowing without my income, and their poor money management, it would be hard for my mother to make ends meet. Within two years my parents lost their house to the bank. They followed me to Vermont. By that time, I had settled in my small town and worked at a daycare. Eventually I took some early childhood education classes because I was good with kids and I wanted to have a positive effect, to do something good, to help one child feel like they mattered.

I started as a cook and dishwasher and soon became a preschool teacher. Ultimately, I opened my own home-based daycare which I ran for several years and even had a waiting list. I wanted kids to have fun while learning and to make every child feel special. So each day I made it a point to tell them something I enjoyed about them. It wasn't always easy – as adorable as they are, preschoolers can be exasperating.

When I happen upon an "old daycare kid" out and about in town now, and they come to me with a smile and hug, I know I made an impact. When I received a letter from the parents of a child that was in my care thanking me for the work I did and telling me what a difference I made in their son's life, that meant something to me.

My goal was to be more like my grandmother and less like my father. I had a bit of his temper in me, and that terrified me. But I knew as an adult, I was responsible for my behavior. I made conscious decisions not to react out of anger. It was a simple lesson in mind over matter, but it wasn't always easy. I constantly reminded myself of who I wanted to be and what I wanted to do.

I also knew I did not want to be my mother. The abuse

she suffered at the hands of my father was shocking and atrocious. I used to blame her for not leaving, for not sticking up for herself and for her children. But once I was an adult, married and with my own children, I know at the time she felt helpless. Powerless. She did the best she could with the tools she had. I would often reflect back on my childhood and it would firm my resolve to make sure I succeeded.

I couldn't control everything, but I could control myself, what I did, and how my kids lived. My kids would not know the horror of that life. They would not know the sting of a belt or wonder if they were unwanted.

I knew what kind of person I wanted to be and strived to become that person using role models around me. I drew inspiration from my beloved grandmother, my sixth-grade English teacher and my best friend's mother. From Carol Brady, June Cleaver, Marion Cunningham and a host of other maternal figures I saw on television. I would be the person I needed when I was younger. I was going to be the parent I wish I had, the parent *I* needed.

I knew without a shadow of a doubt because I made the choice to have children, they would feel loved and wanted; cherished for the beings they were, flaws and all. I did what I had to do to make sure my kids knew they were first, they were my priority. I wasn't always successful, and of course I have regrets. I wish I hugged them more when they were little, and I wish I didn't always follow the strict rules I set. I wish I knew I was stronger then than I thought I was.

My parenting style might not have been typical, and like any mother, I learned as I lived and made lots of mistakes. But I kept joy and laughter in my home. I was fun, but firm. Food fights and family game nights. Treasure hunts just for laughs, or sometimes tasty treats would be waiting to be found. I vowed I would not spank my kids. I wanted my kids to respect me but not fear me. Though it didn't happen often, when I felt my father's temper flare within me, I put my hands behind my back to make it a little harder for me to react.

I may have been a strict parent, ensuring rules were followed and homework completed, but they knew I was someone they could count on. I made sure they knew they could talk to me about anything and that I would not judge them. And holidays were happy. We had Easter egg hunts and Valentine's Day parties. We decorated for Christmas and listened to carols, all the while munching on white-fudge covered Oreos and drinking eggnog and hot chocolate.

As I matured, I often thought about how my father acted. Why did he do the things he did when I was younger? What made him say the things he said? Why would he want to hurt me with his words and his actions? Did he really not like *me* or was he mad that I called attention to the things he knew he shouldn't be doing or didn't like about himself?

None of that made me stop being the person I wanted to be and I doubt it would have changed how things turned out. Eventually I realized that I had to look at him from a different perspective. Not from a daughter's perspective or a child's perspective. I had to look at the whole "him." When I did, I recognized maybe his own childhood held secrets. I am in no way excusing his behaviors; I am however looking at them with an understanding eye.

Everyone's past holds trauma of some kind, but it's up to us as adults to make sure we don't continue the cycle. After he died, I accidentally stumbled upon a newspaper article from the '70s about how he and some friends had been in an accident. One of his friends drowned that day. He'd almost drowned and spent several days in the hospital. He never spoke of it, and there was more to the story I'm sure. I'll never really know as I never got the chance to ask him, though I suspect he would not have told me had I asked. My father was mentally ill and probably suffered from some kind of trauma as a child as well. He'd often tell me the grandparents I knew were not the parents he had. Perhaps they'd also mellowed with age...

So with those thoughts in mind, I gave him the benefit of the doubt. I repeatedly told myself, "Good people do bad things sometimes – it does not make them bad people," and I forgave him. Not for the way he treated my mother – that was hers and hers alone to do. I forgave him for the way he treated me, how he acted, and what he said.

Although he never really took those words back, those words that hurt so much and stayed with me so many years, scarring my soul and my self-confidence, in my heart I didn't think he really meant them. I grieved his passing, but I grieved more for the relationship I never had but wanted so desperately. As he said, he loved me because I was his daughter, and I think as we both grew up, he liked me. Even if it was just a little.

I've taken my experiences, these inadvertent life lessons, and made a difference the best way I can.

A few years after I closed my home daycare, I landed a job at a local child advocacy center as an administrative assistant. A child advocacy center is a child-focused program where representatives from law enforcement, child protection, prosecution, mental health, medical and victim advocacy, and child advocacy, work together to conduct interviews and make team decisions about the investigation, treatment, management, and prosecution of child abuse cases. Within a few months, I had taken on the executive director role. Now I work for a state-wide non-profit agency that assists with the development and enhancement of the child advocacy center model. I've been with the organization since 2012.

My relationship with my three children, who are all grown up now and out on their own, is exactly what I'd hoped for and pictured for myself. We spend time together because we want to – because we like to. My kids look back on their childhood and remember special "Mommy and me" time going grocery shopping and then out to lunch. They remember playing games together and me making up silly words when they'd beat me. And they remember Mom as someone who busted them out of being grounded and drove them aimlessly around town, all the while speaking with a horrible British accent. There were drive-in movies, road trips and restaurants with all-you-can-eat Sunday brunches.

Have there been disagreements? Sure. Did they always listen? No. But they were given tools and taught to use words to get their point across. To maintain control of themselves, be respectful of other people and their boundaries and to approach conflict with grace. And now there are grandchildren, and the cycle of love and acceptance will continue.

I learned a lot of life lessons over the years; I learned how to be a person people can depend on, because as a child, I was at a loss for someone I could count on.

I learned how to be a good parent by the poor example set for me.

I learned how to be a responsible adult at a very early age from the utter lack of responsibility taken by the adults around me when I was younger.

I learned forgiveness is within if you can reach deep enough and perhaps wait long enough.

I learned that if I could forgive others, I could forgive myself for past mistakes and try to learn from them.

I'm not perfect, and that's ok. No one is perfect. Not everyone is going to like me, and that's ok. I had to learn to like myself and all my flaws, regardless of whether my father, or anyone else, liked me or not. To look at myself in the mirror and be okay with that woman staring back at me. To know she did her best. That she was good enough. She was *always* good enough.

REKINDLED WANDERER

MICHELLE TEEMS

Come closer. I'm going to tell you a secret. Life in your forties is fantastic. Don't let anyone tell you different. Yes, there are more wrinkles lining my forehead and several decided to retire around my mouth. I even pluck a stray whisker that won't stop growing on my chin. Yes, there are aches where once supple muscle held prime real estate. However, the confidence, self-assuredness, and wisdom makes the loose skin, sunspots, and other physical flaws worth it.

Who am I? It's not merely a song from *Les Misérables*. It's a question we all inevitably, and see hopefully, ask ourselves at some point in life. After long contemplation, I identified six core areas that I believe molded me into the kind, intelligent, and supremely flawed woman I am today. My childhood, moving away from home, joining the Army, becoming a mother, body acceptance (which remains an ongoing struggle), and becoming truly independent for the first time.

One of my first memories is of standing on the

morning beach while baby turtles dug their way from empty eggs and through the sand to march instinctively toward the ocean. I recall the numerous noisy seagulls above, oblivious to the reason they swarmed.

I was a sensitive child who grew up in a working middle class family. My mother was a housewife (that is what stay at home moms were called in the seventies and eighties). My father started out in the Air Force and then continued to work for the US Government as a civilian. We lived in a small house. We prayed over our food on the table three times a day and we played outside until the street lights came on.

My paternal grandmother raised six children as a single mom. In the early fifties, my maternal grandparents met during a weekend whirlwind romance when my grandfather was in the Navy. They were married after three days of knowing each other. They had five children and were so poor at times that my mother once recalled eating oatmeal for a week.

My paternal grandmother told me the story of her grandfather in the late 1800s who would ride his horse to court his future wife. They would talk on the porch for hours and then, after dark, he rode the family horse back home in the pitch black night. In the country in those days, there weren't any lights, and he had to trust that the horse knew the way back. He later owned a grocery store, but went out of business because he had a kind heart, would sell to anyone, and allowed customers to barter for goods with items he could never use and were largely worthless.

Born and raised in Florida, it's interesting how I didn't notice the heat and humidity as a kid. I don't recall it ever really bothering me. Now, I can't go back because the humidity literally sucks the life out of me.

My Grandma lived down the street, and in the

summer, I used to ride my bike over and we would watch her big box television. *Family Feud*, *The Price is Right*, *Little House on the Prairie*, Mister Rogers, or even Bob Ross! She liked painting and became a painter. (Creativity runs in my veins. My dad plays guitar, my mom sings, I sing, my brothers were in a metal rock band.) Grandma would pour me a glass of sweet iced tea as a treat. Her carrot cake was famous in the family, but I didn't like nuts then and would suck the frosting off and leave them piled on a corner of the plate, quietly rejected.

I have sporadic memories of elementary school. There doesn't appear to be rhyme or reason to the recollections that stuck with me. Once, another student took my lunch and I got theirs. Mom used to make my two brothers and I superb bag lunches with fruit and ham or turkey sandwiches with lettuce and tomato and cheese, chips. When I opened my lunch sack, I immediately knew I could not possibly survive the rest of the day. What was in that brown paper bag? A ketchup sandwich.

I told the teacher and she said, "Well, everyone is already eating, so you'll just have to make the best of it." I took a bite, forced myself to chew and swallow, put it down, and went hungry until I returned home. It felt like reaching into my stocking at Christmas and pulling out a handful of coal.

One time at night, my Dad returned from a hunt with friends and they had a deer strung up for butchering. I watched, fascinated and disturbed. I remember one of the guys dug out the bladder, and it looked like a water balloon. He threw it over the fence as a joke and it splattered on the concrete.

I am a Generation X child through and through (aka *The MTV Generation*). Music played a huge role in my life, and it started with old-school MTV. I saw MTV at its inception, when there were only about five videos on repeat. It was glorious. "Video Killed the Radio Star" is the one I remember, but soon to follow were many hits, a lot of them one-hit wonders. I still listen to many of those wonderful songs, over thirty years later. Martha Quinn, Nina Blackwood, and J.J. Jackson were not mere VJs, but friends. I have no idea what shows are now playing on the music channel that doesn't play music, but it was kidnapped by reality television at some point. I hate reality TV.

Duran Duran fueled many of my early teen fantasies, and I had no carnal knowledge to create full-blown reveries. But I still tried, and around 1987, I completed my first draft of semi-erotic fan fiction. There was a pool is all I remember. Nick Rhodes (the keyboardist who wore the most makeup) held the top spot as my favorite Duran Duran member .

Some of the terms used to distinguish my generation are "latchkey children," slackers, cynical. We were exposed to the most divorces of any previous generation with more Moms working outside the home (not to insinuate that was the cause of the divorces). Now that we're middle-aged, we're supposed to be moderately happy and well-adjusted, according to statistics.

We had great music, including grunge and hip-hop, and great movies. Prince's *Purple Rain* changed my life. Prince was the coolest dude ever, and I crushed on him before I knew what it meant.

I can remember when the first VHS tapes came out and you could rent them from a store. For me, it was *Star Wars, The NeverEnding Story, Goonies, The Princess Bride*, and *Grease* (which were all life-changing movies). Then I wanted to be in a John Hughes movie several years later.

I also recall recording *Star Trek: The Next Generation* on

blank tapes off regular cable television. Mixed cassette tapes were also popular. My parents were religious, and they didn't allow me to listen to radio music. So I got blank tapes and recorded the songs I liked off the radio. I always hated how the DJs would talk and talk and talk right up until the second the vocals came in. But beggars can't be choosers. I would hide the tapes under my mattress.

I grew up in an age with no computers, no cell phones, no tablets. We had a Commodore 64, but the only game I remember playing was *Gyruss*. I used to type my college school papers on a typewriter. One of them was about vampires. When you needed to call someone and you weren't in a house, you used a pay phone. I remember when a dollar would fill up a little brown paper bag with candy from the corner gas station (and we walked there without parents).

I feel nostalgic when remembering that time period. In an age where everything appears recycled, it was a genuine and classic era. No CGI, no SnapChat filters. Senior pictures from Glamour Shots was the only time a picture was touched up.

Today's young people are introduced to the live action version of *The Little Mermaid* while we watched *The Journey of Natty Gann*. I remember when there were only a few television channels. Shows like *Family Ties, Growing Pains, Little House on the Prairie, Cheers*, and *The Cosby Show* were popular. You didn't have hundreds of shows to binge watch on streaming channels and no fast-forwarding through commercials. Everyone watched *The Muppets, Charlie Brown*, and the stop motion Rudolph/Santa movies. (Santa, you're an asshole!) Before and after school, and on Saturday mornings, my brothers and I would watch *Scooby-Doo, Inspector Gadget, G.I. Joe, Looney Tunes*, and Hanna-Barbera. I would collect the comics section from the Sunday newspaper to read.

In high school, my hair was embarrassingly big. Why did I engage with that wall of hairspray silliness? I was incredibly unfashionable for the time period because we didn't have money to invest in fads and trends, but hairspray was cheap. Even if money for new clothes was an option, I wouldn't have known what to buy.

Another factor that solidified my love of music was in the fourth grade, when I was nine. My teacher would play records if we were well-behaved. "*Hungry Like the Wolf*" by Duran Duran, "*Angel of the Morning*," and "*Queen of Hearts*" by Juice Newton and more. I think that was the year I got food poisoning from a ham, lettuce, and mayonnaise sandwich. We always had homemade lunches, and since we lived in Florida, the possibility of ripening foodstuff was quite high. Too shy to say anything about my nauseasness, I made it almost all the way home before finally puking on the floor of the bus. I don't recall whether I felt guilt or shame when I imagined the driver discovering and cleaning it up.

In fifth grade, I became obsessed with *Grease 2*. Not the original *Grease*, but the sequel with Michelle Pfeiffer, Maxwell Caulfield, Lorna Luft, and Adrian Zmed. The movie was completely under-rated. "Score Tonight," "Cool Rider," "Let's Do It for Our Country" were musical gems. Prove me wrong. My friends and I would play Pink Ladies at school. I always picked Johnny and Paulette.

I also fractured my dominant wrist roller skating, which gave me a fear of physical sports, and ended my interest in anything athletic. On the flipside, this began my self-taught voice training. I ended up with an operatic vocal range. I chose another path when I moved to New York City with a friend and pursued partying instead of my gift.

My ear drum burst during this period, and I recall laying on the couch in the living room on a heating pad, and my Mom allowing me to watch "V" and "V: The Final Battle." The mini-series and its sequel, about reptilian aliens masquerading as humans, starring Marc Singer, Faye Grant, and Jane Badler was a life-defining moment for me, and no doubt a huge influence on my love for science fiction and fantasy.

The eighties proved a powerful time for me, in terms of rites of passage and imprinting on music and movies. I began a lifelong love affair with music and film and still consider myself a connoisseur. These two art forms gave me confidence and helped me survive puberty.

I had a "two Coreys" phase in sixth grade. My friends and I were fangirls for Corey Haim, Corey Feldman, River Phoenix, Wil Wheaton, and Sean Astin. *The Goonies, Lost Boys*, and *Stand by Me* were very personal, like friends. I decided I wanted to become an actress. I remember feeling so confident and carefree during this time. I could do anything!

That year we had sex education class and they allowed the girls to order a free "starter kit" with pads and tampons. A month from turning twelve, my first cycle arrived during the summer before junior high school. I remember waking up, going to the bathroom, and seeing reddish-brown spots in my underwear. I sat in my room thinking for seemingly hours before I finally attained the nerve to confide in my Mom. She informed me that I had started my period and then called my Dad to tell him. I was mortified.

Thus began puberty, the worst time of my life. I had another friend who ended up pregnant at thirteen and her parents arranged for an abortion. This event made a big impression on me and might be one of the reasons why I remained so scared of intimacy as a young adult.

Life was emotionally rough during this time. I had a year of home school and a year of private school before returning to public high school. Sports were everything, so I floundered through an awkward basketball season, running up and down the court, occasionally getting the ball and doing nothing with it. I was a catcher during softball season. I remember very little about this time because I never fit in. I had superficial friends and a couple of sporty girls in a grade above who I imagined pity-friended me.

During tenth grade, a miracle happened. A friend from the church youth group said, "Hey Shelly, put your locker by mine. It's right by the choir room."

The theater door stood directly across. Thus began my high school career as the fat and sarcastically bitchy drama queen. I managed to befriend the popular drama geeks my first year. As a junior, a friend and I performed a duet scene for district competition where we portrayed females who realize they are more than friends. The scene ended with us kissing (we blocked the scene where we didn't actually kiss, but the audience couldn't tell) and the gasps from the audience back in 1990 were satisfying. We got a Superior rating at district, but the Principal wouldn't let us go to State because she thought the scene might be too controversial and cause trouble. We felt like rebels who challenged the status quo and engaged in an activity that fought stigma.

Show tunes dominated my singing life. I knew *Les Misérables* by heart and could sing every part. I also loved *Cats*, *Jekyll & Hyde*, *Chess*, and *Into the Woods*. I would literally sing in my room every day for hours. If I hit a note wrong, I would rewind the cassette tape, and do it again and again. My drama teacher picked *West Side Story* for my senior year. I auditioned for Maria, sang *"Tonight,"* and nailed every note.

I shocked everyone. After a rousing applause, the choir teacher immediately called me to the back of the room where she and the drama teacher sat during auditions and asked, "Miss Teems, why was I not aware you could sing like that? Tomorrow, you are sitting in soprano."

The next day, I moved from Alto II to Soprano I. I could hit a high G. Then they gave me the role of Anita, a part for a great dancer. Dancing was my nemesis ironically, but my Spanish teacher approached me after seeing the play and said, "Everyone did a wonderful job, but you had the best accent. You did great."

We would sneak in the auditorium occasionally and spend the night. I was awkward as a teenager and presented a sarcastic and confident image, while inside, insecurity and self-loathing brewed over. I graduated with average grades, but that summer I played Golde in *Fiddler on the Roof* during summer theater. One night, during the song *"Do You Love Me?"* I watched a huge cockroach crawl across the stage right by my feet and didn't break character. Fifty points to Hufflepuff for staying in character!

Acting on stage and singing during high school remained a monumental phase in my life. Misery and angst filled my entire being, but singing and performing on stage never failed to comfort and envelope me in joy and confidence. Life means living in coexistence with bliss and sorrow. Part of the excitement of reaching your forties is the luxury of looking back and seeing your past experiences through a new prism of understanding and forgiveness.

Leaving The Nest

In the winter of 1994, I moved to New York City with a friend who acquired money through an inheritance. He paid the rent on an apartment for a year. It was the chance of a lifetime and the first time I left home outside of a youth group camping trip to Tennessee. A time of wonder and hard life lessons, I had no clue how to be a roommate or a good friend due to unrealized and untreated emotional issues. And because someone had always taken care of financial tasks for me, I didn't understand you share responsibilities with your roommates. I learned things the hard way through unpleasant confrontations and every confrontation proved severe because of my inexperience and emotional fragility.

I lived in Alphabet City in a loft apartment on Avenue C in the East Village. Kurt Cobain died, and I remember it vividly because my roommate had a collapsed lung. We stayed in and watched the news all day.

It might have been ignorance or simply the reality of Manhattan back then, but I never felt unsafe. It became my home, in heart and hearth. I realize in retrospect that my creating an independent life in a giant metropolis like New York City while only knowing one person was extraordinary. I walked outside on my own, navigated the city, journeyed to interviews, and scored jobs by myself. I worked as a telephone operator for a catering and delivery service. I worked temp and got to relieve the secretaries at what was then Bantam Doubleday Dell and got free books.

I hustled as a barista and waitress at a busy gourmet deli off Madison Avenue that is now closed. I served Drew Barrymore, who sat with a young man, ordered matzo ball chicken soup, and ate a bite of it. I got lots of autographs, including ones from Dianne Wiest, Mary Stuart Masterson, Sally Kellerman, and Gavin MacLeod. Gwyneth Paltrow came in before she won her Oscar for

Best Actress in *Shakespeare in Love*. A scene from the movie *Ransom* was filmed right outside, and I made Ron Howard a cappuccino. This was before cell phones, so people weren't snapping photos or asking to take selfies with celebrities.

At dinner with my roommates in Soho one night, during the *Seven* time period, Brad Pitt and Gwyneth Paltrow picked up take-out. Bravely, I walked out, calling, "Hey guys!"

Kindly, they turned around and talked for several minutes. When I worked at a diamond manufacturing company, I rode up in the elevator with Robin Williams, who ended up buying his then-wife the jewelry she wore at the 1998 Oscars.

I lived on St. Mark's Place in an apartment the band Deee-Lite, whose biggest hit was "Groove is in the Heart," previously occupied. One day, while cleaning a drawer, I found scratch paper with lyric notes from a song off their debut album. While clubbing one night, I talked to a member of Deee-Lite who told me a couple brutally murdered each other in the bathroom of the apartment and that a pentagram was burned on the floor in the living room. On closer inspection, I identified faint but clear traces of a pentagram branded into the wood floor.

A cult also tried to convert me. One day, as I walked home, a young woman approached me and started talking. I thought, *Well how nice is this?* She gave me a flyer for a party and asked me to come. My roommate and I smuggled beer into a huge apartment that appeared to take up the whole floor of a building.

Hipster types stood around talking while others played guitars. We were punks and chugged the beers, stashing the empties in plant pots. Once they started trying to separate the males from the females and take us to separate areas, we picked up major creep vibes and deserted the party. I wish I could remember what they called their religion.

One night while clubbing on Halloween, we watched Michael Alig parade around with his club kid entourage. He dressed as a trauma victim with fake blood and bandages on. Another time at *Limelight*, I watched a club kid in drag smoke a pipe and state loudly, "I have to crap," then proceed to pop a squat on the floor and prepare for excretion. Friends rescued the clubber then guided them over to a garbage can, which proved to be the obvious next best choice for an impromptu toilet.

I developed an eclectic taste in music and attended many amazing concerts, like The Smashing Pumpkins, No Doubt, Tori Amos, The Beastie Boys and A Tribe Called Quest at Madison Square Garden, Bjork, PJ Harvey, Bauhaus during their 1998 reunion tour, The Creatures, The Sundays, Jewel, Dave Matthews Band at Giant Stadium with Beck, and The Fugees. I had tickets for Scott Weiland's solo album tour the day he first got arrested for heroin, and the show was canceled. I had a CD Walkman I listened to on the subway. DJ mixtapes were popular.

I left New York City due to an estrangement with my roommate after years of existing in an unhealthy, codependent friendship. The trauma, betrayal, and heartbreak I felt would follow me for years and impede future relationships. I closed my heart and emotions down to protect myself from ever feeling that level of pain again.

Another wonderful part of getting older is looking back and viewing those years from a wiser perspective. I realize part of the responsibility for that toxic friendship lay with me because of impeded perception, untreated depression, insecurity, and inexperience.

Years later, I ended up spending an unforgettable summer in Alaska on a cruise boat. I worked on a huge pontoon that carried about a hundred and twenty people out in Glacier Bay every day. In just a few months, I witnessed major changes happening to the glaciers.

I watched a humpback whale swim nearby, observed a pod of orcas, moose, horned and tufted puffins, seals, black and brown bears. Once or twice a week, I worked at a bed and breakfast. One night, I rode my bike home and stumbled upon a small black bear. We both startled and quickly went our separate ways.

The beaches in Alaska were amazing. The tides changed the shoreline almost daily. Hundreds of eagles hung around the shore, many were brown juveniles. Wild salmon berries and rhubarb grew by the roads. I even witnessed a huge wolf walking through tall grass one day from my window. Days were only dark for about four hours. On the boat, we would fish pieces of iceberg from the water off the deck for tourists to look at and touch.

Once, I even put on a huge orange cold water immersion suit and jumped from the boat into the water for training. The huge suit proved difficult to move around in. A male I had a crush on dove in and helped me swim back to the boat where my crewmates pulled me up on a metal nautical Jacob's ladder as part of the training. This physically challenged me and even though it was required training, it still took courage. (I think that guy liked me too, but we sadly never pursued it.)

Working as a timekeeper for the firefighters at Yosemite National Park was another meaningful job I procured. I watched all the cute liberal hipster guys every day and imagined one of them liking me, but most were taken. I hiked to Upper Yosemite Falls and drove to Tuolumne Meadows. I beheld all kinds of black bears with fur ranging from dark to light brown and even blond. I rode the bus to work and regarded the stunning scenery with awe. One afternoon, I returned after dark and started walking home with my little flashlight. I noticed dozens of eyes observing me, the light-reflecting tapetum lucidum in their peepers caused a glowing appearance. I freaked out until I realized it was a herd of deer.

I started having gallbladder attacks that were horrible. The pain proved so bad, at times I couldn't sit still. I lay awake for hours, waiting for the pain to pass. I switched to soy yogurt and almond milk because even dairy skim milk triggered an attack.

Joining The Army

In 2005, while living outside Yosemite National Park, at age thirty-two, I decided to join the Army. An unusual age to decide to pursue military service and become a soldier, but my choices were usually unusual. First, I required surgery to remove my gallbladder.

The surgery was outpatient and the experience of anesthesia appeared to reveal to me, at the time, what I imagined death was. Disarmingly, the experience behaved like a light switch flicked off. I woke slowly, coughing, and sluggishly remembered what transpired. After the hospital's pain medication wore off, the recent infliction proved so excruciating, I could barely make dry toast in the first twenty-four hours. I watched all the *Lord of the Rings* movies while bedridden and doped up on Vicodin. I asked for a picture of my gall bladder when they removed it, and they gave me one. I expected to be able to see the stones, but the organ was intact.

Because of the operation, I had to wait six months before I could report for basic training. I started preparing and lost forty pounds. I ran with my Dad in the dark at four in the morning before work so I would pass the physical test before reporting for duty.

First stop: The Military Entrance Processing Command (MEPS). I spent the whole day talking to doctors and undergoing physical exercises to make sure there weren't any visible signs that I was unfit to move forward. My group had to strip down to bra and underwear and do the duck walk, fall to our knees, and perform other fun and exciting exercises. One bewildering moment was the discovery that two females didn't bring proper underwear. Perhaps they had a g-string on, but the problem identified itself when the doctor informed us white granny panties were mandatory for his examination of our fitness.

In the year prior, I prepared, did reading and research, so I possessed tons of white underwear and socks, tidily rolled in Ziploc bags. I offered the girls each a pair. They ended up being in my unit. One of them cried in her bunk the night after our first day surviving screaming drill sergeants.

Transportation to the unit was in a packed cattle truck like sardines with no handles or rails to hold on to. If lucky, I snagged a seat on tiny wooden benches lining the walls or grabbed a handrail before another private did. As soon as I stepped off the cattle truck, a drill sergeant pounced, screaming half a foot away from my face. I followed instructions and ran inside, pursuing the bodies ahead of me, where an impossible task to accomplish was assigned, and when failing, my whole unit was "smoked." Getting smoked was the act of engaging in strenuous physical activities like pushups, flutter kicks, bear crawls, crab walks, until certain that death loomed but a breath away.

One female decided to change her mind and wanted to quit. Another threatened to kill herself. Her mattress was pulled off her bunk and ended up dragged every night to the door where night guards watched her sleep until the drill sergeants decided the private wouldn't hurt herself. We all rotated through a night guard shift.

On the first day, for showers, we all stood naked and walked in a line with two female drill sergeants yelling, "Hurry up, private! You ain't got all day. Move it, move it, move it! You're done! Get out!" With only a minute per person, no one got very clean that evening.

Many physical and emotional tests were demanded of each person, and for whatever reason, I maintained a high level of motivation and stayed positive for the nine weeks of boot camp. I stayed focused and did whatever I was told to get through it. I met good friends and almost everyone was younger than me. One was a 5'10" tall, nineteen-year-old who could beat a lot of the males, was strong as a horse, solid as hell in all ways, and ended up my Battle Buddy.

I got a toothache once and went to sick-call, where a person performed a sensitivity test on my tooth, and because I passed his test, he sent me back to my unit, distraught. The soldier behind the front desk told me to keep coming back until they did something about it. I went back the next day and thankfully, a doctor saw my x-ray and comforted me by saying, "Well, I've been doing this for about thirty years, and in my opinion, it looks like you need a root canal." I don't know what that other guy did, but I felt vindicated.

One time, after we were in the field for five days, wearing our vest plates, which add another six or eight pounds, I went to sick-call for severe back pain. Because I could bend over and move my body back and forth, the doctor decided he had a malingerer on his hands. He said, "In my day, females couldn't join the military. You wanted to join, now you need to be a good girl, go back to your unit, and suck it up. You're okay. You might have a little pain, but that's normal. You deal with it."

I got a prescription for the classic military cure-all 800 mg of Ibuprofen. They handed the pills out like candy. Thankfully, that incident occurred at the end of basic training and my back got much-needed rest. It wasn't the only time I experienced misogyny in the military.

I went into a small concrete room with a squad that served as a gas chamber. We had protective (gas) masks on and were ordered to remove them when asked a question from the drill sergeant. Questions like, "Where were you born?" or "What's your birthday?" Then, we could put the mask back on. Somehow, I managed to get through this trial with no trouble. I didn't breathe in deep and only shallowly. Some people came out of that room with ropes of snot hanging from their noses, coughing and crying.

Another time, though, I was in the field and a drill sergeant set off a gas grenade right near me and I suffered a full dose directly in the face. Everyone took off and I left my weapon behind. Yeah, I did that. Thankfully, another person grabbed it and returned it to me outside. Another screw up happened when I left my mask in the port-a-potty and a drill sergeant found it. He tried to throw it up a tree and luckily, it fell. He made me low-crawl around for a while until I received permission to retrieve it, properly humiliated.

The last thing I did during basic training was a 9K ruck march. It was about forty degrees that day and raining. Afterward, I went to a range with barbed wire and had to low-crawl my way across a field with live rounds going off over my head while patriotic music blared over loudspeakers. I crawled my way through slush and made it. Mud covered me and cold temperatures made it worse. A ceremony at the end made me an official soldier. The dining facility (DFAC) served steak and shrimp with blueberry cheesecake the next day.

I began school training as a 74D (seventy-four delta) which meant a Chemical Operations Specialist. One very cool thing I got to do was experience a live nerve agent chamber. I removed my clothing, including bra and underwear, and put on disposable clothes that were burned later. I spent half an hour or longer making sure I had a proper seal on my mask. The drill sergeants made a huge deal out of preparation and threatened to use the NAAK (Nerve Agent Antidote Kit).

"Now privates, if you take your mask off or don't have a proper seal, we will use this on you." They explained how to administer it. It's an autoinjector you place over the outer thigh and slap down on, causing the needle with the antidote to jab through clothing and activate.

I entered a room with a Humvee and netting, boxes, etc. that resembled a military setting. Two people entered, looking like something out of a horror movie with huge syringes full of nerve agent and super-duper imposing rubber vinyl aprons on. They walked in like mad scientists ready to experiment and then squirted the agent on the hood of the Humvee. I used my equipment to decontaminate it. When I left each room, I dipped my rubber boots in a cold bleach shallow water tub. After going through a few rooms like that, I removed my clothes, fed them into a shoot, took a shower, and left. I had a perfect seal on my mask and thought it one of the all-time best things I did in the military.

I didn't stand out during basic training. I tried to blend in. But somehow, I ended up the last person appointed Platoon Sergeant before graduation. Many people got appointed. Some would get fired the same day, some lasted a couple days, a week. I ended up with a drill sergeant coin and got selected to participate in more training after occupational specialty classes for the M93A1P1 Fox NBC (Nuclear, Biological, and Chemical) Reconnaissance Vehicle. The vehicle is self-contained with air-conditioning, and I learned how to take soil, water, and plant samples and how to identify and mark areas of contamination.

When deployed in Kuwait in 2006, my platoon had CROWS training (Common Remotely Operated Weapon Station). An installed screen in the front displayed a camera that swiveled on a mount on top of the vehicle and a joystick controlled the trigger on an M2 (.50 caliber) machine gun. The mighty weapon was a heavy two-person carry and got incredibly hot after firing.

The temperature read one hundred and thirty seven degrees and we were firing the monster in the desert for training purposes. So hot, I could hardly move, even the water in the bottles was hot. Sometimes, in camp, our Platoon Sergeant would score ice for our cooler and I would get cold water and Gatorade. The little pleasures in life were appreciated. The training that day ended up being cut short due to the hellish heat.

Being deployed was boring, although I am a thousand percent okay with not being deployed to Iraq or Afghanistan. Compared to those deployments, Kuwait was a breeze. But because there wasn't as much of a threat, I got downtime. There was a small food court that had pirated movies and TV shows the Kuwaitis would sell. Yes, I bought them unapologetically. I was not a hospital show person, but I watched *Grey's Anatomy* and loved it. I also happily discovered *Supernatural, Lost, Desperate Housewives, Nip/Tuck, 24*, and others.

The bathrooms outside the post, on Kuwait property, had no doors, and I had to squat over the low toilets to urinate. There was a hose you could wash your ass off with. No toilet paper, no hand soap, no paper towels to dry hands off, but there was a sink. There were no females around but US soldiers.

On post, the bathrooms had curtains, but were separated from the showers. What really sucked was getting ready for a shower and then having to use the bathroom suddenly. There was a communal undressing/changing area and the showers were always hot because it was hot everywhere. Sometimes I just wanted a cold shower, but never got one.

I never imagined becoming a soldier. I view it now as an act of courage, bravery, and selflessness. I have a track record of trying new things successfully. I confess this because if I could do it, anyone could. I am an unremarkable person who has done a few remarkable things. I am truthfully not much different than anyone else.

Becoming A Mom

The Valentine's Day weekend of 2008, I got pregnant from a one-night stand. It wasn't an ideal situation obviously, but the experience provoked a reevaluation of my life choices. I made the decision to learn to respect myself more because I deserved it.

A couple of my female friends were pregnant at the same time. One morning, while walking during physical training (PT), a General came up to us and said, "You recently got back from deployment, didn't you? That's what a lot of females do, get knocked up so they can get out of the rest of their time. You have an obligation to stay in a physical condition ready to go to war. I don't approve of females doing this." We were flabbergasted. We informed our chain of command and the incident was brushed under the rug. He was untouchable.

I was thirty-five years old when I had my baby by C-section on October thirty-first. I've always thought the word *surreal* was pretentious, but the experience was truly surreal. I got to the Army hospital at about eight a.m. They would not give me anything to drink, even ice chips. The operation didn't start until three-thirty p.m. They had me on an IV and insisted I couldn't get dehydrated, but I still snuck into the bathroom and scooped water in my hand and drank it from the faucet a few times. I know when I need water.

I got a catheter, which I didn't feel at all, so they must have numbed me by then. I got a spinal and had zero feeling in my body from the stomach down. It was bizarre. The first thing I tried to do was move my legs, and, obviously, I couldn't. They had me restrained on a table with my arms out like Christ on the cross. A huge blue blanket was raised in front of me, hiding everything that happened below my chest. All that, plus an oxygen mask, and a moment arose where I thought a panic attack would possess me.

I talked myself down. A medical student with the doctor performed the operation. My Dad snapped a photograph of my newborn held up by the doctor, blood and all. The actual operation lasted only about six minutes.

I tried to breastfeed my tiny human. I ended up with mastitis. The midwife told me that women who have C-sections automatically have reduced chances of success since natural birth takes hours, which sends messages to the body to kick start the milk-making machine.

About a week after the operation, I found myself crying with my baby sobbing in my arms, and I finally said, enough is enough. I didn't want her balling every time I tried to feed her. My Mom bought me a breast pump. Then, I began to heat wet kitchen towels in the microwave every twenty minutes and massaged my breasts, which were painful. I would get about an ounce of breastmilk each time. So, I supplemented breastmilk with formula until I had to report back for Army duty six weeks later. I tried.

My darling descendant woke up every two hours, drank a couple ounces of food, threw up most of it, and got her diaper changed. I held her for about twenty minutes, and then she fell asleep again, only to repeat the process. I imagined a stilted, bedheaded walk to the loony bin in my near future.

You're told to "sleep when the baby sleeps," and I did that. But two hours at a time was torture. I thought to myself, *what have I done?* Of course, the feeling passed, and she began sleeping four hours at a time, then six, then eight.

Sometimes I stared at her, amazed that she came from me. I felt clueless and didn't know anything about motherhood outside of reading material. Being a parent in the beginning was much harder than basic training. The mind, body, and soul was tested in ways I never imagined. I gained an infinite amount of respect for stay at home mothers.

I needed to work for a break and catch my breath. I don't think people should be shamed for this. A lot of mothers say, "It was so hard to go back to work after having little Thomas." I did not feel that way. I love my child to the moon and back, but I needed away-times. Especially as a single parent.

I did everything for her – change her diapers, clean up her vomit, comfort her when she was distressed, follow her around when she learned to walk and crawl so she wouldn't hurt herself, assemble her toys, make her laugh. I am proud of myself for being able to take care of her needs and protect her, all by myself.

I take credit where credit is due. My child flowed easily through milestone transitions. From crib to toddler bed, from bottle to sippy cup, she rode the wave of childhood gently. She never needed a pacifier, and I don't judge others for implementing them into the raising of a child.

I swaddled her and she slept peacefully. When I stopped, it was like coming off medication, decreasing the swaddled body parts by days instead of doses, with her arms out, and she would jerk in sleep, startle, then fall back asleep.

I never let her "cry it out." I would go and sit in the room with her until she fell asleep, listening to soft CD lullabies, or I would sing to her. My wonderful mother wrote a nursery rhyme that we still remember and can sing, nearly twelve years later.

> *Close your pretty eyes*
> *Go to Sleepy Town*
> *Night night, night night*

Short and sweet. My child rarely woke up crying. She was able to soothe herself back to sleep, if she did wake. We never did "time out" either. I tried it once, and we both looked at each other like *what is this?* and it was the first and last time.

My grand parenting strategy revealed itself to me: distract and redirect. I oriented myself to her. I didn't try to force the circle into the square. I tuned my gears to her, and that negated almost one hundred percent of any potential issues. She was never "wrong." When she climbed on the dishwasher, I would talk to her.

"Climbing on the dishwasher is dangerous. You don't have anything to hold on to and you could fall down and get hurt. Ouch! It would hurt and I don't want you to get hurt. So let's close it and…"

We would play or walk outside. I lived in a forest during the first two years of my offspring's life. Flowers, trees, water from the hose, birds, and dogs were daily companions when it wasn't too cold.

And when it snowed, on went the snowsuit and boots, and I would let her go and explore, following close behind.

Learning To Love Myself

When I was barely a teenager, I went home with a girl from church to hang out. We walked and talked around her neighborhood, filling up time with jokes and anecdotes. A man pulled over to us and stopped. With his window rolled down, he leaned over and said drunkenly, "Hi girls. I'm looking for a street called cherry. Do you girls know where Cherry Street is?" We both seemed to notice the flaccid penis hanging out of his pants at about the same time and ran off screaming, "Gross!"

I had my first real crush on a guy in the seventh grade, and he was nice. We talked on the phone and I knew his interest resided with my friend and not me. I gained weight during puberty. But he still put a sincere effort into friendly talk with the fat girl.

Ironically, a skinnier me ran into him years later as a server at The Olive Garden. I could tell he was interested, but he didn't ask for my number, and I was too afraid to make a move.

In high school, during auditions for *West Side Story*, I stumbled upon a conversation with a few drama kids I wasn't close with and overheard one girl say, "Shelly can't play Maria. She's too fat."

It was the first time I realized that fat girls couldn't be the ingénue. The roles I could hope to get would be limited because of my weight. A little bit of my spirit died that day, but I still practiced.

When I moved to New York City, I lost a lot of weight the first year. I got cute and started to get more male attention. I think men intimidated me and the idea of sex scared me. I fell in love with my gay roommate too, so that was problematic. Romance eludes me.

Living in Manhattan in the mid-nineties, this guy worked the deli counter of a gourmet grocery store I worked at, and he liked me. I had zero attraction to him, but he eye-sexed me every day, all day. He stared and looked. I felt extremely uncomfortable and it was gross and aggressive. The guy who worked next to him said, "Knock it off, she doesn't like you."

But he wouldn't knock it off. I finally told the owner, and he walked right up to the guy in front of me and yelled, "Leave her the f*ck alone or you're fired!"

After that, the guy treated me as if *I* had done something to *him*, like I wronged him or got him in trouble for no reason. I saw him on the street one day in passing and he gave me the meanest, dirtiest look.

I landed a secretarial job at a diamond manufacturing company and the old yo-yo weight monster reared its ugly head. I gained weight. I went from standing and hustling at the barista job to sitting at a desk for most of the day.

I visited a friend at the cafe later and the same owner came up to me and said, "You got fat."

I told him to get lost, only with many curse words. He grinned and walked away. I heard he passed from cancer and the store closed. The food was delicious.

I damaged my lovely body after gaining and losing weight several times. Now, stretch marks and flabby skin mark me like a brand. I turn away from mirrors if I can because I dislike my body. I avoid sleeveless shirts due to the stretch mark scars and my flappy arm wings.

In truth, it is another boon to reach my late forties and proclaim, "Healing has begun!" Healing of my mind and a correction of perception. Never lose hope. Acceptance of self is attainable.

For me, it is only recently that I started to untangle the weight from the depression. A correlation may once have existed, but no longer. I have a body worthy of taking up as much space as needed. I am as worthy of existing in whatever form I need to take as any person who lives in an "acceptable" body type.

At one point, because of depression, I loved my body so little that I didn't care if a poor diet or alcohol put me in an early grave. Depression lies. It went hand in hand for me – the food, the weight, the depression. Bad habits and self-destructive actions were acceptable options. Now I realize how perfectly God made me. Everyone can do and be better, but we are so much more okay than we think when it comes to our value as human beings.

I missed out on swimming with my child because I refused to wear a swimsuit. I stupidly worried about people seeing my body when the reality was the vast majority happily swam and splashed, oblivious. Don't make the mistakes I did. Put the damn bathing suit on and splash joyously with your friends and family!

I despise traveling by plane because I don't yet possess the financial capability to buy first class. When forced to fly, I always try to sit in the window or aisle. The definition of torture is a middle seat. I always try to make myself as small as possible and sit as still as I can so as not to disturb or touch anyone beside me, so they won't feel exposed to my fat. It can be painful.

I missed an opportunity to see the man from Alaska I had a crush on because of shame over my weight. He visited the state I now reside in, but I couldn't even speak to him on the phone. Don't do this, reader. I implore you to live and love yourself! It is a skill you can master before your forties, I assure you.

In American society, a woman's worth is often measured by her attractiveness, how tidy and well-behaved she is in public. There are people who are quick to judge a female if she does not shave or wear makeup or dress the way they think a female should dress. I have been judged for my tattoos before.

People are judged by how hot they are on a scale of one to ten. No one bats an eyelash if a male dates a younger female, but there are words to describe females who do it. Cougar. MILF. Movies are made exploiting older women's sexuality while a fifty year old man has a twenty-eight year old wife and not a word is spoken. But when a female does it, it must be because she has an overactive sexual appetite. It is wildly skewed - women should stay young and look young, while men become Silver Foxes and age gracefully.

An old roommate used ten thousand dollars of her school loan for a boob job and sat around with her mother dishing hatefully about celebrities. I once listened to them fat-shame Pierce Brosnan's wife, wondering why he married her. Maybe because he loved her and took his marriage vows seriously?

Some people cannot understand why Hugh Jackman is married to his wife. They cannot comprehend that not everyone wants plastic surgery and that true love lies on a spiritual level traveling through the skin and to the heart and soul.

Here is another example of the pervasive negativity surrounding the female body. A young woman from the Army, on Facebook, once shared a picture of a woman at Wendy's eating a burger and fries, and posted, "She does not need to be eating here. That is gross and so unhealthy." What business was it of hers what the woman ate? This kind of behavior is hateful and disturbing. There is no place for cruel people in my life. Be free to cut loose toxic people. I did and life is so much greater.

It became difficult and nonsensical for me to keep telling myself *I hate me and my body, but everyone else should love themselves!* I really do want people to know they are worthy of love and they are beautiful exactly the way they are. Part of my reawakening and maturing was the realization that I am worthy and deserve love. But I must respect myself before I can implore others to do the same.

I fantasize about a world where everyone is accepted for who they are. In recent times, I felt invisible. A middle-aged, overweight white woman doesn't get much attention. I say that I would make an excellent spy because no one would notice me. Invisibility is my superpower. I'm working on changing that misperception. I have a self-deprecating sense of humor I use as a shield.

It is no secret that "women of a certain age" can be viewed in a negative light. With a shift of perception and a step into a new paradigm, I now know that I can still be whoever I want to be and no one can tell me I am worth less than a younger or prettier woman.

Society seeks to divide us. But we all have gifts and knowledge to share. As the years progress, we move into different phases, and it's vital we share what we know and lift other women up. This is one of my missions. Not competition or envy, but being truly happy when other females succeed. It's not a negative reflection on ourselves or a loss to congratulate a sister for succeeding. We can all succeed and we all have a place in the world to triumph and prosper. And if we don't see an opportunity, create one!

REKINDLING LIFE

During Thanksgiving week of 2010, I drove to a new state with my Dad and two year old child in a blizzard to begin my new life. I drove my 2004 Honda Civic Hybrid while my father sat behind the wheel of a U-Haul. At one point there was a complete white-out and my dad blared the horn because I almost drove off the road.

I accepted a great job offer, and, through providence, happened to see an ad in the local paper for a rental house and moved in. The house was small and old with the washer in the kitchen and the dryer in the tiny bathroom. There were fruit trees in the backyard – apple, peach, and pear.

I didn't think twice about making this decision, but now I am able to pat myself on the back for beginning this adventure by myself. It took bravery to live alone in a state with no family or friends. The closest relatives, my parents, lived twelve hours away. While ostensibly, I am tough on myself, I can say that in prior times, I successfully conquered challenging life events.

For now I have settled down. Raising my pubescent fledgling remains my top priority. The state I have lived in for ten years is unique. Grocery stores and gas stations recently started selling five percent beer. Before, it was the 3.2 percent kind. In the state-run stores, they don't sell any cold wine or beer, mixers, gum, or snacks. Beer is sold by the bottle. When dining at a restaurant, one must order food before one is served a drink. There are no half price specials, Happy Hour, or shooters, etc. You can't buy a lottery ticket here.

I am an introvert, but don't struggle talking to people when forced into social situations, yet finding friends and meeting people has been incredibly hard. I lead an unconventional life by my state's standards. There aren't as many single moms, and I never married (and therefore had a child out of wedlock). I stand out as different once people talk to me.

At a playground once, a youngster approached me playing with my child and said, "Women shouldn't have tattoos, that's what my daddy said." I responded, "You shouldn't talk to strangers. Where are your parents?" They were watching a baseball game. We ended up talking more, and I know he was repeating what his parents believed and probably needed a little attention. So I gave it to him while playing with my daughter.

I existed in survival mode for almost a decade. I cared for my sweet tot, paid bills, did errands, cleaned my home, and even went back to school to take nine accounting courses. My idea of self-care involved reading and drinking. I'm still working on good self-care ideas and implementing them.

I suffered from depression off and on for years. I devolved to a dangerous point and then was blessed by God with a life-saving experience that allowed me a new lease on life. I am here for a reason and have a purpose. I am happier now than ever before. A marvelous revelation I received in my mid-forties is the fact that I have half my life left! A different life, with different goals, likes, and dislikes, and able to begin a new career if I want! It was exhilarating to realize this fact.

There is more excitement in living my life than ever before. I still work on loving my body, but have no hate for it anymore. I am learning to love who I am, and my solid belief is that God created me perfectly. It's pointless to compare myself to others when we are all here on separate, valid journeys. I wish a well-traveled path for everyone that is paved with river stones collected in friendship, flowers planted in love, trees seeded for prosperity and health, and sun showers that bathe each human wanderer in the gift of self-love.

OPHELIA'S SONG

RENE URBANOVICH

"Poor Ophelia, divided from herself and her fair judgement"

— *(ACT 4 OF HAMLET)*

∽

I'm fifteen years old. I'm sitting in the waiting room, mesmerized by the myriad of black and white framed glossies hanging on the wall, one after the other. There's Bernadette Peters, Bette Midler, all smiles and scribbles, *Thank you to Doctor Von Leden*, followed by cursive signatures that no one could decipher were it not for their identifiable faces. These are famous singers, I think, and I, *unfamous*, am among them.

I've arrived.

When the receptionist calls me into the office for my diagnosis, there is no dread in me. There should be, but I'm so excited to be in Westwood, California, in a fancy high-rise building, following nurses, filling out papers and inhaling eucalyptus breathing treatments, that I'm somewhat detached from the awful diagnosis I'm about to receive. His desk is enormous in the middle of the room, and I sit across from him, alone, as he peers through tiny wiry eye-glasses at my chart. He wears a lightbulb on his forehead, his white hair sprouting in all directions from under the band around his head, same with his white goatee, unruly there upon his chin as he speaks the words that would change my life forever. Now, at fifty-six, when I look back, I am charmed by my former self's innocence— or is it just plain ignorance? Does it even matter?

"Tsk, tsk, tsk," he begins, shaking his head as though I'm a trashy teenage mom or some strung-out drug fiend. *Must be bad*, I think. *Shameful.*

"You have nodules on your vocal cords," he growls, with a heavy German accent, still shaking his head. Telling a singer she has nodules on her cords is akin to telling a runner she has bone disease or is missing a foot. But I don't receive that message; what I feel is a vetting. I go to the same doctor as Bernadette Peters. Nodules must mean I'm a real singer.

My drama teacher is the one who sent me here, to the famous voice doctor of the stars. Mr. Naschel, or just "Larry" to his favorite students, had called me aside during rehearsal and handed me a scrap of paper with his name and number. I wouldn't go so far as to say he'd been actually worried about me, but we were a week out from final dress and I'd been struggling to eke out any high notes for days on end. It was in his best interest as a director that the star of the show hit her mark.

That particular night at rehearsal I'd been perched on Sandy's fifteen-foot-high bedroom platform with the spotlight on me, where I'm supposed to sing "Goodbye to Sandra Dee," the climax of Act II, then reach up and pull out my pony tail, letting my hair loose to display my new wild side. But instead, with the microphone to my face, I sing "Good baah—-a——SHIT!" My voice had cracked so noticeably in front of all of my peers that I screamed an explicative that amplified throughout the 1400 seat auditorium. "SHIT!" a word I hadn't used since I'd joined the Evangelical Christian church six months before. "SHIT" because I'd surely be in trouble since cussing on campus— let alone on stage into a microphone— warrants some sort of reprimand or punishment. But all I got was that scrap of paper. Since I didn't have a driver's license yet, my best friend Janet, not my mother, drove me in her mom's yellow AMC Hornet a week later and we sang "Open my Eyes Lord," and "Why Should the Devil Have All the Good Music" bouncing in the front seats sans seatbelts the entire two hours through traffic.

Larry had begrudgingly cast me as Sandy, telling me he hadn't wanted to give me the role because I had too much attitude. My audition had been so stunning that he'd had no choice, he'd confessed, throwing my attitude out the window in order to produce the best show possible. Mr. Naschel had connections with Broadway performers which meant his friends, the two actors who played Jan and Kenickie, generously came to work with us on blocking, original choreography and acting chops. Some of the cast had even met the writer, Jim Jacobs, at his home recording studio to lay down tracks for the dance scene with Vince Fontane. No company had ever been granted the rights before Burroughs High School in Burbank, and for that, we became cocky. To think, we were in high school working with Broadway pros and acting like it was nothing to write home about. Larry, all five feet four inches of him, constantly yelled at us with this put-on, Saturday Night Live type screech: "People! There are people waiting in the wings!" as a sort of threat to do our best or we'd be replaced. Even I was not indispensable, the leading lady. Poor Larry, trying to reel in all that ego and contain all that brandish youth.

Little did I know that this would be my only claim to fame: playing the first Sandy in the first off-Broadway production in the history of Grease. *Of course* I had high hopes for Broadway since Grease was the Hamilton of its day. The 1978 blockbuster was the highest grossing musical movie of all time, setting the stage for a revival that would spread like wildfire across campuses and theatres all over the US. I was no newbie, myself, having been cast in a couple L.A. performances as a child, even landing a feature in *Carousel*. I took up ballet when I was eight, after crowds of people praised my God-given ability showcased as the sugar plum fairy in our elementary school's *Nutcracker*. I still have the photo of me—a sparkling beauty in my pink sequined tutu, red lipstick smile, with throngs of folks looking up at me in awe. I also had played Ermengarde in *Hello Dolly* at North Central Michigan College summer of 1980 with the world-renown Young Americans, which is where I'd screamed for nine-weeks in exchange for that same awe and connection with a live audience. When I belted out "Summer Nights" with the full company and full band in Grease, I'd reached the pinnacle of my career —I just didn't know it yet.

The capacity for childhood hope is limitless. For some, passion is as natural as sleeping and the faith required to fulfill a dream must outweigh the logistics, the execution of it. But who can know these truths as a teen, when having to borrow a friend's mom's car isn't seen as a setback, but a small victory? When taking a needle of cortisone to one's vocal cords 72 hours before opening night becomes normal protocol, and when the emotional ramifications won't rear their ugly heads until one's prefrontal cortex is fully developed at twenty-five (and by then there'll be babies to take care of) that is when reality will pierce the dream. A great awakening will begin, from innocence to knowledge, and maybe even wisdom, if one is lucky.

My parents wouldn't allow me to go under the knife, assuming I was still young and I'd be able to bounce back without a major medical procedure. The standard treatment for nodules, aka hard calluses, is to remove them through surgery, followed by six weeks of vocal rest. Instead, my high school choir granted me a $500 vocal scholarship so I could learn how to sing correctly. First, I had to be silent for ten days. Beyond that, I had to quit singing until new habits formed to replace the old ones. Being young and expressive didn't help me transform very quickly. I got accustomed to the intermittent hoarseness that often accompanied my tone, in fact, it defined me, and I was unabashedly proud that I never let my injury stop me. I became the resident expert on the voice due to my growing experiences in and out of the doctor's office. I didn't even bat an eye that I was known for the exact inverse of what I had dearly wanted to be known for. Everyone recognized me as the one with nodes, who destroyed her voice, who damned her career, and wasn't I the one with so much promise, who had landed every lead consistently, who sung the paint off the walls in the pop shows and at the Queen Mary with the Young Americans? A pity, the shining promise dampened so early on. What now?

I grew up in a chaotic household with lots of energy and an air of creativity. My mom wove our kitchen curtain herself, a mass of macramé, beaded and methodical in its patterned allowance of sunshine—day in and day out. As a child, it never occurred to me that not all homes in the seventies donned such crafty, handmade decor. Not to mention, not all dads personally laid their kitchen tile, countertop and flooring. The germinating, multi-colored sea-monkeys on the countertop were just one concrete actualization of this creative influence. They slept amid the stench in bottles and jars, like immobile pop-rocks or decorative mosaic chips until one day, they would suddenly burst into energy-tadpoles and dart around the discolored water. They were alive, wildly soaring across their mini-universe for all to see.

My mom kept jars of turpentine on the brown-tiled countertop full of upside down paintbrushes left to soak. Bald Mr. Christy, my mom's art school classmate with the twinkling blue eyes, would often set up his easel in our celery green living room so he could practice drawing live models. The charcoal made her look sterner than in real life, but we four children accepted these technical flaws and said nothing other than how beautiful the renditions were. This was our mother after all. Sometimes my brothers ransacked the kitchen as she posed. Most of the time the house was upside down anyway, resembling the paintbrushes.

We painted, we wrote poetry, we sketched, we sculpted, we sang, and we dreamed. The lumpy foam sculptures, the easels, the potter's wheel, the kiln, the drywall tape, the smell of perm solution, the electric wood saw, the whirr of the sewing machine—these were all accepted normalities in our house. Clean dishes were a novelty and having company only meant clearing the costumes off the couches so we could offer a place to sit down.

This was all I knew.

This upbringing gave me the hunger to create, the

confidence to audition and to act. To try and to succeed. All of my siblings adopted art in some form: I became a singer/songwriter, my brother Nick grew up to be a professional artist and published author. My sister Tina, a photographer, a chef and a gardener; my brother Tony builds robots for theme parks and studios. The creative voice oozed from each of us in ways that need not be sung. Like my mom always said, breathing and being creative are synonymous.

The year I lost my voice was also the year I found the Lord. Not an intentional swap, nor visible, but one I can trace now and make great sense of. The Jesus movement of the 1980s was too much to ignore. All of my friends were attending Bible study and church camp, and I fell in step out of a hunger for the divine and a need to belong. With my theatre opportunities diminishing, my need for community grew. Suddenly, attending church services, reading the Bible, enmeshing with others who shared the same love for God took the place of collaborating with artistic sorts and devoting myself to the arts. Since I was an overachiever, I was absolutely determined to fulfill the expectations of a godly woman until the day I died.

My love for God seemed to surpass my love of the arts, so much so, in fact, that I vowed never to sing another secular song as long as I lived. I was enthralled with the idea of eternal meaning in my songs, so I sang to glorify God with all my heart.

I remember my pseudo-Catholic Dad propped up on the couch one night, probably after a few rum and cokes, trying to talk some sense into me. He drew a picture of a pendulum with his finger in the air, pointing to a definitive line down the middle of this imaginary apparatus, depicting a center point.

"In the beginning," he explained with his big green

animated eyes and overly certain voice, "you may be over here, swinging far off to the right." I rolled my eyes, as most sixteen-year-olds will do when their parents attempt to set them straight. But I rolled my eyes mostly because being Catholic, I highly doubted he could possibly understand what it meant to have a relationship with God. After all, most religions were humans reaching out to God, but born-again Christianity was the opposite. It was God reaching down to us. My dad went on to push the invisible pendulum to the other side with his big burly Italian fingers. "Then when you're older," he claimed, "You'll swing this a-way, and a few years later, that-a-way, until one day," when his fingers stopped their frantic swaying in front of my face, "you'll end up right here!" landing smack in the middle of his air drawing. I knew he was wrong; I would *never* sing for my own glory, only God's, but I didn't argue. It would be easier to pray for him than argue. As was our playful parlay I said, "Go to bed, Dad!" and dismissed him.

An obese fitness coach.
A crippled gymnastics instructor.
A voiceless singing teacher.

The heinous irony might stop a student in their tracks. But at nineteen, I didn't see any big distance between mastery and inexpertness. I wanted to help others evade the pitfalls that no one had helped me avoid. After all, what were those vocal directors and acting coaches thinking when they watched me thrash my voice night after night in Michigan? Why didn't anyone step in to share proper voice hygiene with me? How could my colleagues fail to notice that my voice had all but disappeared, making it impossible to sing harmonies with me or hold a conversation that wasn't a whisper fest? I was determined to share my story with the world. I went to both high schools in my home town and gave seminars on the dangers of yelling and screaming. Carrying a VHS camera on my shoulder, I'd record students' performances and point out the strained notes on playback, reiterating how injurious the chest voice can be when a non-trained singer gets cast and all she wants to do is prove herself.

My shame became my badge. My journey to the center of the voice presented a damaged beginning, but using that damage to benefit others unexpectedly seemed a perfect side-gig. I'd still pursue my craft, but not without taking a handful of people with me, a little like Dorothy from the Wizard of Oz.

It is a well-known adage that those who can... *do* ...and those who can't...*teach*. This was too big a pill for me to swallow, because somewhere in my mind I still thought I'd be a singer. I took on private students in my mom's living room at the age of twenty and so it began. Once I got married and started raising babies, teaching was my job and singing was *just a dream*. Too busy with dirty diapers and sandboxes to tend to that dream, I forced myself to accept this fact, secretly holding out for the occasional Sheryl Crow or Sean Colvin story where thirty wasn't a dirty word—and where experience in the industry could, once in a great while, outdo youth. I honestly thought that I still had time. In the meantime, I worked on songwriting, sang at church, weddings and funerals and taught voice classes for studios and theatres around town.

∽

Raising a family delivers instant identity. With four kids, there is no time for soul-searching. Being a mother was a bit like playing a part—I knew my function. It was a fitting role for me, especially when I could sing them to sleep or break into song mid-bath like in a real scripted musical. "Sit Down, Sit Down, Sit Down, Sit Down" to my standing toddler in the tub (from *Guys and Dolls*) or "Goodnight my Someone" at bedtime (from *Music Man*). I didn't allow "Shit Richie, shit, shit Richie" from *Chorus Line* until the kids were teens, which is about when I confessed to them how I used to sing "Tits and Ass" from the same show at the dinner table just to make my grandma blush. At larger family functions, sometimes I'd perform "Cabaret," and everyone would assume I was faking tears for Miss Sally Bowles when I'd cry. "As for me, as for me, I made my mind up back in Chelsea..." but really, I was crying for my former self, because I somehow knew and agreed with the composers that life is a cabaret, my friend, and all we really have is the arts to keep us human. God, I missed theatre.

After securing babysitting for all four kids and clearing my classes for a week, my husband Jim and I flew to Denver to pump up our skills as we had committed to planting our own church. One of the break-out sessions had to do with writing, so I joined that particular class while Jim went off to learn how to script a funeral or something of that sort. I was excited to delve into a field I had left behind so long ago, this time with a Christian angle. The teacher, who was a pastor of a congregational church somewhere in the Midwest, actually admitted in front of everyone that after a long week of counseling and prepping sermons and caring for his flock, he loved nothing more than sitting down at the computer and writing. Not only did he write for the joy of it, but he wrote *mysteries*. My stomach dropped. I felt sick. I left. I couldn't imagine how a pastor could justify spending time and energy writing for entertainment, or pleasure, let alone pen something as frivolous as mysteries. My best friend, still Janet, pointed out: "Perhaps the irritation you feel toward this man reveals a deep wound in you. He should be allowed to write. You shouldn't judge him." She was right. This accidental leak of negative emotion revealed the danger of my too narrow system of beliefs and begged to be explored. Why was I so disgusted with this man, never having engaged in the slightest dialogue, never having read his work?

One Sunday afternoon soon thereafter, I met with Neal, our senior pastor. We sit in his office, sunlight bursting through blinds, across from one another, the enormous desk between us.

"I'm wilting," I cry. "Artistic people like me are wilting, and no one seems to care. What about us?" I can't quite put my finger on the reason I am wilting, but I know that I am. I feel so different from nearly everyone in my church family—like my personality is a liability and I must self-edit at all costs. Here I am, finally having mustered up the courage to ask a question —what about us? — and while Neal feels compassion for me, he offers no answers.

The years spent caring for my clan required a ton of energy, but I still managed to record a full album of original Christian tunes and perform at a few coffee shops. I'd fulfill my household duties, put the kids to bed and escape to the studio at night, returning as late as 2:00 AM. Whenever I'd lose my voice, which was all the time, I figured it was lack of sleep. Once, when I was scheduled to solo in church for all three services, Jim had invited our friends Geoff and Shawneen over for dinner the Saturday night before. I struggled all day trying to rest my voice: steaming, swallowing evening of primrose capsules, humming and hydrating. My neck muscles were so sore I couldn't spare a single word to our guests. I put Band-Aids across my mouth to keep myself from chiming in the conversation. What a hostess!

Sometimes, I would use a whiteboard to communicate, and on occasion, I'd just hold up a series of signs: Tacos for dinner, and Knock it off! and Be NICE! My throat felt like a vice, especially at night after using my voice all day in the studio, talking to the kids, yelling at the dog. My words were so full of rasp that talking on the telephone was inefficient. Lip reading was absolutely necessary. The strain was constant. But, sounding so tired all of the time held some sort of interest for the people around me. Perhaps it proved how hard I worked with their children during Sunday school. Maybe giving all I could during voice class at after-school enrichment showed parents that I'd stop at nothing, which was a sign of true dedication.

What added to my struggle though, is how my personality would suffer from my inability to speak. I had to practically holler to be heard over the scratchiness, but resting it felt even worse, as I couldn't participate in life. If I whispered, no one could hear me. If I hollered, I felt like a shrieky witch. The pressure was mismatched because it's not like I was angry. I couldn't muster a voice to communicate my feelings. My personality changed because of it and I felt as though I could never be my true self. Plus, it hurt.

My tongue, my jaw, my throat, even the back of my neck. If I could have figured out how to heal, I would have, instead of waiting twenty-four years for a solution. I just got used to it.

When I am about thirty-seven years old, my student, Kimberly, brings in the smash hit songbook *The Last Five Years* by composer Jason Robert Brown whom I hadn't yet heard of.

Kimberly sings line by line as I play piano and I literally feel my heart jump. No — leap! When she reaches the bridge, where her character, Kathy, breaks into stream of consciousness chatter while singing her audition song, I can't contain myself.

"I should have told them I was sick last week; They're gonna think this is the way I sing. Why is the pianist playing so loud? Should I sing louder? I'll sing louder. Maybe I should stop and start over? I'm gonna stop and start over... Why is that man staring at my resume? Don't stare at my resume. I made up half my resume. Look at me, stop looking at that, look at me! No, not at my shoes, don't look at my shoes, I hate these fucking shoes! Why did I pick these shoes? Why did I pick this song? Why did I pick this career? Why does this pianist hate me? Why am I working so hard, these are the people who cast Linda Blair in a musical Jesus Christ, I suck, I suck, I suck, I suuuuuuuuuuuuuck!"

"Oh Kim! Where did you find this amazing song?" I cry, tears glazing my face, giddy.

"On the internet," she answers. "I have lots of time to google new musicals, and this one is so clever. There's only two people in it and the wife tells her side of their marriage starting at the end, and the husband tells his side starting at the beginning. They meet together on stage at the same time only once, in the middle of their relationship."

"Brilliant! I exclaim. Oh, I know that it's brilliant in my bones. *It is brilliant*! Musical theatre will never be the same, and neither will I. And that is all it takes.

This session with Kimberly puts me right back in high school, in Young Americans, on the dusty stage, with footlights, hair-spray, pancake make-up and pin-drop anticipation, surrounded by people who shared my blood. Musical theatre is in my blood, it always has been. I now possess a new mantra for spilt milk: "I suck, I suck, I suck," and bubbling up inside of me, the passion of my youth begging me, entreating me—COME BACK. I can stay away no longer.

I have to sing.

I'm thirty-eight years old. I'm sitting in the doctor's office at Cedars Sinai, vocalizing into an apparatus that measures my intonation, surrounded by an ENT, a voice therapist, an intern and a nurse, all gathered around me to compare my laryngeal stroboscopy films with my ostensibly smooth singing voice.

"You have not one but two sets of nodules on your cords," Joanna Cazden, the therapist declares, "but apparently, your singing is not the problem." Her voice is calm as she delivers this travesty.

I turn to my friend and colleague, Gerald, (also a voice teacher) who I'd brought with me for moral support.

"Well, that's a relief," he says, half smiling.

"Which part?" I'm embarrassed now, wishing I hadn't invited him along. I try to hide it, but tears slip out anyway. "How did I get another set of nodules when I sing correctly?"

He touches my shoulder.

"That's what we'll be working on," Joanna reassures me then gives us a list of the many possible causes of voice dysfunction, among them acid reflux. The nurse and intern ask me what seems like one hundred questions about my health, my habits, my diet, my exercise, my medical history, even my sex life. It seems there's a mystery here that warrants everyone's attention and concern.

This would be the third time I'd have to be traumatized by this news. First at fifteen, then at thirty, and again at thirty-eight. The second time, Dr. Kemplar at USC had wanted me to wear some concoction around my neck and down my throat to measure my PH balance in my stomach acid, to test my esophageal sphincter. For three days! There would be fasting, which was a deterrent in and of itself (I'm Italian), and too many jaunts through traffic, warranting babysitters and costly co-pays. I'd never followed through with the process, blaming the logistics. I'd sworn to hunker down and rest my voice at the very least. I tried. I really had, but a few years later, here I sit in West Hollywood, so ashamed that I want to crawl under a rock even though the staff is genuinely impressed that Dr. Von Leden had treated me at fifteen, as he was co-founder of the strobe we used for my tests. At least I am not the only one confused as to why these recurring blisters persist so. Gerald and I leave, but before we get on the freeway, we gobble down some spicy Mexican food as a last hurrah since avoiding spicy foods has just been prescribed for my recovery.

My husband and I had just signed the lease for our new church building and one Saturday, several church friends joined us to paint the walls golden, hang the funky candelabras and run the wires for the PowerPoint projector. We had purchased a cordless mic headset so I could lead the congregation in worship songs, which I am testing out when Andrea, my newest friend, throws out a suggestion.

"We should use the church for our songwriter circle!" Andrea and I had recently been acquainted at the first songwriter meeting a few months prior, where fledgling artists could come together for inspiration, feedback and accountability. That night, when the meeting ended, we wandered out to the parking lot of Barnes and Noble and engaged in a chat, keys in hand, car doors ajar, moon overhead, that lasted for three hours. Immediately, I found a companion, a sister.

"Perfect idea!" I agree. "This space could double as a black box, or theatre." As we develop our church programs, we make sure to include community events such as songwriter circle, and parks and recs pre-school singing courses. Andrea and I work together on reclaiming our artistic footing after slaving away for years in our kitchens, and secretly, I really like the way she prays using the words, "Mother God" in front of everyone, even those who would eventually leave our church because of it.

I possess so many photos of my vocal cords I can practically fill a photo album. One summer, I'd carried two 8 X 10 color enlargements in the slip cover of my plastic notebook for a workshop in Virginia to use as teaching aids. One night after dinner and drinks, my fellow teachers and I had been pulled over by a cop for an illegal U-turn. I'd sat in the back seat, innocently resting my notebook on my lap; when the policeman shined his giant flashlight on me, fixating on those shiny, pink, round vocal cords, his eyes bulged out of their sockets. I'd felt I owed him an explanation since vocal cords look a hell of a lot like vaginas.

"No, they're not what you think!" I'd defended. "They're my vocal cords!"

It's usually a waste of effort to try and find any humor in defective vocal folds, but this joke found me. I'm not going to lie. I like the way they look —something in me is drawn to the similarities between my femininity and my art, but putting significance and meaning to this would take me some time, and cost me more tears than money.

"What the—?"

I had just shown Gerald the collage I'd made of my vocal cords. Using copies of my vocal cords, little white circles with small openings, I'd reproduced about ten of them and painted them different colors and rendered leaves and stems, making them look like flowers. To anyone who hasn't seen photos of this body part, it might look like a science fiction plant. The flowers are spread across a lush green field below a bright blue sky.

"Do you know what it is?"

"Are those vocal cords?"

"Yes! Mine! It's called "cultivating" 'cause I'm growing a field of vocal cords."

"I want a copy for my studio!"

"Okay," I say. I show him the other two collages constructed from the photos of my vocal folds. One is made to look like a road, a V opening to the unknown. The other, a face, using the opening for eyes, the V shape for the nose and the pink circular part for the mouth. The face is oddly haunting, searching. It's a bit off-putting. I can tell by his reaction.

"Since when do you paint?" he asks. I know he is just curious. Being from the south, he can't be rude if he tries.

"I'm in therapy with the lady from Cedars," I tell him. "I'm obsessed with healing. Painting seems to help me since you can't put words to all of this mess, you know, and how I got here."

"I should try it," he says, "but I'll stick to making drinks instead." He squeezes blood oranges into a martini glass and hands me another.

"Something has to go," Joanna says, handing me a cup of tea, sitting down next to me. After my stint of voice therapy at Cedars, when my hard-earned $5,000 ran out, I began driving thirty miles to Joanna's house in Burbank for voice lessons. Over the course of twenty years, I had studied under thirteen different voice teachers. The way I'd viewed it, all the lessons I had ever taken had served as research for my job, which is how I could rationalize the financial burden on the family as well as my multiplicitous lack of consistency. "It's not like a marriage!" I'd reasoned. Why would anyone stay with the same voice teacher for a decade or quarter century when they could play the field, so to speak? I justified my bouncing around saying I didn't need any more constraints on my life. Joanna thought about it differently—perhaps there might be another motive, an unconscious drive for my capriciousness.

"I want you to commit to coming six more weeks no matter what."

"I can try!"

"Well, let's see how we can make that happen, because it won't just happen."

"I'm down!" I enthusiastically comply. I want to heal,

to do what it takes, can't she see this? Does she not know how difficult it is for me to even get here? The sacrifices I've already made, the shuffling of children, the ding to my wallet, the stress of rubik's-cube scheduling?

"You can't add to your already full schedule," she continues, her calming voice coaxing me into some kind of accountability. "If you commit to coming for six more weeks, something has to give. What will you give up?"

Her house is nothing like the suburban tract houses in my neighborhood. Joanna's furniture is artsy, her garb goddess-like, loose and flowing. She has candles lit and hippie curtains separating the studio from the kitchen. I am disarmed by the sharp contrast between Cedars' sterile environment, where she'd exuded a clinical air, and her current warm and nurturing demeanor.

I rack my brain for something, anything, that I can give up—after all, basketball games, ballet classes, teaching hours, church services, shopping, meals and laundry barely leave time for brushing my teeth.

"I wish I knew," I whined.

She tries to brainstorm with me.

"What if you raise your rates? That way you can teach less and spare a few hours to tend to yourself, instead of everyone else."

"Instead?"

"In addition."

When I start to cry, which is nothing new, I ask her, "Are you a Christian?"

Without missing a beat, she nods, mentioning "Not your brand, but yes!"

I keep crying, which is sure to ruin our lesson. I always say there are only three things that can mess up a lesson: hiccups, laughing and crying.

But she knows better. She tells me, "Cry."

In fact, she lays me on a massage table face down and pulls my hands to dangle over the side. She targets the spot in my back from which point I am to breathe—deep, deeper, deeper, and as my tears pool up on the vinyl, she herself groans.

"Now you," she instructs, "Express."

She guides me as I wallow in my grief sounds, encouraging me to get to the bottom of my breath, to squeeze until I am empty. I feel primal and exposed to be grunting such unplanned, unfamiliar, and ungodly sounds. Here, on this collapsible table, in front of a non-congregant, the pastor's wife, the devoted mother, the dedicated teacher, all disintegrate and I am left with Rene. Me.

Joanna's hands press into my back, holding me steady.

"So much for singing," I say when all the snot is wiped up and I regain some composure. When she asks me to join her for a nine-week workshop in the mountains to work on this breathing-groaning technique, I go from crying to laughing. "You've got to be kidding!" In what universe would a mother-of-four who runs her own business and serves at church even consider a two-night workshop let alone forty-two overnights with a bunch of speech pathologists?

"She doesn't know me at all" I think, as I drive away.

But I am wrong.

"Well, you hit your high C!" Joanna exclaims from behind the grand piano in her Burbank cottage. "How long has it been?"

"I've lost track!" I say, stunned.

"I thought something might be wrong, Rene, but you just take a very long time to warm up."

"Yeah, months!"

We don't do a lot of singing during our sessions. In fact, the previous week, we had focused on breath, sprawling out on the floor like sorority sisters. Playing with the expanding ribcage and the rise and fall of the diaphragm, we'd created a bond, a new intimate exchange. Joanna noticed that whenever I spoke, I talked rapidly and forgot to breathe. Each time I would take a short, catch-breath, she consistently would call me out.

"All you have to do is pause and breathe more often," she had prescribed, "and deeper." She convinced me that I need a reserve of air in my lungs and reminded me to replenish that reservoir as often as possible. I agreed.

As was Joanna's style, she'd start with the physical and move to the metaphysical.

"The word for breath is RUAH, which also means spirit in Hebrew," she began.

I could accept this readily because it is found in the bible, not from Sanskrit or some wonky New Age territory.

"And there is enough breath for everyone in the whole world, right? We don't need to ration our personal supply."

This would impact me profoundly and later I'd proclaim how I'd love to get a tattoo of the word BREATH on my wrist to remind me to breathe, to remind me of the ample, available spirit of God. When she'd gently suggested that this reservoir might also be a well for my own spirit, my own filling, I'd only nodded my head. But, remarkably, slowly, I began correlating the power of God with the self.

A week later, I rush to get out the door, then I get gas, then I miss my offramp. I arrive late, but Joanna doesn't make a comment about it, as I'm certain I would, whether it be any one of my students--adult or child. Is she beyond the constructs of time, I wonder. Or maybe she doesn't take as many students as I do. I teach nearly every lead in town and I have a wait-list.

After a warm up and review from last week, Joanna shows me slides of damaged vocal cords then settles in beside me with a cup of herbal tea.

"The vocal cords need a certain amount of air in order to vibrate correctly. When the air supply is low, they compensate by creating their own tension. They squeeze closed using *muscle* to maintain the vibration instead of air. This pressure is detrimental to the instrument."

I stare at the pictures on the screen—the red-bruises of abuse making welts on the soft fabric of the vocal folds.

"Take that to the spiritual level," she whispers.

"When I stop breathing or don't allow myself the space to just be, then something in me compensates and creates tension. I'm in crisis all the time. If I can just learn to do less and pause more, I could stop this cycle."

"Right. Perhaps pushing through your life using oomph and working like a dog to meet the needs of everyone around you is detrimental to you."

"This is a crazy parallel! You can't make this shit up," I say—deliberately swearing to prove myself.

"I know, Rene. But there's even more."

She sits me down to watch a series of moving X-rays of the diaphragm. Seeing the inside of the human body in action is like magic to me—the lungs are always just imagined in my head, reproduced by graphics or frozen on the page of a textbook. These are real lungs expanding, deflating, inspiring, expiring, white and black, fuzzy and full of motion. The fact that someone willingly exposed himself to hours of radiation in order to further singers' understanding of the vocal instrument moves me to tears. We watched several times over, and while I had thought I already knew how to breathe, I hadn't been able to plumb the information to the depths.

"So, notice how we singers breathe," Joanna summarizes. "Up, down… both. The diaphragm goes up and the obliques go down. Up and down, up and down." She puts my palms together, one on top of the other, with my elbows out. "Push both hands, one up and one down. Feel that tension?"

"I do."

"So, if I tell you that the freedom of the tone and the ability to sustain that tone derives from this opposition, like right here in your hands, what could that mean in life?"

"That freedom can't be experienced without going through the opposition?"

"Right. Being free of manipulation can go a long way, Rene."

I cry all the way home, where I run to my journal and write it down before I forget. I am late for my eight-year-old's 2:00 pick up, but the world still turns.

My voice is gaining clarity as my mind gains clarity. We are making progress. Real progress. My strained head and neck begin to relax, little by little. Joanna gives me a cassette recording to work with at home.

"It may be a bit far out and woo-woo from a fundamental Christian's perspective," she cautions, "but I need to know what you think of it, I need your feedback."

I promise to do it, out of obedience and the need to be needed.

With my headset and Walkman tape player on, I follow each prompt in my bedroom with the door locked. Yoga-type music floods my senses and I hear her voice, her soothing sage-like voice, over the hum of strings and melodic waves.

"Walk into a room. See the walls on all four sides, six feet high, two feet apart, soft, white and cushion-like. Lay your hands upon the walls and feel their texture, their lenience, their give. These are your vocal cords. Imagine yourself caressing the entire wall, gently stroking them. Tell them you love them. Tell them thank you for all they have done for you. Tell them you recognize the damage you've caused by abandoning and abusing them. Tell them you're sorry."

"I'm sorry," I weep. "I'm so, so sorry," and something tells me that they forgive me, something tells me that they'll stop hurting from now on, something tells me that I am going to heal. All they ever needed was my love to set them free. So, I close my eyes and send imaginary green light upon the whole of them, offering peace and tranquility. I breathe and groan and I let go.

After producing a hundred shows for my students, I decided to turn my efforts on myself and put together my own show. We would have a musical director, a five-piece band, and professional first-call back-up vocalists, all performing ten of my original songs in a new genre: Jazz. Like the pastor at the conference had given himself permission to write, I would devise my own means to sing, enlisting our little church building as the venue, in spite of certain Christian brothers and sisters calling it self-glorifying. Charging only $30 per ticket for gourmet appetizers, drinks and a CD recording of the event, we would raise $3,000 to benefit Leukemia, which would help to give the efforts real purpose (after all, it would be a long time before I'd be ready to sing for the sake of singing).

"You'll need to stop drinking wine for three months," Joanna tells me when I share my objectives with her at our lesson. "Keep hydrated and rest your voice."

"I can do that!" I agree.

When I come back a week later with excuses and doubt, Joanna lays me back on that table, to groan again, yes, but also to introduce me to something known as self-care—a word that hadn't yet permeated our culture on Instagram, Facebook, or Twitter.

"Since you're not ready to bolster yourself as a singer," she begins, adding the list of demands on me at the time—school assignments, parenting four children, dealing with a church, managing a marriage, teaching private students five days a week "—and with so many things tugging on you, it's no wonder—we have to call in extra forces."

Fortunately, I'm face down again, so she can't see my freaked-out response.

"Mmmm hmmmm." I wait.

"I want you to imagine a guardian angel."

"Okay," I agree. I can do that. It's not like some magical, occult crystal rock extra force. It's biblical.

"Your angel must have a face. Not like Michelangelo would paint, but a real face," she instructs. At first, it takes on the face of many people: Joanna, Janet, Andrea, my mom. Those who nurture my essence. Then I think of giving it the face of Rene as a sixteen-year-old. The one with unwavering faith in her self-worth and all the confidence in the world. The one who hadn't been crushed by the church, who hadn't yet succumbed to contorting to her boyfriend's whims or the tremendous pressures of motherhood. After musing on it for a bit, which Joanna encourages, I choose my brother Nick, the artist at Disney who understands my temperament and the struggles I face as a lone artist in a structured and stringent environment. He also has come from that free-spirited household with the scent of rubber cement and the feel of clay persistently under our fingernails. He had helped my mom make a mold of my face out of latex when I was sixteen, holding the straws up my nose. He'd been there for it all.

"Okay, I've got it."

"What does she look like?"

"Well, it's my brother Nick. He's an artist."

"Perfect." She is rubbing my shoulders and the back of my neck. She firmly places her palm on my right shoulder, making a warm and firm impression, saying, "This is where your angel lives. Anytime someone asks something of you, you've got to clear it with Nick. He will be the one to say yes, or no. He's got your back."

I thought it was pretty funky, but it does actually work. Late night coffee, favors for neighbors, a glass of wine, extra car-pool, desperate audition prep—Nick says no. He's always saying no. Nick protects Rene in her frenzy of helping others. My voice would be in tip-top shape at the time of the concert. According to Joanna's plan, no one in my circle ever blames Nick, and to my surprise, no one even pushes back at my new ability to refuse. To say no.

This freedom thing becomes addicting and I start to put myself on my own calendar. I go back to college and decide to study Creativity, which leads me into worldly psychology and secular philosophies apart from my religious background. Everywhere I turn, every book I crack seems to undergird my own personal experiences. From Shakespeare to Jung, across the sciences and the arts, some serendipitous force leads my discoveries, which I ultimately will share with the myriad of female students who seek me out, whose voices are also injured or lost, employing the same grace that Joanna has shared with me.

Still helping to run the fledgling church of about 100 people, leading worship, assisting with child care, cleaning toilets and running evening meditation service, I somehow manage to do my homework and feed my brain. It's a lot, but I am driven.

One day, at a routine church meeting, something clicked in me. My husband, Jim, and I are side by side, and he turns to me in shock when I raise my hand to challenge the motion made. While everyone at the table had raised a right hand "AYE," I sheepishly uplifted my arm for "NAY." The elders had been discussing a woman named Tina, disapproving of her relationship with a man whose divorce is not yet final. The same elder to motion her excommunication had just benefitted from Tina's gracious availability when last week she'd been called to babysit his five children for four days because of a crisis. Choosing to stick to their tenets of morality at all costs, legalistic regulations over love, they vote to excommunicate her.

Suddenly, I hear the elders talking like Charlie Brown characters and my body heats up with an unfamiliar fire. Out flows my desperation, bleeding…from beating…those bastions of impossible ideas…panicked, I erupt, from the depth of unconscious…screams, uncontrolled. My soul seems inside out… my essence out for all to see, to hear, as wailing emits a raw but decisive, unfamiliar me. Jim holds me, walks me to the car as I holler, thrash against ritual and tradition—fight against our once well-oiled machine of intactness and proper-ways-of-doing. He drives me to the pumpkin patch where my tears wane and I smell the autumn changes in the dirt, beneath mid-season trees—

half bare and half orange, with leaves falling all around me, I breathe.

Could it be that in studying Shakespeare's Ophelia, I realized my own disconnect with my life? For Ophelia, it was the court, and for me it was the church and the patterns in my marriage and family that could no longer be sustained. I become fixated on Hamlet's lover, utterly moved by her untimely death. Everyone knows it is Shakespeare who penned, "To thine own self be true." I wrestle with what this means for me.

Ophelia begins the play as an intuitive female with an ability to speak her inner voice. She's discounted by everyone around her, suppressed, and silenced. She is so busy validating others, trying to be the version they want her to be, even taking on their struggles, that she cracks. Ophelia goes crazy. Her dutiful, compliant nature causes this great disconnect. She drowns from constant disregard, the disregard from others, yes, but also her own neglect of her true self. Even the gravediggers discuss the "self-offense" she has made by allowing herself to be killed as the water rises to overcome her. Passive to the death.

I can't believe that this story is five-hundred years old, that I am not the first woman to suffer from a lack of boundaries. Through Ophelia, I realize how I, for so many years, had been slowly drowning and that it is up to me and me alone to reclaim my essence and find my voice. I recognize that my voicelessness is not brought on by the church alone. After all, Christ is quoted as saying "Love your neighbor as yourself." How had I missed this? It is a given that we love ourselves.

This would not be my one and only breakdown, but the first of many.

We have evolved to value women's voices more and more with each new generation. My opinions and expressions are far more pronounced than my grandmother's and my mother's; my two daughters have a stronger sense of self than I did. They are able to identify their truths and share those truths with fewer break-downs than their mother. My mom didn't have the luxury of a breakdown; she would have been locked up, as was customary for that era. Too many women were diagnosed as unstable and prescribed Valium or a minor tranquilizer, called Mother's Little Helpers, simply because they were unable to hide their emotion, their authentic selves. Overprescribing these psychopharmaceudicals was just one way of silencing women's voices.

Each generation of women must navigate the cultural milieu of the day; we are products of our culture. The additional enormous pressure of the rigid fundamentalist church may have protected me from many horrendous mistakes; the tradeoff for a tidy lifestyle was the stifling of any personal discoveries and the diminution of my development as an individual and artist.

I had to split from my composed, compliant and gracious self to scream my truth. I wish I had possessed the maturity to be appropriate with my opinions or complaints. I've come to realize that these psychic breaks served to open me up to my inner truth, bringing clarity to myself and to my students who still perpetuate the cycle . I'm fortunate that my family has given me a safe holding environment, fortunate that even my husband had the ego-strength to accept me at my worst, take my suggestions and criticisms, offer me the salve of apologies and even major transformation.

That same year, one of my students starred in a play at CalArts, the liberal college by my house. I solicited three women-friends to attend with me so it's more fun. My life as a voice teacher goes beyond piano drills inside the four walls of my home studio. Attending amateur show after amateur show can be draining, so I'm always hankering for company and ways to make it worth my efforts. This particular performance is in a small black box with raised seats on three sides of the stage below. The cast consists of all females and they tell a story that some of us are aghast to witness. *The Vagina Monologues*. It changes my life.

After howling with laughter and wailing with tears, the four of us end up at the Hyatt for appetizers and drinks, literally in a state of shock. Most of us are church-going innocents that had never given any attention to the labia, let alone female oppression. We could barely keep our heads above water with PTA meetings, shopping lists and cleaning the baseboards. My newest friend, Andrea, is the only one of us able to string a sentence together in an effort to make it relevant. The play opens with women talking about how much they love their vaginas and ends with a chorus of orgasms. Yes, orgasms. Everything lands as all good art intends—making us uncomfortable enough to question our deep assumptions about ourselves.

I take to reading books on the divine feminine with Andrea and further explore how vocal cords don't just resemble the vagina in photos, but also in function. Vocal cords are feminine. They are delicate, but strong. They have GIVE. They are an opening, like a vagina, an opening not to the physical realm but to the spiritual. The conscious and unconscious interplay is much like the man and the woman during intercourse. The vocal cords must be treated well or they won't perform well, much like the vaginal walls will reject or throb in pain when the channel is not tended to. Everywhere I search, even the bedroom, I find abstract and concrete truth regarding my intense vocal journey, a passage that leads me closer and closer to my authentic voice.

Somewhere along the way, in my self-designed academic coursework, my professor/mentor Shamms Mortier assigns me a book on physics. Furious that I am forced to study science—something out of my realm of understanding, I beg him to let me off the hook. "I've already fulfilled my science requirements! This is not fair!" (I clearly *am* learning how to speak up!) Following his intense reassurance, I pour over this book, *On Creativity*. And later, as he suspected I would, I gobble up anything I can by David Bohm, known as a spiritual physicist. This particular section from *Science, Order and Creativity* gave voice to what I had been grappling with, but I hadn't possessed the maturity or enough critical thinking skills to connect the dots.

"The principal difficulty with the religious approach, and indeed with any attempt to make a formal definition of the totality and of an individual's relationship with it, is that it tends very strongly to produce rigidly fixed ideas. These are very heavily emotionally charged, so that they prevent the free play of the mind, and thus bring about destructive false play and the blocking of creativity...To claim an absolute truth about the totality implies an absolute necessity and therefore disposes the mind NEVER to yield, no matter what evidence may be found to the contrary. In the face of such an attitude, a genuine dialogue is clearly impossible."

In digesting this, I realize that when a genuine dialogue is impossible, a person is then silenced, voiceless. Joanna's fancy footwork gingerly invited me into a dialogue wherein my voice could be recovered and heard. As with all confirmation bias, everywhere I turn, I notice folks adhering to dogma, not listening, diligent in their agendas. I keep quiet, but it is an intentional withholding, and one that doesn't last for long.

When my undergraduate coursework nears the finish, Joanna suggests the voice dysfunction track for speech pathologists at CSUN, a mere forty minutes from my house, which would earn me a Master of Science in Communicative Disorders. She even offers to help me get started in the field, hoping we could work together in future scenarios. But after studying Creativity for two years, pursuing my own voice, I chose to study literature and the humanities, knowing I long to explore writing more than I desire to be a better teacher. For my business, the science degree makes more sense, but I am already so successful it feels like it's time to follow my heart, not logic. I found myself earning a Humanities degree which fortifies and amps up my passion for all things art, philosophy, music and literature. Here, I found my voice in the artistic sense—without singing a note, immersing myself in the things that have always called to me. While scripture and doctrine can be one person's calling, mine is for mystery, for emotion, relationships and is rooted in the arts.

Looking back, it is painfully obvious that my inner voice had been the cause of my suffering, but it took Joanna's keen wisdom and sharp insight to delicately point that out. It took advocates like Andrea, Janet, Nick, Gerald and Jim. My injuries had been spiritual, manifesting in the physical. Joanna, like Glinda the good witch from the *Wizard of Oz*, tried to teach me this without puncturing my faith or challenging my love for God. She'd called me Dorothy, the wounded healer, because while I'd unabashedly shared my quest with others, advising and guiding with love and tolerance, I'd been too busy to turn my powers of love and tolerance on *myself*.

Ironically, I dissed the church around the same time that I rediscovered my voice. My husband and I closed up shop and spent a few years off the rails, out of the box, going to plays, traveling, partying and sifting through some pretty profound anger. The wise words of my Italian dad did come back to me once we'd settled back down in our marriage, co-raising a grandchild this time, the pendulum having swung back and forth, and resting smack dab in the middle. He'd predicted this so many years ago, but my youthful passions had clouded my view. As I age, I realize I'm not the only one whose childhood dream morphed into an unforeseen adulthood reality, which makes me feel less humiliation. In the studio, I try to infuse a bit of wisdom during our lessons so that my students' inner voices are part of their training. Asking them, "How did that feel?" or "What do you want to sing? It's **your** decision" preps them for independent choice and cues that they may not be encouraged to follow elsewhere.

I'm still working hard on tending to my inner voice. The old Rene wants to put a bow on my journey, throw in some redemption for a happy ending. But the new Rene sees the beauty in ambiguity now, much like poets see loveliness in fog, knowing the worth in accepting what is. Midlife and menopause have ushered me into the grand stage of reconciliation, and I've had to acknowledge that a large part of my journey was indeed silent and stifled, dormant and docile like the early phase of the sea monkeys on my mother's countertop. But one day, that burst of energy incited me, a living creation, and I darted around amid the murky water. Unlike poor Ophelia, I am able to keep my head above the troubled waters, and recognize the forces that, in the past, pulled me under are not life threatening. Every day, I can set out to create, to paint my life in full color, to live intently through metaphorical songs which reflect my deepest self and honor the eternal breath and spirit within. I have not been hoarse once in eighteen years, after suffering for twenty-four years prior. I use my voice from morning until night, nearly seven days a week. I squeal, I laugh, I holler, I whisper, I chat on the phone, I sing.

I sing.

LESSONS IN BEAR HUNTING

RHODA WEBER MACK

Here is what I learned later, when I went bear hunting: I was not as fearless as I imagined. I shrank from facing the bear. He was always more complex and more broken and paradoxically wiser than I could face. I did not open myself, but curled into a familiar, self-protective silence.

If I grew up silent, it was because I was a middle child on a farm in the foreign land of the Pennsylvania Lutheran countryside, isolated from my own Mennonite culture back in the homeland of Lancaster County. If I grew up silent, it was my stories published in the national church publications, the plays I wrote and directed in high school and indie summer stock that spoke for me. But the fields of home were bounded by the unknown, and I was curious. The late 60's were breaking all of us open in terrifying and exhilarating ways, and I was too naive to be afraid. That came later. The fascination with openings, with what lies beyond the known took me out of the safe fields of home, wide-eyed and open to the pollinations of the 60's. I went looking for the bear.

I met D at a friend's college-and-old-friends potluck

party, where, like the buffet itself, there were too many threads in the cultural currents to tie a houseful of unrelated guests into a cohesive gathering. But then, from across the room, one voice rose to tell stories of living among wolves in the exotic new science of ethology. and the room fell silent to listen. Later, as we all walked out into the meadow of stars, naturally pairing up, I found myself walking with the storyteller. He was football-shouldered but lean, with haunted eyes and a wide, sensitive mouth. From that night on, we were inseparable.

Because I had been raised inside the bounds of linearity, rigidity, and the unquestioned rightness of the strait and narrow, I was driven by a hungry curiosity, and in the sudden opening to all possibilities that the 60's expressed I was first wide-eyed, then unable to judge, then pulled under. D's family was a new culture to me, and I learned new words: Ashkenazic, holocaust, *ich bin Juden*, pogram, refugee. I learned to see Israel, not as the prophetic linchpin to the end-times, but as a refuge for the hunted. I was open, eager to welcome another world. I saw with new eyes the tortured Jew hung at the focus of worship in Christian churches, the horror of ritually drinking "blood". I absorbed it all, agnostic to everything new and all I had been taught. My own family welcomed the stranger among us with open arms, because paradoxically, against the grain of mainstream culture, if he wasn't one of our own *gemeinschaft*, at least D was Jewish. One of God's own.

D's family was wrapped in a slow motion time bomb, but I didn't understand the meaning of the wreckage. Who knew, back then, that WWII had shipped PTSD home with the survivors? Who could understand, in the full triumph of the mighty male businessman riding the roaring 50's, that D's father, who had survived D-Day at Normandy and all the horrors that followed, who came home to launch innovative industries, was a lit fuse? Who could understand that his cutting, hateful rage toward his eldest was breaking D's sensitive, compassionate and idealistic spirit? Who could understand—until D did later—that a WWII machine gunner who had seen all but six members of the First Infantry First Division mowed down could not allow himself to love his first-born son, because everyone he had loved had been lost?

In a dysfunctional family, one person is often designated to be the crazy one, both as the sacrificial scapegoat and paradoxically as the trickster/healer. D stepped up to both roles, taking the brunt of the rage and the devastating denigration. But I only understood all of this much later. What I knew was that a towering, legendary, decorated war hero was tearing out my beloved's heart. I began to understand the haunted look in D's eyes.

What I knew was that my foundational disposition for social and environmental justice clashed with the conservative Republicanism of D's father. What I knew was that the counterculture's all-embracing spaciousness of being was directly contradicted by the linear vector of competitive progress with which we were told we had to make a livelihood. I balanced unsteadily between competing narratives about what is true in the world. In my widening lens, where everyone had their own fierce, contradictory truth, I understood less and less how to form the sense of it into a singular vision. My tongue lodged in my throat and choked me. I no longer knew what I knew. I could no longer speak for myself. My voice became soft, barely audible. Sometimes my voice wandered off in mid-sentence and I lost the words that could complete the sentence. I wasn't sure what I had meant to say, or if by mid-sentence it was even true anymore.

I spoke instead with my hands in the fiber arts, resist

dying into the fabric my visions of a world too large for words: organic forms hovering over a trackless landscape, or the sea as a plowed landscape beyond the waveforms of the hilly shore. But I couldn't launch it into a livelihood.

Like Forrest Gump, D's timeline was woven through the movements and happenings of the '60's. He saw it as his time to step up into his father's footsteps, to repudiate the inaction of the WWII Jewish resistance, to act on his idealism. After a second or third whiskey he was primed to tell stories, and he did. In the early days, some stories were corroborated by people who had been there too. Later, when adult responsibilities had fully entrapped him, the stories took on an exaggerated edge as if, by being larger than himself, he could finally gain his father's love. It was hard sometimes to tell where the truth wandered off into hyperbole, but truth is fluid when you are trying to match a father's towering heroism. When our daughter found the parable of his life story in the movie *The Big Fish*, his reaction was—well, and wasn't the old man right about those unbelievable stories he told?

We flailed, trying to crack the riddle of right livelihood while a new consumer lust partied under the disco lights, and the hard swing of Reagan's orthodoxy was redefining the Right as right. D chose, improbably, the practicality of craft. Welding, to be specific. Railings for the suburban building explosion. Ironwork which became art, but that came later. I was the draftsperson, laying out the geometry of stairs on the garage work table, managing the backend office from the house, phoning customers while I hushed a child. D could lay a flawless weld bead in any condition, but his dyslexia couldn't sketch the design ideas in his mind's eye. I did the design work, and D's hungry neediness absorbed the credit. We were a team.

We were also poor, scrambling without weekends or

holidays to make enough to nearly pay the bills. I knew how to make the leftover London broil from a Sunday dinner with the in-laws flavor our meals for a week. At the family table, I slipped my share of protein to the others. I got skinny inside and out. I fed the bear.

I had no time anymore for the one thing that defined and sustained me. I no longer had time to write, and the need for the words to flow choked me. I scratched through notebooks and abandoned the novels that rotted as my mind outgrew them. My notebooks hunkered, unprocessed, in stacked shelves. Writing became an insubstantial fantasy escape and not something practical that could— what? put food on the table?

I dreamed one night of an eight-foot woman carved of black stone standing outside our bedroom window, nearly featureless but for the mouth which once had been a spring. A stone wedged deep in her mouth had stopped the flow of water. In the dream, I arranged for the statue to be moved for storage to the barn owned by Langston Hughes.

"What happens to a dream deferred? Does it dry up
Like a raisin in the sun? Or does it explode?"

That dream lodged itself deep as confirmation and secret sorrow. I recognized that I had come to stand in the lineage of women before me who had surrendered themselves and their dreams to the raw demands of necessity. I understood, at a new level, the dream my mother told us, one bitter morning, of running after my father as he drove away in our 1940's black Chevy, calling out "Mercy, mercy, mercy!" We replayed that scene on the stone slab sidewalk, with the designated "Mama" running after "Daddy" on the tricycle, flailing arms and calling for mercy. I wonder what my mother felt, watching from the kitchen as the cruel sum of her life played out in the laughter of her children.

Viola herself had been the youngest in a family of six, with an ambitious father who was battling his own demons of worthlessness as an orphan to become one of Pennsylvania's top potato growers. She remembered wagon rides to Philadelphia market with her Papa and a load of potatoes, then coming home with Chesapeake Bay oysters and other astonishments. A lithesome wisp of a girl, Viola had been picked out of the line-up at Saturday Night Young People's Meeting, ostensibly a godly church service to focus youthful energy, but essentially a dating app, by my then-handsome, meditative father from the stony red-dirt fields on the wrong side of the county.

He moved his bride into a broken-down wreck of a farm with sagging floors and no inside plumbing, the best his back-country father could afford for his eldest son. I wonder what she felt, watching her bridal Art Deco bedroom set from Philadelphia moved into the ragged house. I wonder what she felt when her four sisters-in-law whispered about her haughty wish for a refrigerator, when a springhouse was good enough for any wife. I wonder what she felt when her husband searched for a new farm for his young family, a farm fertile but small enough that he could devote his weekends to the Lord's work, how she felt when he found a once-grand stone farmhouse with the original log cabin, a whitewashed springhouse and a two-seater outhouse, a shockingly far hour away up north in the next county. I wonder what she felt as her body broke under the burden of bearing eight children, and doctors misdiagnosed her crumbling spine for a woman's hysteria. I remember, with the grief of hindsight, that I had little sympathy when she asked to be committed to the county insane asylum. My father bought her a country tonic of peach brandy, and she stayed with us, her thin mouth curled in secret bitterness that softened as they grew into love, and the updated farm showed its fertile potential. Later, finding her notebooks boxed in the attic, I read her schoolgirl ditties and understood that she had had her own dashed dreams.

D's mother, too, was a model of the crushed and suffering woman. She had been doubly abandoned, first by a mother who died in childbirth, and then a father who saw her as the cause of his wife's death, and who passed her off to unwelcoming relatives. She was anxious and fragile, cursed with an anxious intuition for looming catastrophes. Marriage promised safety for her. As he did with everything else, D's father took control of her choices and opinions, and she surrendered agency for the promise of security.

Because we lived nearly across the street, I saw how D was expected to continue the role he had played since early childhood, how she relied on D's steady presence and reassurances. To be the responsible one, without thanks or authority or respect. To be in charge as a child while his father worked unholy hours building a business. To be watchful for danger, to ease his mother's panics and to patiently reassure her. To consider everyone's needs but his own. But D was the archetypal helper. "If I had a magic wand, I would be waving it all day," he would say. All his life, like the good soldier, like the expendable grunt, D had stepped up, and now I too was a player in the family drama. But I had his back.

When we had nothing, I gifted him with Wallet Poems, slipping them into his thin wallet for Father's Day, for his Virgo birthday, or in a particularly hard time. Sometimes, that and a quiet hand on his back was all I had to give.

. . .

RHODA WEBER MACK

WALLET POEM III <Rattle of snare drums, up, coming to steady beat>

Hey, when
was the last time I
winked a note
into some corner
of your morning?

Hey when
did we start eating only leftovers?

Hey when
did the sheets start collecting all these crumbs?

When
were the future, ourselves,
and the snap of the passing moment untoothed
by the jaws of what must be?

Hard truth and a day's short pay
erode like a rip tide at
one's footing; habit and
the forgetting of dreams block
off the passages to anywhere
but where we stand.

So here we stand, marking
our limits, like rocks on the shoreline
eroded to bone.

Well here is
a small toss a
fling of change a

> *motion of surprise a*
> *hoot in the wind a*
> *nudge upcountry a*
> *shout of Who knows! a*
>
> *little Joy.*

And for the long year when everything seemed to break in our hands:

RAINY SEASON RIFF

> *Time was*
> *we ran like wind and water.*
> *Kids don't know. The kids they don't know.*
> *They're fearless. They go bear hunting.*
>
> *Time grinds its wear*
> *into the easy pathways.*
> *Time carves its name into canyons.*
> *Time silts the shadows.*
> *Time takes its course.*
>
> *She loves you, or she doesn't;*
> *it's all the same meatloaf.*
> *The wind picks up in the east;*
> *they say it'll rain steady till Friday.*
>
> *Time takes a weekend.*
> *The water is rising in the basement.*
> *The rain slants a sleek grey curtain*

> *across the window. And the truck won't start.*
> *He's wet and cold in the Carhartt,*
> *streaming mud and rain in the kitchen.*
>
> *The kids, what did they know? They went bear hunting.*

And another, when the way forward seemed to have no opening:

PROMISSORY NOTES <single drumbeat, sustained>

> *Later*
> *We'll slip into something comfortable.*
> *We'll kick off these combat boots.*
> *Later we'll ease these brittle bones*
> *into something warm, a healing bath,*
> *a night on the terrace*
> *up on Bully Hill.*
>
> *Well, I still remember where we're going.*
> *We've imagined it so hard I can almost see it there*
> *shining above the waves on the island*
> *where it's Sunday all week long (hmmmm mmmmm)*
> *with a little (be-bop de be bop)*
> *Saturday night(be-de-de bop)*
> *live edge.*
>
> *Oh and these boots. Yes*
> *they can keep on walking*
> *into later.*

D kept the poems in his wallet like found money until they were shredded, rendered unreadable by the salted body sweat that seeped through the leather.

We outgrew the garage and bought a large three-story 1890's barn, a former commercial creamery icehouse with history, charm, and squirrels in the 18" deep sawdust-insulated walls. We broke out of the narrow blue-collar world of ironwork as a fabrication skill, and built our reputation combining historical references with innovative techniques. We scrambled to stay above the flood of the new, cheap imports from China that mimicked hand-built work.

Like his father, D was an early adaptor, a lateral thinker whose mind leapt the divides of disciplines, from ironwork to art history, period style, harmonic proportion, and graphic design. I was gatekeeper and bookkeeper, corralling the wilder ideas and nurturing the good ones. We launched a craft school, and students flew in from around the country. From the second floor office, I could hear the ringing of ten hammers on ten anvils down in the back studio classroom, and the heartbeat thrum of the mighty power hammers. When the hammers rang in rhythm below me, I knew the class had found its beat. D moved among students and found the one with the broken heart, and he gently eased the pain as he worked one on one. He was almost happy then.

But mostly, D was hangry. It was all too much for him to hold together. The family motto of "Prepare for the worst" stopped before the second part "and hope for the best,", and it began to frame our lives. I bore his anxious rages; I stood between him and the world, as his mother had done for her husband. I fed the bear. The mood swings between hunkering despair and creative euphoria became wider, and I held the broken pieces of him together. I understood the psychic wounds, but he was too wily for the therapists I convinced him to see, turning on his charm to heal the healer. He convinced the doctor to sit on the examining table, while he asked, with a trickster's tease, his own medical questions. The doctor too, was charmed and missed the diagnosis.

One memory remains like the singular meme of our partnership: D is standing in the doorway to the back studio, looking in on the workshop in session, and I stand at the front door of the fab shop, reading his posture and his face across the hulking machines and work stations. The glance between us tells me that he is okay for now and what he will need next. A passing student registers that look between us, smiles reading the gesture of understanding between us, and in that moment I feel happy. To the outside world at least, we are the A team.

D self-medicated, and one of his medicines was playing the role of the trickster healer. He made phone calls to colleagues across the country, waving that magic wand, and man-to-man they opened their secret lives to his disarming humor and kindly attention. D was beloved, embraced in the brotherhood of men that stood fierce and fearless at the forge. They sought him out, pulling up a chair at his work-piled desk to pour out the anguish of the breaking marriage, the suicidal son, the deadbeat client, the scheming partner, the legal trap of a bad contract. He listened, he counseled, he pulled out resources and prescribed solutions with the astute strategies that could have healed his own broken childhood. At home, where he self-medicated, he released the raging bear.

But he didn't know how to release my voice when he needed all of me, and that broke him too. Coming from a culture of quietude, I was terrified of loud voices, anger, and hurtful honesty. My inheritance of pacifism mistook keeping the peace at all cost for the price of a killing silence. My own low threshold for conflict matched a partner who had none, and when at last I burst out in self-defense or counter-argument, it would be overblown for having been held in so long. We faced off, tense, oppositional, bound together in mutual frustration and desperate need. We were yin to yang, spinning in retrograde to one another's core. Sometimes we canceled one another's forward motion, and sometimes we doubled the other's trajectory in a slingshot of high energy. We both imagined escape, but there was no way to finance a second household, so we lived in the same house, in the same bed, living the motions of marriage with the heart gone dead. We were all we had, bound together irrevocably. I was learning the hard lessons of bear hunting.

AFTER THE CEREMONY: AVOWAL <triumphant processional as the couple leaves the altar, with horns and bugles, and the voice of the narrator is unheard in the calls of the well-wishers>

> *They say what won't consume kills you longer.*
> *Well, I am consumed all right.*
> *I'm consumed by this luv.*
> *It eats up my waking. Too early.*
> *It eats up the shape of the day,*
> *the mood of the morning,*
> *the possible present.*
> *It crouches over the roofline in a posture of hunger.*
> *It stalks the ghosts in the attic and pours out of*
> *   drawers*
> *where old projects are buried. It eats me alive.*

> *\<quicktime honky-tonk BUH-DAH BUH-DAH*
> *BUH-BUH-BUH\>*
> *I'll just be a minute. It will just*
> *take a minute swish*
> *the sink feed*
> *the cat send*
> *the message grub*
> *the garbage soak*
> *the shirts break*
> *the appointment.*
> *You can do it all on a run, or in slow motion.*
> *It doesn't matter. The dishes will always be in the*
> *sink.*
>
> *< BUH-DAH BUH-DAH BUH-DAH-DAH>*
> *When I have a couple of free minutes I think*
> *I'll go plant me some forget-me-nots.*

Love and memory: I was raised to think that faithfulness and staying the course are non-negotiable virtues, that there is always a way through, and it turned out that the way to the open air would have been to push back, yes, but also to open myself. I was afraid to do either one. I wrapped myself in a protective, careful silence.

If my throat was closed, it was because I did not trust my own judgment. Painfully, from a shuttered distance, I heard the sound of myself not being able to finish a sentence, speaking hesitantly, haltingly, breathily, forgetting in mid-sentence what my mind had sprung up to say. When a visiting artisan took me out for lunch, he told D afterwards that he did so because he was fascinated to hear my broken language.

Mercy! Mercy, mercy.

This was the mercy that found me: the closed women's group I had been wistfully watching from my lockdown of 24/7 workdays invited me to join, and I was astonished and grateful and terrified. These women saw me as the powerful woman from the metal arts studio. A hammer swinging woman. What did they know? I was welcomed to create a new history of myself from a nearly blank slate. But when I spoke, the words strangled in my throat. How could I speak? I didn't know what I thought or felt, and my identity was pressed like a dried flower in the files of contracts and emails and the architectural drawings I drafted.

But this group of women with powerful personal stories and a long shared history invited me in without judgement. They took turns bringing rituals, gifting one another with the places our hearts wanted to go, Month by month, unknowingly they steadied me, cupped the weak candle-flamelight of intuition against a windy world. I learned that I was allowed to laugh again, full-throated. And I wondered if D, the trickster, might have done some background nudging to arrange my invitation, knowing how desperately I needed a life outside of the studio that had trapped us both.

NIGHT MUSIC: WE TAKE DANCING LESSON
   <sweet slow violin, tremulous and haunting>

> *We were taking waltz lessons on the front lawn of*
>   *the farm,*
> *you, and my siblings and I, all of us*
> *shoeless in the dewed grass, learning the steps,*
> *under the night lights by the barn*

and it wasn't Vienna
and it wasn't moonlight,
but your hand was against the small of my back,
   gently guiding.

Our fingers laced in a gesture of mutual forgiveness
as we turned in a coupled tandem
in that field of our dreams.

But still our feet, yours and mine,
swing off-center,
too wide, misreading
now, stumbling, we sidestep
one another's intention.

NIGHT MUSIC PLAYS UP AND DOWN MAIN STREET
<Fugue, weeping fiddle, blues-harp>

For years when we went on vacation, she said,
Michael would sleep off the first three days.
On the fourth day, with two left and the clock
   running
I would begin hysterical crying because
I couldn't face going back.
<blues harp muted>
On the way home we would talk about
how it would all be different, this time.
And so it would be
for a week or so.

<Bagpipes, a Celtic dirge>
The day after Mr. Ames clipped the garden hose,

between coffee break and lunchtime,
to the car muffler,
in the garage behind his dry cleaning establishment
while he sat listening to talk radio,

yes, on the day after,
Hilda was in, extra early,
framed in the plate glass of the storefront.
All day she stood like a statue steaming shirts from the rack
while the traffic wound by like a stream of mourners,
down the block from our studio,
All day her hands worked from memory while she looked out to the street.
She didn't seem to see our furtive glances,
the quick takes at her face and the hose still dangling its obscene connection. Her hands were busy all day.
They had to be.
She was looking straight through us to what had killed him.

<Drumbeats, aggressive bass over 4/4>
You'd think if you were angry enough, things would change.
Things would be different
it can't go on like this
no more
no way
not on your life
you betcha
you got it?
don't get it?
well gotcha.

BOOM BOOM BOOMBOOM

No way.

<Blues fiddle, slow and sad>
You think what hurts you won't kill you. Not yet.
Not today.
You got time. Think it over. Maybe sometime. Just
not today.

<Black gravel-voiced woman singing>
Well, I got news for you brother.
Tomorrow's gone be too late.
Well, I got news for you sister.
Tomorrow's gone be too late.
If you think you can live through Monday
Gonna need another slice of wedding cake.

<Voice-over, the lecture hall>
The essence of blues music is tragedy. Life is ragged
and unendurably hard, yet in the utter heart of
darkness the human spirit shines undyingly
through.
Or the foibles of the heart test the limits of life's
resilience and love's capacity for compassion.
Or, the rushing impulse of the moment betrays the
unspoken intent of steadying love, and what
flashes is not what lies holding and unknown
below the surface.
Or, looking for the bottom line, we sink into a
miserable mire.
Or, life gives us a party and spits us out with the
garbage;
our hair matted in the grease and chicken bones

while everyone shouts and eats cake.
Or any way going, it's a fatal attraction,
and there are no winners. Look around you, honey;
there are no winners in this game of love.

Ay ay ay and we are so encumbered
that we cannot work with what is in our hands to be
    done.
This is the point where together we turn, turn, turn
    away,
alone together.
Slamming shut that door to my interior:

If YOU ever YOU always
Why don't YOU YOU never

Tossing the crooked stone at YOU from my own
    dark bag of rocks.
Tossing the crooked stone at YOU from my own
    dark bag of rocks.

<Heavy Metal Dissonance, elbows and forearms
    crashing on the keyboards>
Nightmare: the house is burning around your bed.
Can you, still dreaming,
rouse a sleeper's unmoving legs to safety?
Or you are falling,
and there are catch holds on the cliffside if you could
    just grab hold.
But your hands won't move or
even worse, they do
and your fingers shred themselves on the catch holds.
Or your body has become a corpse, with the flesh
    falling from your arms

*in great grey clumps, and if you could only
if you could move to prove that you are alive,
the flesh would firm and ripen to rosy life.*

*But how to awaken-- CRASH!
how to grab hold-- BASH!
how to stand up-- SMASH!
how to stir*

*<Black gravel voice wailing>
Well let me tell you sister,
tomorrow's gonna be too late.
I gone down to the kitchen,
there's no more slice of wedding cake.*

*ASHOKAN FAREWELL <fiddle low and
    melancholy>
Fact is, Michael thought they could still work it out
six months after she was living out of a suitcase in
    someone's beach house.
One morning he awoke late, to an oppressive heat;
the calls of the birds were silenced,
the white curtain barely fluttered
and then the mourning dove called low from the
    wires.*

*<Sweet riff, blues>
They say what doesn't kill you traps you longer?
Well, Hilda's still steaming shirts in the window on
    Main Street.
She's cleaned up the garage out back
and it's a storefront now
with a faded sign saying For Rent.
Michael and his wife are working it out.*

they've found a safe distance in their love;
she's at the beach house permanently
and he has the empty house home office all night
  long.
The blues all have a bittersweet edge;
you wake up in the morning and you're still here
somehow intact, more or less, to work it out.
The dishes are still in the sink.

<Jazz saxaphone riff>
I understand hanging on.
I understand there is this plot line between us,
this hungry necessity,
this living to be done.

Bring up the drums, bring up the alto sax, bring up
  the mandolin:
I got this rhythm going,
I've got this primal pulse pounding

<strong drumbeat, rocknrollnwailn guitar, bass
  beat>
WOOWOO
WHA WHA WHA WHA WHAM

Down in the growl and the wail I hear a sweet and
  terrible persistence.
I hear the black blood pounding deep in the
  heartland of sorrow.
<Jazz saxophone riff>
I understand the sweet in bitter.
I understand how the walking blues
carry your feet through four four, half-time,
the back-it-up beat of rhythm and blues,

the easy rhythm of mooooovin grooooovin
halftime party time cakewalk anytime
gonna keep you moving through the blues.

<She slides to the mic in a red dress.
She has bells on her ankles.
She has rings on her toes
and her hair hangs in long gray strands about her
    face.
She grasps the mic in both hands and she looks into
    your eyes.
Bring up the sweet dark sound of the clarinet,
    honey.
Bring up the high sweet sound of the clarinet.
Bring up the husky strong voice.>

Cause I'm gonna holler out!
Cause I'm gonna sing.
Gonna name my Avowal,
Gonna give that baby wing.

Break the violin on the altar of this sacrament.
Cause I'm going bear hunting (drum drum drum
    drum)
I'm going bear hunting (drum drum drum drum)
I'm not afraid.

Bear claw on the altar
blue forget-me-not on a white plate.

When at last D consented to see a doctor, the cancer had already spread. We went to Maine for a holiday on the ocean in a hiatus between treatments, and on our way to the Ogunquit Theatre to watch Buddy Holly die, we laced fingers with a simultaneous thought glancing like a flash of light between us. What we could choose, and all that we had, was to live in this moment.

As soon as D spoke the thought aloud, we both looked across Route 1, expecting the ocean to spread like infinity, sparkling beyond—and there it was, but between us and the sea was the long stretch of seaside cemetery. The crisp white lines of headstones: this was our moment.

"Whatever is happening," counseled one of my wise women friends, standing in our kitchen with her weathered face and the long grey braids that had her mistaken for a native elder, "take joy." It was audacious advice. It carried me like a hymn through the days that followed.

On the last full day of his life, I had driven D to another doctors appointment, and as we pulled into the parking lot, I noticed that he was wearing mismatched boots. I shouldn't have mentioned it, but I did. Too proud to go in mismatched, D reached down and unlaced them both to walk into the medical center in his white cotton socks. So I slipped off my own shoes too, and followed him in. Later, the photo of two pairs of empty shoes, D's mismatched boots beside my lime green mary janes, became our daughter's iconic shot of her parent's life together.

That afternoon, when hospice delivered the morphine patches and the ominous oxygen tanks, my eldest and I charted a desperate calendar of caregiving so that I could both be at home and keep the business alive. There was not enough of me to wrap around the neediness. I knew how his pride rejected the oxygen tanks, that the story he clung to was that—in a vague someday—he would ride a motorcycle to Newfoundland and oblivion. But there was the machinery of dying, wheezing now in the bedroom. In the dark D turned to me in the bed. "Help me," he said. And I could not. I was empty. In the morning he rose, showered, shaved, and lay back down in bed to ask me to help him dress. As I slipped the briefs up over his hips, he thrust an arm overhead, reaching, and took a last deep breath. It was June 6. D-day. He had breached the beachhead.

D had compiled a list of personal contacts, pages and pages of them, and when I called, nearly everyone said, "I'm coming." There was only one place to accommodate so many, the place where D's life had bled out: the studio. I called the party world owner who had always set up our tents for workshops and events, one of D's multitude of friends. I called him on short notice, in the season of graduations, weddings and Father's Day parties of early June, and he choked for a moment before he said, "Don't worry, I'll be there."

While the stakes for the double white party tent were getting hammered into the studio parking lot, supervised by the company owner himself, and I was busily curating the upstairs showroom in D's honor, one of our sometime-patrons, a difficult and moneyed mystic, drew me into the little design office saying, "I've only come for a few minutes. I know you have a lot to do right now, but I come with a message of love."

He had a story; he had just been to a small monthly gathering of fellow mystics with a healer-sensitive to whom I had once taken D, and through her D had sent me a message. "I was afraid of dying," our patron quoted, "but there was nothing to be afraid of. I have joined with a band of brothers, and we can do more here to help than I could have on the other side." It was absurd and unbelievable, but it was also uncannily true. It was what D would have

LESSONS IN BEAR HUNTING

said, the one whose phrase when he felt the pain of the world was: "If I had a magic wand, I would be waving it all day." And now, perhaps at last he was.

The morning of the funeral was a retelling of the movie *The Big Fish*. Volunteers took over directing traffic on the village streets to guide the streams of traffic. Someone had flown across the country with a hand bell that he had stayed up late to forge, and the bell passed along with the microphone as person after person rose to ring the bell and tell the story about how he himself, as D's confidential friend, had personally been the recipient of many attentive phone calls. After a while someone rose like a betrayed lover to reclaim the bell, saying, "And here, I thought I was the only one!" Laughter spread like a ripple in a collective shift of recognition.

Later, after the potluck feast, after time to roam D's showroom-museum, after the hand-written notes dropped into a slotted box, after the wide circle toasted with whiskey or apple juice as a blacksmith friend took the box outside and lit it afire in a hand-crank forge from D's collection of old tools, after they all turned to leave, I followed my heart's impulse and held a pot of violets, my mother's flower, over the smoky aroma of burning blacksmith coke and sage. I plucked the blue-black blossoms one by one and dropped them with an empty mind into the flame.

Bear claw on the altar
blue forget-me-not on a white plate.

At first, I dwelt in that sacred pause of death and loss and new beginnings. In the green gold of midsummer morning light, the curtains stirred in the upstairs windows open to the cabin woods as I met my day. Take joy, I remembered, and it was the steady hand on my shoulder as I drove the fifteen minutes to the studio, reminding myself to *Breathe, breathe. Be.*

Remembering, improbably, to smile.

Each morning of that long hot summer, as I unlocked the office door to duty and disaster, I murmured a mantra. *Keep me whole, keep me centered, keep me well.* It was all I could do. Then I would swing the door open, and the dossiers and contracts and half-written estimates would rise from yesterday's piled desk to swirl like a flock of angry birds around my battered brain.

> *Take joy then,*
> *because either way it is a hard haul to tomorrow.*
> *Take joy anyway*
> *because that may be all you have left,*
> *hard as the shell of a seed,*
> *and irrefutable as weather.*
> *Oh stinging wind, I place my face to yours*
> *and kiss you.*

I was on high alert, sometimes with a phone to each ear, adrenaline surging, calling on line two while listening to voice mail on line one. Punching a phone number into my calculator while I paid bills and moved money to cover them. But I felt a steady hand on my back, and when I quieted myself into the subtle rise of joy, I was empty, and I rang like a bell. I was learning that when there is nothing left to go on, emptiness opens to a gift. I began to hear the voice of my day, quiet but distinct, a simple nudge toward what is to be done, now.

Walking On
There were signs everywhere, pointing and subtle,
>*quietly waiting to be noticed or not:*

the way the leaves shivered on the trees as I thought
>*of something,*

the glance of the sun against a wall,
the lift of the snow into my shovel light light light,
the rock that pings against the windshield
and so breaks my lurching thought line,
the motions of small events, the files that are done
>*with me,*

and so have made themselves absent from the
>*desktop,*

the email that refuses to be sent, and as it turns out,
needs rethinking.

Everything speaks. Everything has a voice,
all all all in a faint steady hum or quiet ssss or
>*distant roar.*

It raises the skin on the back of my neck, trying to
>*listen.*

It shivers me.

Oh yes, and sometimes the Door
is just a door,
Sometimes the Curtain winks and says nothing.
But the red light is always the Red Light,
which, like the ringing bell,
chimes a pause in our intention.

Listen to this day, for in all its turpitude and
>*pain and*

reek of hell in so many small pinched places,
this day is alive, and speaks.

It was the voice that walked me through that first hard winter of biting minus 20-degree polar vortexes and deep icy snows, the winter of no jobs except the single project-from-hell, and the one broken, steadfast employee that I refused to lay off even though my funds were hemorrhaging. At home I cut the thermostat to 45 degrees and set the faucets to a slow drip. On weekends I chopped firewood and huddled over soup I had cooked without electricity on the wood stove. I eased the truck down the crooked icy driveway in 4WD and steered out of the snowbanks. I listened to silence for the subtle nudge, and trusted the voice.

Take JOY through clenched teeth 3 x day on an empty stomach.

I woke one morning hearing the words for an improbable craigslist ad, and I posted it. Just like that, the next owner flew in with his girlfriend, cocky with his new M.A. in Blacksmithing. I watched that blooming young woman, with her own jeweler's aesthetic, stand back silenced as he struggled to resolve a railing layout when both she and I saw the design solution. *Run while you can,* I thought. Later, just in time, she did.

For sale or for the taking: one life's work, plans, hopes, visions and ideas, all yours now, for the asking, for the scrap heap, for the making of something new, yours now, all yours, and I lay claim to none of it. Highest bidder takes all; that's how it goes. This was not the ad I placed, but it was the one that posted itself to my life as the young buyer discarded everything outside of his fresh grad school aesthetic. So began the slow task of dismantling everything we had taken a lifetime to build: the well-tooled old-school studio, the treasury of classical and innovative house jewelry samples, the historical record of architectural adornment. There was the auction, the giveaways, the freight-car-sized dumpster twice filled with the pyre of our personal history.

> *I. Monday Evening: On the First Day of Inventory*
> *And on the first day, light and then darkness.*
> *That is all.*
>
> *I had solo time in the fab shop to document,*
> *   annotate, photograph,*
> *just the big machines this time,*
> *and in the camera lens I find your tools, your*
> *triumphs of the hard-won find, your*
> *carefully purchased allies, your*
> *1930's Bridgeport, your*
> *vintage Clauser and Ellis. Your*
> *presence moves in and out of the camera lens,*
> *   turning*
> *the light blue and golden*
> *in the old overhead fluorescents:*
> *what you seized and held onto, and what seized you.*
>
> *On the first day of inventory,*
> *there was a little light.*
>
> *II. On Discarding the Objects of a Lifetime*
> *Here, take this sheaf of drawings for instance,*
> *thick with memory and tedium and triumph.*
> *Look, remember when we built this one,*
> *a jewel in someone's courtyard*
> *where the guests pass by with*
> *their cocktail glasses and their chatter and*
> *never notice the fine curl of stalk in iron, the crisp*
> *   line,*
> *how the design folds back onto itself as,*

breathlessly, the elemental iron unfurls.

*Now I drop these blueprints of concept and
    completion
with quiet blessing into the grandchildren's scrap
    paper drawer.
Look, see how you can make a
book out of these blueprints, how on the back side,
the blueprints form shadows of trees as gates
awaiting the lions and bears of your animal
    kingdoms.
The prints will end up crayon-scrawled and
    trampled and
I know that. I drop them anyway. Amen.*

I saw something then in the ashes. I saw how everything transmutes into something else. What was valuable became worthless, while the smallest objects shone with new importance. The studio show pieces whose iterations had sold so many projects were carted away to hide someone's oil tank, while the long desk that had held my burden of paperwork was reborn, gifted as a sewing business workspace for a young migrant. Curiously, the things I gave away made me the happiest as we stood together in a moment of mutual serendipity.

In cosmology, what comes from nothing is an explosion. From this something comes something more, newly begotten. Don't try to hold it; it will burn you. I know, because I have held onto the remnants, but old sweat and bitter work leaked through my fingers, and I was undone. The burning pyre of my yesterdays was a baptism by fire, a holy purge, a stripping to the bone, and I was newly, nearly free of myself.

Now, scanning the event horizon, I search for first principles. Hold steady in the eye of the hurricane, yes. Hold the center calm in the rumble and roar, where the tide rises, yes. And here comes the next wave. Here it comes, riding high and wide. And dangerous. Here it comes.

Ride it hard when you need to, yes. Hold your breath when you need to go under. Hold on to nothing but the sea itself. Be the still point, gathered and focused; be the wave, riding the crest and trough of the generous and merciless current.

Yesterday's yes shatters on the rocks. The dark is sentient but unknowable, and sometimes that is all I have. Whatever happens, take joy, the wise woman told me.

Take joy. Yes, and amen.

Something small and somehow perfect happens. The way opens to a largeness, and I slide through. Yes, and thank you. The way is immense beyond knowledge. And mysterious. It is all I can know as I gather my slender raft for the sea.

Now I am in retreat, not the retreat of defeat or backing away, but a retreat *into*—into myself and a centering quiet. My life gifts me with quiet spaces, rooms by the sea or in a college library, a spare bedroom, green parks with a table and a view. In unexpected places, my life gifts me now with labyrinths of stone or greenery or brick, and I walk the maze, circling forward and back but always, always toward the center. Weaving the circle, my being spreads wide in all directions, and Presence opens to the other, to you and myself merging into the great immeasurable. Take joy, yes and amen.

Standing at the center of the labyrinth, there are some things I know.

What I am most afraid of: Revealing myself.
Shattering the mirrors of deception to stand naked.

What satisfies me: Acting in freedom

What distracts me: The easy path

What destroys me: The winds of change challenging my direction

What I long for: Clear-hearted openness.

What takes me through the day: Habit, yes, but also the grace of subtle listening.

What I notice now: how sometimes the Great Coin spins on the non-edge of matter anti- matter, and will not settle down in my lifetime, or yours. And still I say, Yes.

Pruning my life, I find the full basket crate of old notebooks, where my heart fell silent at the gate of yes, and I open old files to the novel that has grown like Jack's sturdy beanstalk in my absence: how the story we tell ourselves makes us who we are. It's a novel for those of us who have lost the map to initiation into the Mystery. I edit it hard, and find the next one already pouring onto the page.

I am peeling back the layers of the heart now, excavating, opening, and finding the hidden layers. Retreating to center, I am learning that there is always another layer before the kernel. But I am braver now. I am less afraid of my own voice. I am learning how to be vulnerable, how to open my mouth trusting that the words will form, sometimes even sing. And when my words sing, it is not I that forms the note, but the bear rising at last, fiercely open. I am vast as the sea, and small as a seed, and I am no longer hunting the bear. I am the bear.

A JOURNEY THROUGH ETHIOPIA

D. MAGADA

Had I been told at the age of 20 that I would one day live in Ethiopia, I could have believed it. It reflected on my young girl's dream and ambition to discover the world. I was going to leave my small town, become a journalist, travel and make friends all over the world. Like the classical hero Ulysses, I was going to set on a long and intrepid voyage.

Had I been told at the age of 20 that I would one day live in Ethiopia with my husband and our five children, I would have had serious doubts. I never imagined myself the mother of a large family; at the time I pictured my future with two children, a girl and a boy in that order, like all the women in my maternal family lineage: my mother, my grand-mother and my great-grandmother. It was written that way in our family DNA, why question?

Had I been told at the age of 20 that I would one day give up my career to follow my husband to Ethiopia, I would have burst out laughing. That picture was so far away from my youth's aspirations that it was just not possible. I could not become that person. I was ambitious, driven, and above all independent. Never would I rely on anybody for my livelihood, especially not a man. I would earn my own living and be the master of my destiny.

But life has a way to make you do exactly what you swore you would never do, and that's what happened to me too. Two decades later, my young 20-year-old self, hidden somewhere inside me, saw something she couldn't recognize: a busy mother at the Ethiopian airlines counter at Rome Fiumicino airport, checking in to board the midnight flight to Addis Ababa, seemingly overwhelmed with her five children running around her and too much luggage to manage.

It was August 2011, and we were moving to Addis Ababa, capital of Ethiopia, mother of Africa and all Africans, ancient Kingdom of Abyssinia and land of the Queen of Sheba. My husband, proud father of our five children, was being posted there with the UN, and I had agreed to follow him in that venture. We were leaving behind the city of Rome, where our last two children were born. Rome had been the city of my youth's dream, the one place where I aspired to live after a first visit at the age of 20. By leaving Rome behind, I was leaving my own aspirations to make way for my husband's, but at the time of boarding the flight, on that warm summer night in Rome airport, I didn't know that. The call for adventure and novelty overrode all the rest.

"You know you won't be able to work," my husband, Stephen, had told me when his position got confirmed a few months previously. "The Ethiopian government doesn't allow it. No spouse employment for UN staff, it's the deal." I took the information in, not sure how it would affect me. I was accepting to follow him in his career to have more flexibility as a mother and writer. In my view, the many travelling opportunities associated with the move could provide an exciting substitute for a staff job. After all, I saw myself as a free spirit, not necessarily cut-out for the corporate world. I wanted an independent professional career but on my own terms. "I think I can live with that," I replied, thinking to myself that I would have to break the announcement to my mother.

"Where is Ethiopia exactly?... I can't picture it on a map precisely," my mother asked me with apprehension when I told her about our move. Anywhere outside France was already a big step for her, but moving to another continent, to Africa, was beyond her reach. We are in opposition to each other. Where she is settled, I long to escape. I open to the world at large, she thrives in the world she has created for herself, in the very street she never left. This inherent difference has been a source of tension ever since my adolescence. Whenever I want to go, she tries to hold me back. She is my mother, she doesn't need to do it verbally, her power over me is such that I feel her invisible hold trying to pull the reins back towards her. I gather my strength and keep going anyway, constantly living in some form of discreet opposition. It makes every departure hard. Fighting your own mother is like fighting a part of yourself. "Ethiopia is not that far away, only six hours from Rome by plane, we'll be back regularly," I said to her as words of reassurance. "We don't have the choice anyway, it's the mobility policy, we have to move." We may have been requested to move but I hid my own desire to travel behind a work obligation that made it acceptable to her. In our family ethos, work was the ultimate ruler, we had to do whatever was required to make it a success.

As I was discovering too with Wikipedia's help, Ethiopia is a vast country in the Horn of Africa with a population of over 100 million people and an area twice the size of France and four times Italy. It was an ancient civilization going back to Antiquity, and the only country in Africa (with Liberia) never to have been colonized by a Western power. When the Persian, Greek and Roman empires were thriving, Ethiopia was home to the powerful Axumite empire which extended beyond the Red Sea into modern Yemen. Even if it remained one of the poorest countries on earth ranking 174th out of 188 countries in the 2015 Human Development Index, it was rich of a millenary history, a unique culture, a distinctive cuisine, and as many World Heritage sites as in Egypt, and that for me was the main appeal. I was going to live in the land of the Queen of Sheba, how more enticing could that prospect be?

Once in Addis Ababa, my life as a great adventurer pushing her own limits stopped at our house's well-guarded gate. In our new configuration, Stephen was the one with the successful career, travelling all over the country, I was his back-office, in charge of all matters pertaining to our family and household. A clear Ulysses and Penelope division of roles. For him the exciting world outside, for me the tedious confines of the home. But we also had five destabilized children to support emotionally through our move, and I had to take responsibility for their well-being. Parachuted into an alien environment, we were asking a lot from them: to adapt to a new school and house, make new friends, to try and understand new cultural codes, be far away from their grand-parents and cousins, get used to different food, give up their favorite activity for new ones, etc. Like trees, they had been abruptly transplanted and needed to grow roots again to thrive. I still remember their first day of school and the look of awe on their face as we walked into the courtyard to search for the list of classes. That year, there was no excitement or speculation as to who their teacher and which friends would be in the same class. They knew no one. The list was pinned to the wall and kids were pushing in all directions to be first in line to see it. The kids who happened to be in the same class embraced each other with a scream of joy, the others expressed their disappointment at being separated from their friends, mine stood still at a distance, silently watching the scene but inside themselves, a cataclysm was happening. Stephen and I stood by them, full of the understanding that we had put them there and there was no way back. We had to support them through the emotional upheaval we had triggered. He was in a demanding job where his full attention was required, he couldn't do it. Hence, it fell on me and I took up all the duties related to our family and household. Without having planned it, I became a full-time mother.

Seen from Europe, I seemed to have an enviable domestic set-up: a team of staff which included two maids, a cook, our driver Solomon and three guards on a 24-hour shift. On paper, I could do what I wanted. The reality was otherwise. Instead of being a support system to help me cope without family and friends around, it required work. Our two maids, Alem, a mother of four, and Hiwot a young bride, expected me to give them instructions all day and closely check their work. That wasn't as straight forward, since I didn't speak a word of Amharic and they didn't speak English either. They had to perform many tasks no longer needed in Europe which I had listed with the help of our driver's translation services. That included handwashing clothes during the frequent power cuts, thoroughly cleaning the house because of the excessive amount of dust and dirt on our shoes, systematically washing fruit and vegetables with chlorine to avoid parasites, boiling fresh milk because of inconsistent pasteurizing, refilling the drinking water jars, in other words many time-consuming tasks that required labor. I quickly found out that my list system wasn't as effective as I thought it would be. They cleaned the house as I asked, however, they would use washing powder to mop the floor (resulting in a very sticky floor), they kept the same dirty water to clean upstairs (cleaning became pointless), they mixed up the detergents and used soap for our clothes, they didn't use the vacuum cleaner on carpets but swept them with a dirty brush (making them dustier), etc. In the morning, on my way back from school, I systematically found our house turned upside down with the furniture removed, the chairs on the table, the rug outside and Alem and Hiwot moving about in a busy fashion. Often, I didn't know where to put myself. Whenever I tried to sit at my desk, they interpreted it as me monitoring their work and interrupted me with mundane requests such as *Madam OMO*, when the washing powder was finished, or *Madam, 10 Birr*, when they had found a small banknote in my husband's trousers. To whatever I tried to explain with expressive hand gestures, they systematically replied *yes, Madam*, with a slight bow of the head, and kept on cleaning the way they had started. At the time it was pulling my nerves in all directions, so instead of returning home I would stay at the school cafeteria.

Alem and Hiwot had been placed by the estate agent who brokered our rental contract and had been there from the start, even before I arrived. Alem, the oldest of the two, was a soft-spoken lady who invariably wore a long dress covered with an apron and a headscarf, the customary maid's uniform in Addis. She took great pride in the success of her children. Her eldest son was a driver -an indication of social upgrade - while her eldest daughter was at university in the southern town of Jimma. Her two youngest were still at school and in the care of her mother while she was at work. For this reason, she came and finished early and was entrusted with the keys of the house. Her younger colleague Hiwot, in her mid-20s, stayed later. She was a more vivid personality who had the great ability to transform herself when she left our house at the end of the day. In the space of a few minutes, her work leggings, headscarf and trainers were replaced by a miniskirt, a tight top, high heels, bright red lipstick and perfectly done up hair. Most days, her husband, who was our landlord's private driver, drove by to pick her up. We also had a part-time cook, Alemnesh, who came in the afternoon only. She had worked for Ethiopian families before and knew mainly Ethiopian cuisine. As a result, I had to spend a great amount of time showing her how to cook European dishes. Unlike the cleaning duties, I willingly took care of that task. The food we ate was important, not only for its nutritional value, but for the connection it gave us to our country of origin. Dislocated as we were, we needed that comfort. Food is more than nutrient, it is a deep link to our culture and our childhood, and probably one of our first sensory experiences. It thus provides emotional as well as biological nourishment. When destabilized through an expatriation, it is our remaining link to the world we have lost. It is known that migrants give a disproportionate importance to their cuisine to exist in an alien and sometimes hostile environment. My own grand-mother only cooked Italian food (to my great pleasure), even after living in France for half a century. We did the same, dedicating an inflated budget to buy imported food and groceries just to be able to "feel at home." I showed Alemnesh how to make pizza dough (I had found a recipe online), how to prepare fresh pasta using the pasta machine we had been given as a gift, bake cakes and biscuits, make Irish bread (with pre-prepared imported flour) and cook vegetables only lightly not to lose their nutritional value.

I later understood that this situation was the result of centuries of a feudal system that was still somewhat ingrained in society. The people working at the lower steps of the social ladder were expected to show full obedience to their master. The master, or employer to use a more modern term, was seen as all powerful and they had to bow in front of such power. Showing initiative was going too far and even reprimanded. Ethiopia society no longer functions in this manner after 17 years of socialist government and 30 years of a parliamentary system; however, some remnants of the past are still present in social behaviors, particularly when it comes to domestic employment. I was unable to behave as a "mistress" or a "madam" as they called me, because I didn't have the built-in mechanism to do so coming from a more egalitarian social model inherited from the French revolution. The knowledge gap was also wider in Ethiopian society. People working as domestic staff were among the least educated in society. They often came from the countryside where they grew up in extremely rudimentary conditions. Often, they were hired very young and inexperienced, below the age of 16 in extreme cases. They had no washing machine or fridge at home, they didn't even have a bathroom; they were using a basic bar of soap to clean everything because it was the cheapest option. Trying to explain that one detergent should be used for the bathroom while another one was better for the kitchen was beyond their comprehension. We, in the Western World, are the product and the victims of consumerism. From an early age, we have been exposed to marketing and advertising to make us believe that we

A JOURNEY THROUGH ETHIOPIA

need five different detergents to clean a house: one for the bathroom, one for the kitchen, one for the dishes, one for the toilet, one for the windows, etc, and that stayed in our subconscious psyche. It made me reassess my own way of living. I stopped consuming an array of different merchandise and bought the basic disinfectant Detol, which we used for practically everything and was much easier to handle. I was learning too. I also realized that my great luck in life, especially as a woman, was to have been born in Europe in the last third of the 20th century, where we had access to free and universal education and were encouraged to socially raise ourselves. Had I been born in rural Ethiopia, my life would have been drastically different. We may think that we have free will, however, we do not choose where and when we are born. That partly dictates our path in life. Mine was one of freedom of choice in an open Europe where we could move from one country to another without a visa to expand our horizons. In a different time and place, the story may have been otherwise. However, with all the reasoning I could mentally construct, I struggled to accept that I had become a *de facto* housewife, mainly concerned with domestic matters. In our new circumstances, I was asked to manage a micro-enterprise at home while my husband was out there saving the world. That was not part of our initial agreement as a couple starting a family. The balance and sharing of roles in our marriage had tilted. I had become a *Madam*. The professional identity I had built for myself over the years, while trying to raise a family to the best of my ability, had vanished overnight on the Rome/Addis-Ababa flight. Where was the bold French girl who left her small town to move to the biggest city in Europe to make it into journalism, despite not knowing a single soul there? Where did she go? Had the traveler Ulysses become his wife, Penelope? That question became a source of inner conflict for me. Inside, the voice of my 20-year-old self would begin to torment me: *"Where is the great journalist of your youth? vanished, is that it? a non-achievement? Look at what you have become, a housewife, une femme au foyer, a Penelope, just following your husband in his career, how unimpressive...."* That voice undermined my self-confidence and in extreme moments, made me feel like a failure. When I was in a good mood, I could joke about it, saying that now that I had the staff, I needed a butler to manage them. Most of the time though, I would lock myself into our marital bedroom and cry my sorrow out. Even then, I couldn't cry in peace. Our chief maid, Alem, would knock at my door to put the ironed clothes back into the wardrobe before she left for the day. *Madam, clothes*, she would whisper. HELP! *Can someone get me out of there?!*

To make matters worse, I felt guilty because as a rich person I had no right to complain. I had all the material comfort many people in Ethiopia couldn't dream of; who was I to moan about my loss of career? "You have a rich woman's problem," a white male friend of mine once threw at my face when I later mentioned it. It was true, I was rich, much richer than I ever thought I was. Coming from a European middle class where most people could attain a minimum level of material comfort, I had always believed I was socially in the middle, comfortable but not rich. More so, with paternal grandparents who had been economic migrants, I did not come from the French ruling class. But now that I was confronted with the wilder world, especially Ethiopia, I was amongst the richest. I had been propelled overnight to a different social class with an army of staff under my command and yet, I didn't have the code of conduct to play that part. That triggered many conflicting emotions in me from annoyance at being thrown into that role to guilt because as a rich person, I should keep my mouth shut and enjoy what I had. But inside, I was suffering from the psychological and cultural trauma of a displaced person.

My husband became my natural outlet. After all, he was my spouse for good and for bad. We had come with his job, why should he enjoy it while I was so miserable? With him, I became even more vocal in my complaints.

-"All I do all day is managing our life, is that what your mobility policy means? You having a great job and me stuck at home doing the back-office stuff? Is that what it means? TELL ME!", I would shout, leaving him, speechless, to deal with his own guilt for having brought us there.

-"What do you want me to do? if it doesn't work out, we don't need to stay, I'll look for another job," he would reply, always trying hard to find a solution, to which I opposed a firm NO. The more I complained, the more he tried to find a practical solution and the more I rejected it.

No, I didn't have the energy to think about moving the whole family again. That was too much. In my despair, I contemplated the thought of moving back to France. I had left my country of birth more than 20 years before and never ever had envisaged moving back. This time, I felt so lost that I needed to return to the origin and reconnect with the person I was then, in the hope of regaining a sense of direction in life. "Actually, I want to go back to France, just myself, without you or the children, that's what I want," I would say. He knew I didn't mean it, I had too much of a mother's instinct to ever let my children down. It was just a half-hearted attempt to indulge in my suffering and draw attention to it. With the stress, I started suffering from panic attacks at night, something that never occurred to me before. I would usually wake up abruptly at around 4 a.m., my chest oppressed with a feeling of breathlessness I could only relieve by tiptoeing (not to wake him up) outside on our balcony. It was dislocation syndrome. My new life in Addis was suffocating me, I needed to gasp for oxygen and breathe fresh air. I stood there most nights, wrapped in a warm shawl listening to the monotonous chanting from the nearby St Gabriel's church, learning to distinguish the Christian orthodox prayer from any other incantation.

Amid our difficulties, I didn't want to admit to Stephen that I was the one who had wanted to go to Ethiopia. When I realized while still living in Rome, that there was no option but to surrender to the mobility policy if he was to continue in his UN career, I started researching potential destinations (I love looking at new places to go to). I don't remember when and how but out of the many possible destinations, Ethiopia came to my mind, as if she was calling me out. I started researching schools and cultural places to visit, and the more I read, the more I got interested. Subconsciously, I had pinned my map on Ethiopia. I communicated it in disguise while in transit in Addis Ababa's airport one day, when, not seeing more than the airport lounge, I texted him saying that I "wanted Addis." "What do you mean, you want Addis?!," he replied, not understanding my cryptic message. At the time, it wasn't even on the cards, but in an interesting twist of fate, it materialized. A year later, as Stephen was required to move, a position in Addis opened. He applied, he was the right person for the job, and the ball started rolling. As our move got confirmed, I was introduced to Rahel, a Franco-Ethiopian friend in Rome, who interpreted it as dictated by some universal spiritual power: "That's no accident, you will see, it's more than a professional move." A few weeks later at my parents in France, my father told me that in his childhood he had a dog called Menelik. I had never heard that story before, maybe it was another indication in disguise that I was destined to live in Ethiopia. Torn apart by many contradictions, I nevertheless felt compelled to stay. I had no choice anyway, I was stuck. My husband was now supporting our family, what did I have to offer as an alternative? Nothing, nowhere. It was all gone. I needed to have a plan and a direction and that is precisely what I lost: a sense of direction in life. Deep inside though, I knew there was more to Ethiopia than my superficial life there. On the other side of this tunnel, there would be a bright light, the guiding light of this ancient country, a country far richer than what I had first seen.

Whether I wanted it or not, in Addis I was part of the expat community, which was socially very active. Many social events which ranged from quiz or movie night to charity disco parties or sports tournaments, were hosted inside the school premises to bring families together at weekends. At the heart of it was the Parents Teachers Association (PTA), which constantly organized activities representative of the cultural diversity, including sushi making, belly-dancing the Bollywood way, modelling in a private fashion show, improving one's painting skills or becoming a full-time tennis player. On the first Wednesday of every month, the PTA organized a special coffee morning, during which one of the mothers (occasionally a father) cooked or baked a dish from her country of origin. It was a special event on the calendar for which parents dressed up. One month we could have an Indian breakfast, another month an English brunch, the following month Brazilian street food, etc. For the occasion, the cook demonstrated her recipes which could then be experimented back home by other expat mothers to the delight of their family. This gathering was also the best place to be kept informed on school gossip and drama taking place, such as extra-marital affairs, sometimes between parents and teachers, career frustrations on the part of the non-working spouse, separation and divorce, as well as less dramatic stories involving teenage romance inside the school. One lady couldn't bear to see her career deteriorating because of her expat situation and was talking about leaving Ethiopia and her husband altogether. Another lady was frustrated at seeing her husband enjoying too much his life of leisure and leaving the financial burden on her alone. As part of their defense mechanism, they were openly critical about their host country. The medical services were poor, the shopping opportunities nonexistent, the infrastructure inadequate, the road manners erratic, etc. Nothing was as good as home, but once at home, they would criticize it in reverse. It was too narrow-minded, too rigid, too organized and not open enough to other cultures. They had learnt to be misfits anywhere they went. Many of these spouses (they were still 90 percent women) had given up their career to follow their partner into unknown territory and had to combat boredom and loneliness as much as they could, given the restrictive circumstances. They were often better educated, had started with a similar if not higher salary, but somewhere along the way they had to give it up. It usually happened in their thirties when they had babies and realized that chasing two careers while raising a family was an almost impossible endeavor in the international or diplomatic service. Moving from posting to posting, they felt powerless and isolated in places where they had little opportunities, no long-term friendship, no extended family support, no social connections, no cultural references, and not even the language of the country. The comfort of the expat circle was all they could rely on to engage socially and overcome the frustration of not being able to work, unlike their working spouse whose office provided a diverse network of social connections and a sense of self-worth.

One Latin American mother named Karla, was an exception and was able to energize that community. She was passionate about Zumba and had recently become a certified teacher so she could teach fellow expats. "My father wanted me to be a journalist, I went to college, I took a good degree, but it wasn't for me, I much prefer to teach Zumba," she once told me over coffee. "*How could you not want to be a journalist? It is so interesting,*" I remember thinking to myself. She organised live zumba marathons for charity which gave her the opportunity to dance on stage and wear an impressive selection of her most extravagant zumba outfits. She was full of energy trying to get the crowd going and was her happiest doing so. We were close to being at a Shakira concert or the Rio Carnival, so festive these events were, and they lasted for a few hours, unstoppable as she was. For her, and that is probably why she was so positive about life, their family expatriation had been a golden opportunity to do exactly what she wanted and free herself from her father's expectations. She was an inspiration to other spouses, who didn't find their situation as upbeat and light-hearted. I was part of the latter group, the frustrated one. Inside myself, my 20-year-old self was making herself heard again: "*what the hell are you doing here? Is that what you are going to spend your life doing now? Yoga, zumba, and sushi making or belly-dancing?...........I know you're not the only one but is that what YOU want?*" I resented being stuck inside an expat bubble. I was here to discover Ethiopia, not to learn to make sushi, for that I would go to Japan. It made me feel socially diminished. In Addis, every aspect of my life depended on my spouse's organization, my right to stay, the amount of time we would stay, the papers I needed (ID, driving license, etc..), the lifestyle we needed to have (compulsory barbwire on the walls, as checked by a security officer). Outside of the expat circle, I no longer existed for myself. I had to fit into a new identity, that of a UN expat spouse and that identity felt tight, like a dress a size too small, I couldn't move at ease. "What brought you to Ethiopia?" was a regular question I had to face in our social outings. There was only one answer possible: it was "my husband's job." Many nascent conversations were quickly interrupted after I replied. If it was my husband's job with the UN, I could be of no use since I was "only" a spouse.

Relegated to my unwanted condition, I would fight back with a "but" and summarize my professional history to regain some form of social credentials. To my great disappointment, it wasn't of interest to anybody. Nothing was. Their reaction was like a mirror throwing back at me the image of the person I had become socially and which I didn't want to be in the first place. Their reaction came to confirm what I was telling myself: that I was no longer the great traveler, Ulysses, but his wife Penelope endlessly weaving at home until the return of her heroic husband. *You see you've become a spouse, a housewife, I'm not lying, they are telling you that too, no point fooling yourself,* claimed the voice inside me. I found courage in thinking about my own mother whose generation had greater limitations, and who, when confronted with her own life choice, fought for her independence and took over the family restaurant. She wasn't supposed to, in my grandfather's mind, she would get married to a respectable man while her brothers would inherit the restaurant. Not in her mind though, she married the man of her choice: an Italian immigrant and she worked hard in the family business. When the time came, she fought hard to be the one to take it over. Now that my time had come, I could not sit there and passively accept my new condition. I had to do something about it. *Mother, you are always there to give me a virtual kick in the butt.*

I am part of a generation of women who didn't think they needed to be feminists. We were led to believe that we had equal opportunities and up to a point we did. We went to college, we played mixed sports, we rode motorbikes, we went out as we wished, we had a liberated sexual life, in other words, we had a post-1970s freedom our mothers never enjoyed at the same age. Why be a feminist? It seemed like a fight from the past. The road ahead was open for us, we would have a successful career without giving up motherhood, thanks to our mothers and sisters who fought for our rights. Here, I want to pay my respect to the French figurehead, Simone Weil, who after a 24h acrimonious debate (she had to stomach many insults), succeeded in passing the abortion law in 1975, and instigated the family planning centers where as a teenager in France I could get free contraception without disclosing my identity. My generation never thought other hurdles would come later in life, when trying to combine a fulfilling career with raising a family, a hurdle that became unsurmountable when adding an expatriation.

I was now in that situation, full of the realization that I could not dedicate myself to a career and be present for my children, not even in the 21st century. One of the two had to give way. That wasn't only due to our expatriation, if anything the latter exposed a basic truth: that the established work structure doesn't allow a woman to serenely have both. She is asked to make an impossible choice. Extending maternity leave or providing more flexibility at work may help, but it is merely a way to mitigate . She still must make far reaching compromises to fit into a model that was not made for her. Despite parity at university, we still don't see many women at the top level in their mature years, they drop out of the race long before. Running a race with a baby in your arm and a toddler holding on to your dress, slows you down, you can no longer compete unless you shake your own children off your legs. Many mothers leave that track to find a gentler walking path, more compatible with motherhood, but they feel diminished on a professional level, and society is always there to remind them of that. No one ever questions a man's desire to have a career and a large family, on the contrary, he is seen as a fulfilled individual. When a woman does it, she wants too much. Why should we, women, be forced to choose between one or the other? Why does it have to be such a black and white configuration? As a result, most working mothers live in a constant state of guilt. Guilt for missing a child's music performance because of a meeting at work or guilt for missing an important meeting because a child is sick. Whatever they do, they are never forgiven by one or the other.

I deeply suffered being relegated to a spouse status, and that impacted on our marriage too. All was well when Stephen was in Addis, he was an involved father, he took our children to the Lycée in the morning, he played football or tennis with them and helped with their schoolwork, doing what many fathers do in their free time. On Sundays, we would usually have a family lunch in one of the many new restaurants. We had a regular rhythm to our life in Addis. However, that rhythm would collapse again when he was called on a mission within a 24-hour notice. When that happened, he had to drop everything, pack his bag, take his passport and jump on a plane and I was left on my own to deal with the rest. To be doing that on and off was emotionally exhausting, like constantly living in a stop and go motion. Go for him and stop for me. I resented it. His return after a few weeks was just as difficult. We had gotten used to living without him, he had to find his place again and fit into a family dynamic that had evolved without him. He did so through menial tasks such as interfering with the cooking or complaining that the house was too messy and getting the hoover out (I am the untidy one of the two) or telling the kids off for reasons I contested. To be doing that on and off was a strain on our relationship. As soon as we were together in the house, we argued or kept at each other's distance, as if the fact of being confined inside the same space was now pulling us apart. It wasn't always apparent, mainly because we had so much distraction with all the children around us, however, it would occur with the silliest things like looking for the remote control or forgetting to buy milk. In an unclear manner, I was using minor points (such as milk running out) to reject my spouse status.

I would say things like: *I DON'T KNOW where the remote control is, why do you ask me all the time, can't you find it yourself, are you blind or what?*

He would say: *why don't you ASK ask me to buy milk on my way back from work, instead of complaining that it's finished at 10pm when the shops are closed?*

I would reply: *and why do I have to be the one thinking about buying milk? Why can't you do it too? Are you too busy saving the world to think about your children's breakfast?*

Our arguments were always the same. They started with a minor discussion such as milk running out and ended up in a near explosion, where we each retrenched to our initial position to avoid a full clash.

I would say: *You don't understand my situation, you don't understand what it feels like being stuck here all the time.*

He would reply: *I don't know what to suggest anymore, I don't know what to say, you take everything so negatively.*

He felt powerless because of a move he was responsible for, and at the same time, he had difficulties dealing with the emotional shifts this situation triggered in me. *"Your emotions are overpowering, there's no longer any space for mine, I can't take it anymore,"* he would say when he had enough. From where I stood, he seemed rather emotionless to me. I couldn't grasp the fact that he was able to move from city to city without an emotional upheaval inside. He couldn't understand why I was so affected by my decision to give up my career, and why I couldn't just let go of it. I felt he didn't give me the kind of emotional support I needed to come to terms with it.

In the face of his exciting job, I was left with my interior monologue, mentally stuck in a dead-end loop. *I am just a support system to his job, he is Ulysses, I am Penelope. He goes out there and triumphantly saves the world and I am holding the fort to give him comfort on his return, his children well looked after, just like Penelope, patiently waiting for Ulysses' return....she was even rebutting suitors, poor Penelope, she couldn't have a sexual life either....*

But *I DON'T want to be Penelope, I wanted to be Ulysses too, I did everything to become Ulysses and I nearly succeeded…*

But I want to be with my children too, I want to raise them myself, I am the best person to do that, I can't delegate, no one will care for their needs as much as I do......

But I had a promising career, I was very good at it, I could have gone far, why did I give it up? It was the wrong decision, I should have thought about it more and now I am stuck in that domestic life in a place where I have no rights...Madam clothes, Madam clothes, Madam clothes, all day, help!...

But I couldn't have done my job without affecting my children, I would have had to get up and go at short notice whenever some news broke out just like him in his job....it was impossible for the two of us to do that...and now it's too late, I'm well past forty, people my age are established in their career... even here, if I were permitted to, I couldn't compete with younger reporters, they can jump out and cover stories, they don't have a family to think of...what do I want to run after? no point even trying, I should give-up the aspiration and enjoy my life as it is, as he says all the time, "why don't you enjoy what you have?"...and what can I say to that? I am in pain because I am living your life and not mine, and you can't even understand that....

Yes yes, I know, I am so blessed to have five children and that's why I keep my mouth shut, but inside I am boiling and in pain.... why do you suffer so much? he asks...Shut up! You have the job and the five children too, you take it as a given to have both, why should I bury part of myself, why should I silence myself?...I worked harder than you at college, I got better degrees, I fought for my career in a culture that wasn't mine, and now where did it take me? Your wife, I am nothing more than your wife, I should print business cards with "wife" as profession, "support system to a UN job" so no one would ask me anymore what took me to Ethiopia...crystal clear at first introduction..."just a spouse"... whereas you, you have gone beyond expectations, you've gone further than you thought, how? Do you ask yourself how? Doesn't it occur to you that what I gave up was transferred to you?...of course, you work hard, of course you make sacrifices for your family, I can see that...but I also see how thrilled you are when you get up and go for an emergency, not having to think one minute about how your household will be managed in your absence and who will look after your children...I see the expression on your face when suddenly you are wanted somewhere, you are needed, it is yours, you have to go...It is exciting, I know that, I have been there before, it makes you feel part of the world, it makes you feel at one with your own time, it gives you that sense of accomplishment, it is you, it is who you are, the identity you have built for yourself...and I, I have lost that.

Our situation was further exacerbated by the fact that

we came from two different cultures and languages. I was the fiery French extrovert; he was the accommodating Irish introvert. I tended to explode, he tended to implode. When faced with the kind of emotional rollercoaster I was going through, he simply froze, like water turning into ice. The more I expressed myself, the more he withdrew inside. Fire versus ice. His way of coping was to remove himself from the problem and stay on a single track at work, mine was to constantly repeat the same complaint because I felt I wasn't heard. We were at a dead end. We are opposite in character. I tend to be emotionally involved when dealing with a problem, replaying the script over and over in my head and feeling the weight of it. He takes a decision practically and gets on with it. He is factual, and as a person he is more comfortable dealing with facts rather than ideas. When a matter becomes too abstract, he loses his way. I am easily taken over by my imagination, in good and in bad. I need to control myself not to let my mind wander through dark thoughts of tragedy, illness or future war, and bring it back to the beauty of the day. He has his mind on the ground, I have mine in the air. Where do we meet? In Addis, I was groundless, I couldn't meet him on the ground anymore. The only place where we would still meet was in the bedroom, and that probably saved our marriage. To add to it, the UN environment was not the most conducive to marital success. The divorce rate among staff was notoriously high, turning divorce into the norm rather than marriage because of the exceptional pressure it put on couples. The work commitment was such that it was made for people with no emotional attachment, who had the freedom to come and go as they wished without affecting anyone. In the case of couples, there was necessarily a winner and a loser, simply because one of the two had to accept to be restricted for the other one to have a complete freedom of movement, or they had to accept to live apart with all the consequences it can have on a relationship and a family. In our couple, I felt I was the loser, the "victim sacrificed on the altar of his organization" as I told myself, but he wasn't the one to blame, it was the system. Unconsciously, Stephen and I were the products of an established model of society, a model that was constructed by men for men. We were stuck in the in-between. We never questioned the fact that we would share parenthood and work life, it was our understanding from the start, but the model we aspired to, particularly in our field, did not fit into the reality of the workplace. We found ourselves squeezed in the middle of a wider structural issue with one having to give up her personal aspirations for the other to be able to progress. Unable to respond well with our limited human emotions, we were left with the psychological suffering it triggered.

Our situation - common to many couples - was exacerbated by our expatriation. It was the story of an early 21st century couple trying to build a life together, considering social constructs, youth aspiration, education and the constraint of globalization, whereby the workplace is pushing couples further and further apart and atomizing families. I was hopelessly striving to be at once Ulysses and Penelope, and not succeeding very well because it was simply out of my control. I wanted to raise my children with the belief that life's potential and possibilities could be fulfilled, and I was the one deeply frustrated by the shuttering of opportunities. How could I become an example to them and not contradict with my own action what I was so passionately preaching to them? Be an independent mind and spirit.

Girls, don't listen to their promises and don't buy into their model, it's a lie, they will tell you that you can have it all, it's not true, not with their structure, you'll exhaust yourself for nothing....Worse, if you don't manage, they will put the blame on you for not succeeding, and you'll feel even more inadequate...Don't, you will find that it is just not possible, not in that model, it was made by men for men...Just relax and find your own path, and find a partner willing to walk that path with you, build a new model together, it is harder but the reward is commensurate for both of you... for the sake of your joint happiness...

ALCHEMY OF THE SOUL

LUCY JAMES

He is sitting beside me. Waiting. Waiting. Impatiently waiting. I know what is to happen next: it's the usual routine. I am staring out of the car window, stalling the inevitable. I fixate on the trees, imagining with all my might that when I turn around, he will be gone. A barn owl takes flight on liberated wings. Beautiful… But he is starting to lose his patience. I know it. His smell becomes more intense with every breath, an animal instinct as my body recoils. I cannot fight. I cannot flee. I can only freeze. He moves towards me. Every muscle in my body contracts upon itself. Soon he will be upon me. I know. Every sinew of my body aches with fear. Revulsion. Now I have been told. I must surrender. I heave at his touch. I know so well what is to come. He has me in his clutches now. I am barely an adult. He knows I hate him, and he resents me for that with deep anger. It is time. He is sweating. I can't breathe. Can't. Breathe. Drowning. Drowning in this sick pit of revulsion I feel for him. Now he is trying to claim what he says is rightfully his, persisting against my resistance. My skin is wet from his sweat. I will smell that for hours, even after I have scrubbed my skin raw in the shower, until the water burns and hurts me. There's nothing I can do now but lie here until it is over. The rough fabric of the car seat is scraping against my back. At least I have something else to focus on. I count down my spine, one vertebra at a time. I think I know which one it is that hurts, but I can check it tomorrow. Maybe I could look it up in a book... Inside my head, I am screaming at him to free me. My arms cry out to push him away. Far, far away from me. So that I can breathe. Breathe. Fly in liberation like that beautiful barn owl I saw. But my body is a dead-weight. I cannot move...cannot...move...

I am jolted awake, back to the present, animal-eyed with fear. That dream again! My heart is pounding so hard that I can almost see my pulse through the darkness. Fear has coiled itself round every muscle and I ache. Wrapping my arms around myself for comfort, I scan the room but the only thing surrounding me is stillness and the dark. I am alone. Yes, I am alone. Alone. As the aching in my body begins to soften and disperse, I comb my hair back with my fingernails and return my hand to my heart. I gain control of my breath. My skin is wet with sweat, but it is my sweat. Yes, I am sure. I lean across the bed to turn on the light, knocking my glass of water over as I do so. I jump at the sudden noise then curse as the water pools around my journal, soaking through the spine. I can see I am safe now. But somewhere along the way, some cruel mutation of time has twisted itself into a merciless spiral that is threatening to engulf me until I am almost completely consumed by memories. Until I almost have to remind myself how to inhale.

ALCHEMY OF THE SOUL

"Enough now", I say out loud. "Enough."

Twenty-four hours later, I watch as my latest lover rises from the bed, thirteen years my junior. I was just beginning to enjoy the closeness of human touch. Just beginning to sink into the glorious illusion of a circle complete. But the young man's sudden movement, his deliberate exit from my bed has broken the connection. I pull the covers a little higher to cover my nipples, leaving the swell of my breasts enticingly real. Through a mesh of tangled hair, I observe him dressing, his back to me. My lips part slightly, and I can taste the red wine that brought us here to my bed.

I watch with rehearsed confidence, perfected over years'-worth of practice. I take in the contours of his virile body, wondering who he really is now that the climax of passion has passed. For a few brief seconds, I watch him fumble irritably with his buttons. Eventually he curses and gives up, leaving his shirt misaligned. He can sort that later. He is ready to leave. He has enjoyed my body deeply and I his, but now it is time for him to go. My certainty and self-assurance were what lured him here in the first place and I hold on to them tightly.

I smile to myself, close my eyes and lie back luxuriously, watching him from the blissful comfort of white sheets and pillows. My hair is dishevelled, and I feel beautiful; an Aphrodite figure, the epitome of divine feminine watching my glorious lover leave, satisfied and wrapped in my spell. But this man, who less than an hour before was lost in the throes of ecstasy at the mercy of my touch, is now hurriedly zipping up his jeans and reaching for his coat. No time now; he will put it on as he makes his way down the stairs. He pauses to look at my body for a few seconds. He mutters something as he touches my shoulder almost imperceptibly, enough to convince me that he will be back another night, then he leaves. The door clicks shut, and his feet are audible against the wooden floor as he makes for the door, down the stairs and out into the night.

I rise from the bed alone. Drawing my fingers through my hair, I make my way to the bathroom, the coolness of midnight heightening my awareness of the room. All my senses are ignited, still feeling my breath and hearing my heartbeat deep inside my chest. I look to the mirror and am pleased by what I see. The hours of sex have tousled my hair into an enviable mane for a woman of my age, and my lips have a plumpness that wasn't there this morning. I turn on the taps to fill the bath and watch the water ripple and steam, just as I watched my young lover dressing for his return to reality minutes before. Bathing leaves me thoroughly satisfied and ready to welcome the type of sleep that only comes in the aftermath of physical bliss. The water picks up and jangles the candlelight into myriad diamond pieces on the surface of the water.

Once full, I watch the water slowly settle into a perfect mirror. A mirror of pure silence. The music I chose for the night came to an end long ago and all that is left is the soporific dripping of the tap, sending the water into tiny concentric circles from a point of liquid perfection. Seven droplets of jasmine oil land in the water and I watch them disperse and unite again on the surface. Gently I lower my hand to test the temperature and swirl the water around. There is something hypnotic about this ritual: the sound, the movement of light, the soothing warmth against the heightened sensitivity of my skin.

I step in and lower my body into the water, feeling every sensation as it wraps itself around me. The candlelight softens my body and reminds me of the way Vermeer painted his women. Ordinary women, plain girls made beautiful by the sweep of sunlight coming in through a dusty window, lighting a stray tendril of hair that crept from beneath the tightly bound cap that held their modesty and allure in place. That one tendril of hair could hold more mystery than the stars; it could take men by the hand and lead them through the dark streets of their mind into caverns of eroticism.

By candlelight, my figure could almost be that of my twenty-year-old self. The new softness has subsided into the light of the candles, and I feel glorious and real again. I close my eyes and surrender to the warmth. The young man has gone for tonight, and I am glad. I want to keep the illusion alive until the next time because waking up with reality would be more than either of us dared to acknowledge. In the night, the spell of illusion transforms my desires. In these moments, I can be whoever I want to be, for him and for myself.

It hasn't always been this way. But as the years slip by, more and more men are becoming intimately acquainted with my body, a portion of my mind, and very little of my soul. Beneath their surface impressions of me burns a flame of deepest violet and indigo that no other person in my world knows is there yet. It harbors an innate intuition, a deep spiritual wisdom, an abundance of creative gift, and an intrinsic connection to something higher than myself that even I do not yet fully understand but know is there.

When I am alone in nature, there is oneness, and when I view the world beyond my boundaries, I ache with the pain of its perfection. For as long as I can remember, even in childhood, I wanted to breathe the equilibrium of beauty and pain, darkness and light, masculine and feminine, where each embodies the other in perfect union. A sunset could ignite my soul with its embers and wrench pain from my heart for all its power and glory. I could weep at the sunrise, transformative in its purity, its dewy newness calling the birds to sing and the flowers to press their delicate, fresh bodies to the sun in an act of purest self-love. I would worship how the sun could be so different, so diverse with every moment. How the light could transform stories of the heart and set the birds free and unfold the flowers from their damp, earthy resting place when the time is right.

I recall that I never quite understood or knew the beauty of my eyes, the deliciousness of my smile, the naïve allure of my laughter and joy in my youth. Yet somewhere deep within my hidden truth, I knew I held the power to mold myself into a beautiful manifestation of life's essence or to destroy myself as quickly as the sun makes its retreat into the ocean in the last few moments of evening. Throughout my life, somewhere in my deepest level of unconsciousness, the choice would always be mine.

Now I rest in a scented bath, keeping as still as can be so that I can see the pure perfection of the candle reflected like the figures in Dali's *Metamorphosis of Narcissus*. That beautiful, traumatised painter, so strong within his fragility that he could show the world his truth, and portray the tortures of his mind through the illusion of art. New to the waking world; the master of dreams and illusion. I draw the water to my knees and watch as it caresses my body and washes over my breasts, peeling away from my skin, exposing the reality.

When I eventually emerge from the bath, steam and scent still rising in tiny tendrils before the candles, I draw a white towel around myself and knot it at the crease of my breasts. I clear the steam from the mirror and look once more at my reflection. No longer do I see voluptuous lips and smooth skin within the forgiving light. I see only my eyes, once alight as though every drop of beauty they received came to life and ignited within them, now filled with deep sadness. I watch droplets of water form and roll down my breast one at a time, each cradling its own fragment of candlelight and trailing down my body one by one. One rolls like a tear into the dent of my collarbone and rests there.

I make my way to the bedroom window now. It is nearly 1am, and the limpid air is like balm on my skin The stillness of the dark is augmented by the sound of a distant car alarm so I start the music again. Poignant notes sway in slow motion with my heart, pulling me with their dance. I close my eyes , and the music weaves itself through my body, moving me slowly, seductively and willingly with its rhythm. It leads like a soul partner, and we complete the dance as one, until the first of the candles fizzles, diminishes and dies. I stop and watch the smoke rise in a single curl and disperse into a cloud of recklessness before disappearing into the night as though it never existed.

I close my eyes again, this time to conjure images of times gone past and count on my fingers the number of lovers who have come and gone from my life over the past two decades, since the day I armored my heart and forced myself to forget how to love. I can remember them all by name and by scent. I can recall something unique, something endearing and exciting about every single one of them. Each had their own way of capturing a fragment of my heart, at least for a little while, until the illusion died, and the same lesson was learned again.

Typically, after a while, they start to see other versions of me that they hadn't accounted for, and suddenly, I am not longer quite so exciting, or enticing, or erotic as they first thought. They have all moved on in new ways. Some are married now and some have found fulfilment through their work. Of others I have no idea, and I wonder if they even have any recollection of the night that they spent with me, drinking deep, full-bodied wine and the hours of ecstasy and tantalizing bliss that ensued. I wonder if they ever think about the sensuality of my hips, my expert lips, the sensual indulgence of my body on nights where every touch was intentional, and every breath loaded with mystery and pleasure.

The music changes to the next track. The air is sharp, and the stars are bright. The moon is almost full; the three-quarter moon that nobody ever really notices. No poet I know of has ever sculpted a three-quarter moon with their words. No artist ever painted its incompleteness. No wandering gypsy has ever celebrated its missing magic or drunk in its vague promise; no pagan rites have ever taken place in honour of the almost-full moon. Yet there it hangs, a vivid reminder of the passage of time, the recycling of life and the opportunity for renewal that eludes us with each passing day. In forty- eight hours, she will be a full moon, and true lovers will revel in her glorious light bouncing off oceans and rippling its way in and out with the tide. Druids will worship her promise, and somewhere in the world, wolves will wander with heightened awareness through the night. She will glow bright and white in the darkness, expecting reverence. But tonight, she is incomplete.

Two weeks later, and my fingers are tracing the intricate spiral of a fossil, pondering the twists and turns of the prehistoric watermark that is etched into the surface of the rock sitting heavily in my left palm. A persistent February wind jangles its way through the harbor yet again, picking up chunks of my hair and flinging them across my eyes along its way. I am in Cornwall, in my soul-town of St. Ives. There is something about this place that brings me home, no matter how long we have been apart. Whenever I return, it is to find those strange little familiarities have been waiting patiently for me all along, constant and unfazed. The same familiar line of houses clustered along the peninsula, dividing the town in two; the same temperamental sea that can turn from glittering stillness into torrid violence in the space of a day; the same wheeling gulls, somewhat intrusive yet gloriously liberating in their flight – all waiting patiently there for my return. Waiting to welcome me back to my spiritual home.

On the surface, it is a holiday maker's town, bustling with families, surfers, pensioners, and children, all competing for the first ice cream or the sandiest spot in the cove or the biggest wave. But, beneath the transience of daily life is an ancient wisdom, a secret that stirs so deeply within the earth and the wind and the sea; it imprinted itself upon my own soul the first time I came here, just like the fossil in this rock in the palm of my hand.

The wind blows again, this time carrying a cutting chill and a five-bell chime from the clock tower. Although the afternoons are considerably lighter now and there is an undeniable quiver of spring inland, the Atlantic air still clings on to the dying remains of winter, weaving it in and out of the fishing boats and pounding at cliff faces, taking unfamiliar walkers by surprise in its sudden ferocity on the otherwise calmest of days. Despite the cold, I feel the uncontrollable urge to remove my boots and socks to feel the sand beneath my feet again. The tide has begun to retreat for the night, leaving behind a solid mirror of sand displaying colourful echoes of the boats that lie waiting for the tide to lift them up once more into their tireless daily dance.

Further up towards the harbor wall, the sand is as soft and light as ever, and it is here that I choose to remove my boots and spread my toes into the grains. Although it is cold, it is comforting, and I close my eyes for a moment to feel its energy connecting with my own and resting within me for a moment. With my eyes closed, my senses become attuned to parts of the town I haven't noticed until now: the smell of seaweed hanging in dripping swaths from the ropes that stretch across from the harbour wall; the jagged cry of the gulls fading away with the night trawler as it chugs its way around the harbour wall and out into the open sea.

Here is the place where I feel free. Freed of the trauma that to this day has plagued my life ever since I moved back to my home-town two years ago and found myself face to face with him on my way to work every single day. Ironically, it was he who first brought me here to St. Ives when I was barely eighteen. Yet here is a glimpse of the freedom I have craved for so long. Freedom to break away from his jealous grasp, from the twice-weekly rape, the threats, the blackmail. Free from the cage that has been closing in upon me every day, pinning me like a butterfly to a board while my life force still pulsated in my glorious, redundant wings. Twenty years. Has it really been that long? Apparently so. Yet somehow, twisted by the cruelty that is trauma, my memories have been closing in on me, their hold on my body and mind growing tighter and tighter until I reached this point where the slightest thing can bring the past to my present as unexpectedly and vividly as that vicious February wind.

Here I am free. This is my place. This was where I belong and I know it instinctively, yet for some reason, life had never brought me here for more than a few days at a time. I pick up my boots and make my way across the sand, glancing back every now and then to notice the bare footprints that I am leaving behind and ask myself why I am not doing this every single day. I need to go to The

Island. I adore The Island with its tiny chapel and ancient views. I make my way up the steps onto the cobbled street and through the labyrinth of whitewashed houses and granite roofs towards that familiar grassy peninsula that is my beloved Island.

I recall a time when I was twenty years old, finally broken away from him, and here alone. It was then that I discovered The Island for the first time. An eccentric-looking figure in tartan and an oversized waxed jacket had emerged from the other side, leaning on a walking stick with a slight hunch that from this distance had lent her a mannish appearance. However, as I drew closer, I saw long grey hair being shredded by the breeze and a wise and womanly sparkle in her surprisingly blue eyes. I recall that there was something about the stranger that captivated my attention and, with a wave of uncanny intuition, I knew before she spoke that this encounter would be a significant one. Sure enough, the elderly stranger stopped and engaged me in a conversation that seemed to begin somewhere in the middle.

"Just down there. That's where she goes. Night after night…but they never found that child." She gestured with her walking stick towards the aggressive black rocks below. Seeing that I was not quite following, she patiently began to elaborate on her mysterious tale.

"She's called The White Lady," she continued, her lively eyes alert and fascinated by her own story. "Long ago it is now, a ship got into distress. Right about there, it would've been. About there, look."

She swung her stick towards the rocks and brought it back down with a defiant thud. "They managed to bring 'er in, though, and got the people out. A young woman was one of the first off. As she stepped out of the boat though, 'er baby fell out of 'er arms and was swept out to sea. Night after night she went searchin' for that child, but she never found it. Poor little thing wouldn't stand a chance down there. They say that woman died of a broken 'eart."

She pointed her stick accusingly at the sea before continuing her questionable tale in a matter-of-fact way.

"But no sooner 'ad they buried 'er did she appear out there again. People 'ave seen 'er – all sorts of people – even the surfin' lads. Just see 'er lantern moving across there on the beach, look."

At that point, there was a dark pause and I wondered what to say next. Then I noticed that the old lady was looking at me with a knowing, slightly lop-sided smile which spread right through the creases in her wise old eyes.

"Things aren't good for you at the moment, I know, but it's going to be alright. You're on the right path."

I let out a bemused sound that was somewhere between a laugh and a sigh, laced with a huge question mark.

"How do you know? How can you tell?"

The eccentric stranger smiled at me.

"Your eyes," she said simply. "There's so much wisdom in those eyes. You're an old soul. You've been 'ere before. Many times."

"Yes!" I exclaimed with more hope and excitement than I had felt in a long time. "Yes, I have! I know I have! I love this place – there's something about it. I live about as far from the sea as it gets, and it's fine, but I've never felt quite *right* there. Here...well, here I just feel like I've... *landed*!"

The stranger had simply nodded as though she had just been told a fact so obvious it wasn't even worth mentioning.

"Not just 'ere," she said. "I mean 'ere, on this earth.

You're an old, old soul. You've 'ad many a lifetime, all over the place, not just 'ere."

She paused again, studying me with an intensity that would normally unnerve me, but which was in fact strangely reassuring.

"You're just searchin', that's all," she said at last. "You might feel as though you've lost your way but believe it or not that's good."

"It doesn't feel too good!"

"Take it from me. It's nothing to worry about. Your soul i'n't in the right place yet, that's all. Start listenin'! Things always work out when we start listenin'."

She paused then and I recall the way she looked at me so intently that for a moment I wondered if she might be a ghost herself. But then she banged her stick on the ground with such conviction that any supernatural suspicions were dispelled in an instant.

"Well," she added briskly, "it were nice meeting you. Enjoy your walk. Weather's calmin' down a bit now."

Without waiting for an answer, she was off on her way.

I stand here for a moment, recalling that mysterious meeting. A group of oystercatchers make an ungainly landing on the shore and begin poking busily about in the shallows looking for molluscs and, as they do so, a cluster of gulls lift in unison and begin to circle around one another, higher and higher into the sky. A sense of peace and oneness pours through me, as though someone or something has just lifted a corner of the veil that has been hiding my light for so many years. The gulls continue to wheel and dive, each one striving to fly higher and more recklessly than the rest. For a fleeting moment, I feel a glorious sense of oneness with everything around me, the birds, the sea, and the highlights around the clouds as the sun begins its rapid descent into the waves.

I pull out my journal. I have come here to heal and to repair, and writing is the one thing that has always allowed me to express myself, although I haven't done it for a while. In my darkest times, I almost convinced myself that my gift was a thing of the past. However, my recollection of the conversation with this elderly stranger – whoever she was – has begun to alter my perspective slightly. She was right. There has always been so much under the surface that I have never shown anybody before. Those long months of trauma and abuse that I've kept hidden from the world, even from myself, until I almost managed to convince myself that it never happened. Until now, my life has been governed by unconscious fear and I have allowed myself to slip further and further away from my soul's calling. But just as this place waits for me, my soul has been patiently waiting for my fear to move aside so that I can truly begin to live.

Without a thought, I begin to write:

> *When birds fly,*
> *There is no past for there is no future.*
> *Only now.*
> *They too must find food,*
> *They too must seek shelter, they too must provide,*
> *They too must risk their lives to fulfil their purpose.*
> *But they glide. They soar.*
> *They have no perception of "what if" or "maybe".*
> *Only now.*
> *Together they soar, separate entities in a collective*
>   *whole.*
> *Glinting in the sunlight. Resting on the waves.*
> *A seamless fusion of individual souls,*

Dancing as one in the wind.

As I look up and out to sea, I notice the wind has dropped and a solid dark cloud has split in two, edged like smoldering paper. Suddenly the source of the fire presents itself in its glorious radiance. I lay my journal beside me and watch until the final sliver of flame disappears beneath the waves. As the sea turns to ink and the gulls become nothing more than shrieking pockets of night, the old lady's ghostly story gets the better of me. I drop my pen into my own pocket, clutch my journal, and head back across The Island towards the comfort of the town. I recall the old lady's words:

"Your soul i'n't in the right place, that's all. Start listenin'. Things always work out when we start listenin'."

The tiniest celestial crescent has taken center stage in the sky. Tomorrow will be a new moon.

Five days later, I return home and that night I have a dream. Not the usual dream; the fear eludes me tonight. This dream is different. It is a vision. A message. A woman comes to me. Her hair is swirling about her face, long and almost black. Almost real, but not quite tangible. She reaches out her hand and I take it. I can almost feel the coolness of her hand in mine – but not quite. I sense it. Deep in the unawakened part of my soul I can feel its energy flowing like a spring into the deepest part of my consciousness. The woman begins to speak. I can almost hear the words but not quite. I sense them. Deep connections form between the woman's words and my deepest intuition that has been fighting for breath amidst the stagnant memories in my mind. The next thing I know, I am sitting beside her. She is wearing a flowing white gown that is spiralling with the air and dancing with the sunlight that rests on its folds. I feel myself lean against her gentle form as she promises to show me my life in an array of spiritual energy. My spiritual energy.

As I lean further into the woman's gentle presence, I feel myself drifting into a slow and gentle meditation. I am aware of my sleep state; I know my body is sleeping but my soul is wide awake. My mind is active but with every breath I take, it recedes into the depths of space until my soul becomes one with all around me and beyond. A red mist begins to move about my form, gently at first, like the ticking of the clock or the chiming of the bell. Reminding me that I am here, now, present in this moment and my soul is truly, truly awake.

"Sleep deeply," the woman says. "Rest your mind deeply and become one with my soul." As the red envelopes my vision, I feel the pain of my last encounter with the unnamed man; the man who I knew so well but cannot bear to utter his name for fear of making him real again. He is always there, always loitering in the depths of my mind, smirking at me as I try time and time again to move on, to love again and to trust again – just as he used to in real life. Every time I allow myself to slip into the heart of another, he comes back into my mind with a vengeance, and drags me into his chains and hauls me back into his toxic cage, one stifled breath at a time, until I become entwined with the black snakes of abuse crawling all over my skin, enmeshing themselves in my hair, gripping around my neck until there is almost nothing left. Nothing left but him. I start to recoil.

"Feel it," says the woman. "This is real only in your thoughts, an imprint in your singular past. But in the eternal cycle of karma, this moment no longer has to exist. You have the power within you to alter this moment. To see it, to feel it, to release it within this energy. Let it empower you once more, then send it away.

This energy is yours. Its roots stretch down to the deepest parts of the earth and beyond, beyond all that is known to you. Rest in this energy and know. Know power. Know strength. Know stability. Know your soul."

The colours change to a swirling orange into yellow and once more she persuades me to watch them form images, sensations and feelings of loss and grieving that have surmounted through suppression and denial of my truth. When the energy turns green, the grief tears through my heart with suffocating power. The woman holds my hand and tells me to feel; observe and feel. Amidst my tears and through my crumbling facade, I know that she is guarding me and guiding me through a journey of self-realisation.

I wake the next morning and lean over to check my alarm clock. It is unusually late. I notice that my journal is open, and the corner of a page has been torn off and placed like a feather on the corner of my nightstand. Lifting myself onto my elbow, I reach across, almost knocking the glass of water over again. Although erratic and hastily formed in the darkness of sleep, I recognise the handwriting as my own, but the words were ethereal.

Life is just a flicker of consciousness in the Universe.

I ponder this for some time. Where is it from? Who wrote these cryptic words? What does it mean? I sit up in bed, push my hair away from my face and read the words slowly, over and again. I begin to recall the woman from my dream. My vision. A woman whose presence was comforting and gentle, who had promised to guide me through the path of my life. These words had come from my hand, but my hand had been guided by the illuminated presence of this woman.

Deep into the following night, from the stirrings of my soul, images start to form in my mind's eye. It has only been a few weeks since I last painted, but lately it has been doing little to satisfy me. The brush strokes are contrived, coming from a rut that someone else had carved; forced in a direction that belies me. It has been several years since I painted from my soul, deep in the night when nobody else was awake, when time takes on a new form; sometimes disappearing altogether. In those peak moments of flow, I am transported to new levels of consciousness where the rest of the human world is happening somewhere far, far away.

My lover has just gone back to his own home, and deep down I know that was the last time that I will hear from him, and that my feelings of connection are little more than ghosts. Although I don't love him, I am strangely addicted to his presence in my life. Maybe it is the hankering after having what I cannot have. Maybe it is the excitement of a lithe body and a youthful spirit that makes me feel young and desirable for a while. Or maybe it is the longing for human touch, a moment to savour the illusion of being in love and loved, without the danger of the entrapment and abuse that my heart believes will come with it. For a moment, I want him to know who I really am. I want to share with him the colours and contours and passionate dances that my paintings portray. I want to open my rapidly expanding journal and share the scrawling writing that, since my time in St. Ives, has been appearing on the page every night before sleep, or every dawn when sleep eludes me. The acute loneliness of post-orgasmic bliss, the tears that escape as it all comes to an end, are becoming almost unbearable. It gnaws in the pit of my stomach as I recall the choices I have made; the promising new relationships that I have fled from, overcome by fear; the children who never had the chance to be conceived. The grief is almost unbearable.

I keep my old paintings in a small, dusty space under my bed, pushed up against the wall, wrapped loosely in an old voile curtain. I lay them now on the floor in front of me and carefully unwrap the sheet, revealing the corners and the creases in the canvases where the paint never quite managed to reach. The first image is laid before me, and my throat catches when I see the perfection that comes from the imperfections, creating something so beautiful and true. I distinctly remember creating this one – or rather, I distinctly remember the day it was created through me, rather like the words on my night-stand. I was unaware of the process or the subject of the painting until intuition told me it was finished. I called it "Reincarnation" - something I had never really thought about before. I was living and blossoming in Austria at the time – a carefree young adult with an insatiable lust for living. It was a small pocket of delicious linear time when the traumatic fragments of my past were dormant, like a long-forgotten, distant nightmare, and the colours of my world were vibrant and full of hope.

I run my fingers along the contours of the ghost-like figures in the image before me. The more I look, the more entities I see emerging from within the lines and the textures. They emerged like that on the canvas that day from a place way beyond my conscious awareness. The colours, earthy and ochre, are reminiscent of the fecund earth in its transition from Summer into Autumn. How apt this is to me now. The spirit of the damaged maiden, lost in the mist of her own youth, has returned to me gradually through my secret world of painting, crying out to be heard, just as these figures reveal themselves to the observer, layer upon layer upon layer. Time is strange.

Parts of my distant past feel as close to me now as the air I am breathing, yet other parts are estranged, as though they happened to someone else somewhere in my distant memory. This night alone is strange, as though I have been living someone else's life. An actress playing the role of seductress. Nothing more. Thinking I was protecting my heart and fulfilling my body, when the reality is I was destroying myself. This night of physical union with my lover feels surreal, as though it never happened. I feel as though I have left my body beneath the layers and layers of denial and pretense that have shrouded it over the years, while my soul travels deep into timeless space where the eternal flame of my truth still burns.

I find my paints and an empty canvas and lay them out across the floor. The smell of the pigment catches in my throat but brings back the glorious tingling of hope and inspiration. I select my colours as though in a trance and squeeze them onto the torn-off piece of cardboard that is my palette. I close my eyes and allow the image to form in new shades of white, cadmium yellow, a dash of cadmium red; the colour of candlelight. Only this time I do not want to paint secretly in the depths of the night. I want to be there to witness the freshness of dawn, the dewdrops that cluster together before the world is awake. I want to embrace the transitioning of Summer to Autumn, with an energy as full of lightness and hope as though it were Spring. I want to create eternity in colour, an image that depicts the cycles of time: the death, the rebirth, the chance of a new beginning. I want my soul to be known.

The feeling of that first stroke on the canvas is authentic and true. The light of my higher self is guiding my hand, sweeping into my consciousness. I have no idea what time it is when I finish, but the birds are stirring in the trees outside and the pink rays of dawn are beginning to push their way into the house. Soon the sun would rise, and the day would pick up where it left off yesterday, before the candles were lit and a young man alighted at my door. He seems so far away now. My soul has led me through the night and now my body is exhausted and spent, but my mind has clarity and my soul is weeping with liberation and joy. I stand and wipe my hands on an old rag that I had forgotten about, discarding it onto the floor. My hands are covered in the candlelight hue from when I abandoned my brushes and allowed the image to flow directly through my hands to the canvas. I step back to observe my soul's work, then I make my way across to the window and cast it wide open.

As time goes by, I learn that the healing process is like a deep valley. When we decide to begin our journey of descent, we go deeper, deeper, deeper down until we reach the bottom and we see at last what is there. Buried amongst ragged rocks and consumed by stagnant waters, we find memories, emotions, fears and cries longing to be heard. Little by little, we pick them out, we feel them, we observe them, and then gradually and at our own pace, we begin to climb again up to the other side. As we journey onwards, way-markers appear before us. We are drawn to people who bring lessons and guidance, some who bring healing, some who bring hope. There are people who show us what it is that our soul yearns for, and people who show us the opposite. Without the knowledge of experience of that which we don't want, we may never truly experience that which we do. Our intuition calls upon us, and gradually we begin to take note and follow. We repeat this healing journey many, many times through different layers, different dimensions of our body, our mind and our souls, until we eventually reach the essence of our true and enlightened self.

Along our journey of transformation, a great truth is revealed: the mind is not only a product of our brain and our thoughts, but it is the conscious energy that vibrates within every waking cell of our body, and we can use it to alter and transform ourselves through our intentions. When we understand this, our all-encompassing mind evolves in a way that really and truly shapes our lives and alters the way that we live, breathe, work, grow and experience our world. When we follow the path of the soul, our mind and our body can together create the perfect fusion of authenticity and wonder, a connection with the universe, with the world around us, with each other and deep, deep, deep within ourselves.

Each time we repeat the journey into the valley of our earthly experiences, we can stand back and see our beginnings from a more evolved perspective, and begin the process again from a higher place of understanding. Each time we embark on the journey, we embrace and absorb more learning along the way. We expand and grow in wisdom until we learn to trust that what we see, what we sense and what we feel is a creation that comes from our own, deep unconsciousness. We notice more of what is around us. We become more aware of the landscape in which we stand. We sense its energy above us, below us and within us, and we grow as one. The more we grow, the more we feel and see and know of ourselves. We observe the oceans glittering in the sun; we watch them dance in time with the wind, following the rhythm of the moon in her never-ending cycle of death, rebirth and fruition. We learn to choose our highest path, mindfully at first until gradually our conscious choices become embedded in our all-encompassing minds, and we arrive at a place where we meet our true self; a place where our highest levels of unconsciousness and consciousness synchronise and become one glorious, authentic, synthesized whole.

And so is the cycle of life: The Maiden, the Mother and the Crone, each one giving birth to the other in our journey to deepest divine wisdom and truth. Sometimes, there comes an intuitive moment of recognition when we sense within the triad a part of ourselves who needs to be healed; the small frightened part who was left behind along the way, who screams for help and who overrides our soul's choices from her place of abandonment, rejection, betrayal, violation and fear. Now, I embrace the Mother phase of my life, and in turn she embraces the Maiden. She heals her with her love, comforts her with her understanding and guides her with her strength. She listens when the Maiden cries, guides her when she falters and holds her through her fear. In her completeness and truth, the Mother looks beyond and calls on the wisdom of the Crone.

Do we ever know true enlightenment until we have first experienced darkness? Without the depths, we cannot truly appreciate the elevation of awakening and light. Until we know entrapment, we cannot know the feeling of pure bliss of flying on wings of white light. Until we know loneliness, we cannot truly appreciate the divine fusion of souls. When darkness and light fuse in a spirit of pure acceptance, a true array of colour bursts forth in a dance of clarity and truth. In the moment when bleak rain cuts through the light of the sun, a rainbow spectrum of color bursts forth. The pinnacle of time where light meets darkness is where the perfection occurs.

Five years later, I rise early and embrace the dawn. Nothing is without colour this morning. The distant fields are blue, the sky is pink, the shadows are long and violet. Only a group of jackdaws rising from a skeletal tree are devoid of color, a stark contrast to the promise of the day. Soon, the earth will be green, and the sky will be ablaze with oranges and reds. The world is stirring, and as the sun begins his ascent to full glory, Venus sparkles her quiet farewell. Later, as the skies turn from aqua to indigo to black, she will shine again in her timeless, eternal wisdom. For a moment I am standing within the presence of my highest self. I smile and close my eyes to welcome the next beginning in the eternal cycle of life.

WEEDS

JOANNE POTTER

I don't know why I didn't record this in my journal, because I remember it vividly—the day I bought my widow's weeds.

That's what they used to call them when Victoria was still queen in England. Weeds, the clothes a widow wore for a year following her husband's death.

Long, heavy, impenetrable, they included a weeping veil whose purpose, I'm assuming, was to hide her puffy face and red eyes. We don't wear these anymore, of course, but we do need a black dress for our husband's funeral. We do need that. And, more than a year before he died, more than a year before anyone knew when he would die, I found one.

I was in Goodwill of all places, browsing for something to wear to a wedding, I think, and there it was. Crepe, midcalf, with little pintucks down the front and a belt in the back. Just the style that looked best on me and a bargain besides. Obviously, however, there's a problem with this. One does not buy a dress to anticipate one's husband's death. It's not done. And for good reason.

How could I even consider it? I knew he was sick, very sick, and had been so for a long time. My common sense told me that, eventually, he would die. But not soon enough to necessitate buying a dress. Not even close. I didn't try it on. I hung it back up like I'd been stung instead, and walked out.

But I kept thinking about it, trying to imagine what would happen if—when, if I was being honest—Dave did die. Would I want to go shopping then? After all, I almost never wore black. I didn't have one thing in which to wrap grief that big.

And I kept remembering the little, almost microscopic, ways that God drops favor into my unexpecting lap, and I kept thinking of the dress. Would it not be better to get it now rather than have to get one later, when I would rather be doing absolutely anything else? I knew it would. Okay, I thought, I'd put it to the test. I'd wait a couple of days and if it was still there when I went back, well, I'd get it.

It was and I did, but guiltily, without telling anyone, and I shoved into a corner of my closet. I didn't want to look at it. It hung there for 13 months, after which I took it off the hangar, wore it exactly twice, for both of Dave's funerals, and got rid of it, casting it out as though coated it with acid.

My widow's weeds, for which, by God's grace, I did not have to shop while broken and weeping, had served their purpose and I never wanted to look at them again.

I couldn't figure out where your breath had gone. It was there a couple of hours before, your chest still rising and falling, reassuring me that it was okay to fall asleep. What made me wake up? I'd felt no motion. You lay just as you'd been, but still. So still.

I think I said your name, hoping, but even then didn't know who I was talking to. You were warm to the touch, supple and familiar, but something was missing. I never thought one could feel the incessant course of blood through veins, but now—that must have been it. I knew then, but didn't understand. It was 2:00 a.m. No sound anywhere.

I lay back down, my hand still on the front of your shirt, conjuring a heartbeat, willing you to stir. All the hours I'd laid next to you, listening to you live. Surely that's all it would take again—a hesitant puff to the back of your neck, a light stroke on your cheek.

I can't remember now when I'd last shaved you, whether your cheeks were rough or smooth. It seems like you'd been soft as a newborn. Maybe that's exactly what you were.

I was supposed to do something, but couldn't move, couldn't stir, much less rise.

How did Bryan get there? Nancy and Knute and all the rest? I don't remember calling anyone.

I do remember Bryan lifting me away from your side, the only one who had the courage, the only one who could have done it. A son's duty.

Did anyone but me hear the roaring, the guttural tearing cry of impossibility? Where did it come from? Surely that ascending animal moan was not mine.

I could see nothing ahead. The future was cut off. All roads impassable. No going either forward or backward. My legs useless, not able to carry me anywhere.

Then someone must have called somebody. The funeral van backed into the driveway.

We washed you. You didn't need it, but I'd imagined it

so many times. I'd pictured a warm, white cloth and a body that cooperated, the only kind I'd known. But you were heavy, unresponsive—difficult to move or turn, more a thing than a man. And baby wipes. Good Lord. I wonder if you hated that.

But I did get to say goodbye to your skin—all of it. Every bit that had once bent so feverishly to me, or yielded to mischievous play, or reached out with familiar comfort. All that skin—the rough, the bald, and the places still fine and baby soft, having remained well hidden.

Your friends helped to lay you on a cart, so slight by then, and covered you with your own blankets. They shouldn't have covered your face.

I stood on the front porch and watched the hearse pull out of the driveway, knowing they were wrong, all of them. A call would come soon. You still lived, of course. You would gasp once, then breathe, and they would call to tell me.

But they didn't, and it was only after you left that the enormity of the void showed itself. It was bigger than you, bigger than us both. Not only your corporeal body had vanished, but so did possibility and future, all we were going to do, all we were going to make right.

It had all run out.

As insistently as we possessed one another, it was never enough. You wanted me to trust you more, and I wanted you to desire me more. We were in danger of being subsumed by that need, always wanted more from one another. Our need threatened to incinerate us from the inside out. Constant and dangerous, it could not long be borne.

No, I didn't trust you. Even you, because I knew the monster inside of you. I'd seen it. The anger, the suspicion, the absurd, violent power living right next to the gentle scholar, the beautiful poet, and the delightful storyteller. I remember your hands—clumps of flesh and bone as capable of pain as pleasure. I hear your voices still—both of them—tender comforts and brutal truths.

But as much as we had, there was never enough. Both of us wanted more—more understanding, more love, more time.

One always thinks there will be more time, and then there isn't. Of all the gifts we gave each other, all the palpable attempts to satisfy, it never happened. It couldn't. And then, all the striving came to an end because time itself ran out. By taking away any future we might have had, God took away the hammer with which we beat one another and said gently, 'You can stop swinging now.'

You stood way too large in my view and I think perhaps, me in yours. There was only so far we could go together.

The fire must have burned hotter than I thought. It incinerated something vital in a flame for which you provided all fuel—spark, tinder, and log—so that, once you were gone, it all faded to cold, white ash.

I have no capacity to love now. No place exists to house it. A spark sometimes rises, but it is only lust and finds no place or reason to become flame.

You mined me well, carved winding passageways no one else had ever attempted, then filled them with yourself, stealthy and complete, so that I would not know you were there until you'd suddenly vacated them. You pulled out so thoroughly that it seemed an instantaneous dissolving.

Now the passages are hollow—spiders scrabble up their walls, drawing long webs without disturbance. I don't understand how the tunnels remain without collapsing, but they do. I hear the wind whistle around their corners. Nothing keeps them open.

You gutted me when you left. Those sinuous halls once filled with light and love don't even echo. Nothing catches their plea.

I am left a ready framework bearing your design and use but with no resident to occupy it. The pressure has reversed. Where once burned enough heat and flame to ignite every cell my skin could hold and more, this cold, covered shell threatens collapse inward for lack of ignition. No wonder I've begun to fall apart.

"He was so young," they said. "He was taken too soon." But you weren't taken too soon at all. We'd done all we could do, both ruined and satisfied as much as was possible. We both knew there was more, but we'd run out of ways to get to it.

And now I do not get you back. Neither do I get youth or passion or decades of shared living. They are all gone. I do not get you except in flavor, in aroma—as though you'd been juiced, made wine, and drunk. Not touched, but possessed.

Even the memory of you still makes me giddy, but I have to live in what I'm given, not what's been taken away. I did not want this abandonment, and was given no time to assimilate it.

His voice came immediately, that first day, as still and small as promised.

"You're mine now."

Why does God always sound like you?

"This is our time."

Your worn out, burned up flesh wasn't even in the ground yet and God was staking His claim. The only voice I couldn't dismiss.

I'd imagined it might come, but expected it to be easy, obvious. I would lay you to rest with regret, but then turn full-faced to God, tears already dried, knowing He'd waited patiently, even planned for these days. I would finally sink, content to be helpless, into all-powerful arms and commune with divinity. I'd actually sometimes considered this the only logical outcome to a, if not God-ordained, at least God-permitted loss as deep and total as yours.

But I'd underestimated the ongoing contest for my attention. You, my dear, were never the only contender. I'd neglected to look in the mirror. And, now that I was no longer occupied with your physical and emotional needs, the real culprit, my most vicious opponent, my own egocentric self, stepped unashamedly to the fore. So familiar. So sure she is always right. So insistent on her territory.

The battle had been waged unwittingly constant, the combatants not innocuous cartoons—not a plump cherub on one shoulder and a horned trickster on the other, whispering kind caution and slippery temptation into respective ears. It was hardly a battle at all. You were gone. I'd already taken back the territory, so God simply waited, perfect and patient. Staked His claim plainly and let all the grasping darkness my own conceit could muster boil up and fester, demanding hot attention, urging immediate decision.

Mine.

My freedom. My autonomy. My self-realization.

Me.

My needs. My future. My choices.

My Life.

Mine.

I belonged to no one anymore. I took no orders.

This was my payback—recompense for years of deference to husband, children, ordained circumstances. I got to choose now. I would make the path and walk in it with all the strength that the adversity God brought to me had wrought.

Your death was His idea. God did this. On purpose, by intentional design. Even God doesn't get to dismantle a life, knock out every support, and then expect the ruin to stand itself up and thank Him.

And then the voice whispered, *"But I do."*

My heart was broken, of course. That happened on the day you died. That's when the howling began—the grinding, relentless gnaw that took the place of your immediate presence. Something inside was falling apart, never to be recovered. I didn't need a doctor to tell me any of that.

But to find out that the wound, the abnormality, the crack in the perfect fabric of my universe went beyond the psychic, well, that was news. My heart has been broken a longer time than I thought. This break however, this swollen, bulging blood vessel, was mechanical, a hard fact of malformation that, if it failed, would bring a quick death. One wrong move, one injudicial action, could break it definitively and for good, sending me into the infinite, to whatever comes next, to you.

Well, now, that was an alluring thought. Even now, I smile at it. And sigh. I could be done. I could rest, finally and forever. Just let go. I wouldn't have to do a thing except wait. I contemplate this and daydream of you. Your arms open. You smiling.

A conciliatory surgeon, careful to assess my degree of potential panic as he spoke, described both the offending aneurysm and the process by which he recommended I give him permission to saw through my breastbone, remove the faulty components, and replace them with dacron and pig parts. My own flesh, swapped out like a carburetor. Pulsing, yielding, life-filled tissue thrown into a dumpster somewhere in the assumption that a manufactured lump of any kind could ever find an appropriate home next to my beating heart. He spoke as if he offered life, but I knew better.

I held up my hand. "Stop. Just stop. What will happen", I asked him, "if I do nothing?"

He leaned back slow. "You will die. Sooner, not later."

I smiled. "Death is already claiming me, young man. The ability to draw one more breath does not define life. If you cut into me now, I may gain more years, but will lose a singular chance. After all, how many people get to choose their own end?"

He didn't move. I'd counted nearly to ten when he stood up, gaze still fixed.

"No one", he said, and excused himself.

And then the other voice interrupted the silence. Again, the inner declaration.

"No one.

You do not get to chose your own death. That is my right, mine alone.

You were bought with a price."

You belong to me. You are mine."

My flesh cried out ownership at the same time as its sovereignty was claimed by another. I watched the easy way out close and grabbed for the last light before it winked out.

Who am I? Whose am I? Especially now, when the answer matters so much?

I've often thought about a soldier on the eve of battle —what he thinks, whether he sleeps at all, how often he wants to simply turn and run. No sane man wants to fight those fights. He has to want them to be unnecessary. He has to wonder why people can't just get along. But the oath he swore, the freedoms he enjoys, all require that he get up the next morning before the light is full, pull his jacket tighter around him, pick up his pack and rifle, and step out with his comrades into danger.

Boldness is not required. Just follow-through. To do what he does not want to do. To act in concert with what he believes right. To be able, should he survive, to look in the mirror and see a man, not a counterfeit. To choose pain. To choose sacrifice. To choose suffering.

Who wants to do that?

No one.

Who does it anyway?

God help me... I do.

Part of the problem is that there's no good death. It's a myth of male romance, a construct that makes men feel good about fighting, that gives something destructive a dignity it not only doesn't deserve, but never achieves.

Death has different faces for sure—some much more horrible than others. Some deaths curl and writhe in agony, offering welcome end to desiccated flesh. Some come by bloodbath, exposing steaming viscera, staining anything close bright red, drying to black. Some deaths look gentle, allowing the slow countdown of diminishing breath or stealing it away in the middle of unsuspecting dreams.

But no death is a friend. We were made to live, not die. At bottom, regardless of our understanding of what may or may not come afterward, we know we were made to live and we fight to stay alive, all the while trying to ignore that we won't.

Still, death holds an allure when life gets hard, as it always does. It calls, or tempts, or promises relief. Everyone has felt it, but the feeling is a lie. Even if heaven brings perfect communion with God and loved ones, we were made to live and struggle, regardless of the cost.

Still, I don't want to live as much as I used to. Death

looks welcome more often now because life costs so much more. I could use a good rest, and relief from the burden of years, but it's a passing desire. In the end, I will gasp for my last breath just like everyone else, afraid perhaps, or perhaps given a reassuring vision of heaven at the last.

Until then, I have to give up having to know why I still wake up every morning. I didn't will myself to life and can't choose to opt out of it. I'm along for the ride and best just settle in, content to not know the reason why. There is still something to do, after all—my minuscule contribution to be made to the great whirling world. There may still be some measure of good life, but there is no good death.

In the meantime, I have to sort out the matter of where to go instead. Have you noticed that no one uses maps anymore? We have electronic maps now, and they are a poor substitute. I have a love-hate relationship with my GPS. It usually gets me where I want to go, but once there, I don't know where I am. It tells me where to turn, but gives me no reference points regarding anywhere else. It tells me whether to turn right or left, but not whether I am east or north of the place. It consoles me with arrival, but leaves me stranded without objective location.

Going somewhere by GPS feels more like an out of body experience than traveling. Surroundings and scenery don't matter—there's no turning right at the old Sinclair station or going past the red barn. Street signs don't matter—the destination isn't two blocks past Park or at the intersection of Mill and Main. In fact, the destination isn't anywhere that would appear on a Rand McNally—it's at the end of a blue line that doesn't even have the grace to stay put. It shifts constantly with perspective and progress. As I get closer, it gets longer, and streets appear at right angles along the route as if out of nowhere.

I don't like it, even if it helps me find places.

I was following its directions again today, the blue line laying out the route bit by measured bit, my car one of a crowd blindly sharing the road with other drivers on a mild fall day. At first, the trip felt easy and companionable. As I left town, however, the other cars peeled off one by one, right and left, Until eventually I was alone, alone on the road with the blue line.

I didn't know where I was—on the road by myself, unsure of whether I was really going in the right direction, and having no one reliable to consult.

It's not supposed to be like this.

I'm not supposed to be alone.

You should be here.

I know we said we'd be together until death, but I, at least, didn't mean exactly that. What I meant to say was that neither of us is allowed to die so that we'll never be separated. Marriage isn't supposed to be together until death. It's supposed to be together forever.

Where are you, anyway?

If you aren't here—and you aren't—then where exactly did you go?

I don't understand heaven. I can't picture or point to it. I put it into my GPS and got a synagogue, a photography studio, and a corporate office 52 miles away. While you were alive and so very much here, I didn't need to find heaven. I lived it, or at least often enough to satisfy. It was as though you carried heaven on your back.

But you're gone now and I can't find you. I sound way too much like Mary's plaintive cry at the tomb—They have taken away my Lord and I don't know where they have laid him.

I've lost my way. I can't find you and don't know where to begin to look. Christ says "Follow Me. I will lead you home." But I don't want Him.

I want you. Back. Here. With me. Young and Strong and Here. Just Here.

There's no blue line for this. I told you—this thing is just no damn good. It doesn't lead to the one place I want to go.

But I had to go somewhere. So I did.

I let the surgeon bust me open, healed, then went to Italy. I lived for a month in a fourth floor walkup in Florence a block from the Uffizi and another block from the Arno. I spent days in cathedrals and museums and little winding markets. I wrapped myself in tales of Medici infamy and drifted daily in and out of neighborhood churches to the melody of the nostro padre and abbi pieta. I stood morning and evening in front of the duomo, marveling. I flung open shutters that faced the alleyway, taking in at every hour the smell of wine and garlic and old stones. I found beauty there, and God, and the full breath of new April green, but not you. After the month was over, I came home.

They say that smell is the most evocative sense. For years, you smelled like smoke. There was not only the smell of it, deep brown, smooth and acrid at the same time, like a familiar dog or a dozen different kinds of leaves. There was also the vaporous result of it, the wisps that rose around you in slow strands as you puffed, thinning as they moved. It was a leisurely dance that renewed itself with each exhale, obscuring the unrelenting blue of your eyes and occupying your mouth in what looked like moments of thought, but were more often pauses between them.

You stopped smoking in June of 2009, stopped casting up your pipe's little cloud and I could see you unobscured every moment I chose to look. One would think that the end of the smoke made the view of you more often clear, and it did for awhile, but now that you're gone from physical sight, the image of you begins to dissolve into another cloud. Where once I saw you clear and immediate, now the edges of you look touchable at first, then break up and float away. They have become in reality uncatchable and, if truth be told, undesired. You are dissolving, too, but rather than into benign air, into the smoke of the mean, the crass, the ordinary.

This is what is happening—my memory has begun to exert its authority over content, willfully selecting pleasure over pain, ascendance over the broad gray of everyday.

After all, in life you prickled, even wounded. Part of your allure was your razor—the way you sometimes wielded feeling and opinion as truth. The way you were right so often that it became expected custom. The way you proclaimed and decreed.

Now, though, your weapons, so long unsharpened, have sublimated their pointed ends to soft prods and I do not stop them, wouldn't even if I could. Time and memory have disarmed you. Recollection of hurts and unease are becoming wisps while I'm not looking and just floating away, the way you did. Damage and disorder leaving for good and not coming back. Memory lacking destruction but leaving comfort. The confusion of aggravated love gone like smoke.

Memory and remembering.

They are not the same.

Memory looks back, turns over and fondles moments past, sometimes long past, for comfort, for reassurance, sometimes for confirmation. It also, without permission, reconstructs. By its very nature, memory is not reliable. It depends not only on desire, but on mechanical brain parts, neurons and synapses, and as their connections break down, memory gradually fades farther and farther back into the past, becoming dim without permission. Memory, sharp and bright when young, needs no incentive to crumble and recreate itself according to its owner's personal preference.

There is no help for this. Given enough time, memories reveal more about the desire and history of the brain making them than about the actual events they purport to preserve. We make and re-make memories involuntarily into comfortable refuges or cutting punishments but, either way, they are ours and those that people them with us are consigned over time to increasing fantasy.

Remembering is different. Memory is the struggle not to forget. Remembering is current and active. It happens right now, in the front, not the back, of the mind. It is today's, not yesterday's work. I remember to take the dog out. I remember a birthday. I remember tomorrow's dentist appointment.

Action follows remembering. It brings me something to do. It builds up. It admits and provides for a future. It is a light just beyond the glass; I open the door and reach for it, gather it in, and it becomes the days of my life.

Memory fades by necessary attrition. From time to time, it rises on its own for good or ill, but not entire and not forever. Pieces of memory constantly disassemble themselves and float away, carried beyond resuscitation.

I don't remember being two years old, or five, or almost anything under ten or so. There are photographs of those days, and I recognize my juvenile features in them as round, fresh versions of my own, but I reach back and can't grasp anything concrete. There's one picture in particular from what must have been my third birthday that frames a little girl with a Buster Brown haircut and a purple dress with a white round collar in front of a cake with a ballerina on it and three candles. The little girl is plainly delighted, and I think that surely the memory of that day would have lasted, but though I remember the picture, I can't remember living the day—not the feel of it, or the sounds of the singing, or blowing out the candles in a single, trembling puff.

It must have been around second grade that I lost my snowpants. It's just a flash, really—standing in a coat room that smelled of old wood and wet children, wondering how I was going to explain the incident to my mother, who would surely be angry. I would have been about eight then. And there's the time I ran into the box of my brothers' model train tracks and the connecting prong from one of the track sections stuck in my leg. I remember running up the basement stairs, track flopping up and down and blood dripping from the wound, blaming my brothers the whole way.

There isn't much else, though. Even from high school. Thousands of my own life's days all gone, escaped without as much as a whisper. Other people possess distant memories. I don't.

Lately, I did some reading about how memory works—the mechanism of passing electron charges from neuron to neuron through synapses and how the storage and retrieval of information can be corrupted or lost through decay. Good memory, assuming that memory is more physical than psychic, depends on the health of the neurons being connected. What's wrong with mine? Are the spaces too big? The charges too weak? No one seems to know why some people remember and others forget but I know one thing: I was not gifted with good memory..

You are dead now, now victim to my faulty memory. Dead in the removed third person, not in the intimate second. I can hardly speak to you any more. Your face, once so close and open, has turned away to embrace its own future. I am left to mine.

My web of memories has become a scattering of islands without connective tissue. I have lost the intimacy of them. Pictures exist there as isolated situations and experiences, no longer woven together. They come from a distance now. I don't carry them in a pocket anymore. Instead, I have to retrieve them from a folder in the next room, available but not as close by.

These days, remembering never has anything to do with you. It deals with, well, it deals with today. You live in my yesterdays. It's true that many of those yesterdays were wonderful and I will still bring them out and hold them in my arms. They still warm, even when they wrench. But now I have learned, sometimes at least, to put them down in a safe place and, in remembering what must be done today, find reward there, too. The reason for my life can no longer be keeping you alive.

Parts of you are gone, become third person and still loved, but drifting ever farther away. To the memories that remain I still turn back for a look, even while walking forward, and wave a sweet goodbye. I have to go. I'm remembering today. Yesterday is fading fast.

Most of the time, frankly, it doesn't matter. I take pictures, write journals, keep notes. It works. Until now, a sub-par memory has only amounted to inconvenience, something done poorly between others done well, fair recompense to balance the cosmic scales. I could live with that. It seemed a good bargain—until now—until all I have left of you is memory.

At first, right after you died, the memories seemed nearly as corporeal as flesh. It was easy to keep you with me. Memory was fresh and came with all the senses—taste, touch, smell, all of them. All neurons were firing, every connection made strong. You stayed alive and with me every minute, vibrant, and alert. You were gone, but still with me every day, so real. So real.

No wonder I didn't believe you died. To everyone else, you were gone, but I knew better.

Then, as they always do, the memories started to thin, dissolved like your pipe smoke, drifted right through grasping fingers. It took a few years to realize it was happening. It was so gradual. I was so accustomed to summoning your presence into life with just desire and a minute of concentration.

And then I couldn't. Not all the time, of course, but often enough to give pause. I was losing you a second time, and this time my degrading synapse activity was giving me nothing in exchange.

And that's where I'm left. Reaching back for a past I connect with less and less. I still intellectually know a lot of what happened—where we were when we did this or that, who we shared days with. But I can't remember how they felt. I can't feel them anymore. I can't feel—you.

You're gone and I'm going to have to let you die or retreat into delusion. If I try to hold on, your persistent presence will degrade into a kind of madness. To retain whatever sanity I have left, I've developed a desperate mantra, repeating it as often as reality starts to slip:

You're not coming home.

Ever.

I will never know your flesh again.

You are gone for good.

Vanished.

Evaporated into thin air.

Dead.

Dead.

Dead.

It's not only you I miss. It's the possession of you, the

comfortable familiarity of well-known skin only a short reach away.

Skin is a lovely thing. It not only covers all of our important physical parts. Its curving warmth and plump, smooth continuity speak immediately of intimacy. I touch you and you become mine.

Skin is territory. Touching it is dangerous, titillating, satisfying. I miss that.

All around, every day, humans touch and are touched. Fingers slide down an arm or around a waist or over a crowning nipple. Someone traces the curve of a face or hands cradle one another. In our time, you knew my skin and I yours, committed it to automatic memory not by intent, but through free, repeated exposure. I had it once. I had you, inside and out. You didn't belong to me, but I had you, close and winding, most intimate when taken-for-granted casual—the proximate blush, the accidental stroke.

My skin is grainy now, and spotted. It is pleated and crepey or crisscrossed by lines in the same way that occasional water traces paths through a desert. It is old. I am glad you aren't here to see the ruin your absence has made of me, how I dried up when frequent, familiar touch fled for good. You were part of me and even my skin knows it.

Skin knows its own. I'm glad you had me when I was plumped with young oil. What is left of this skin now, dry as tissue, I keep to myself.

I'm getting old quickly.

The burden of years weighs heavier now. It is a drawstring sack carried on my back, often opened and added to, but never relieved, then slung again over my shoulder.

The sack arrived years ago, its first occupant the cataclysmic understanding of sin, and increased its load with each sorrow and loss. But this last, this scooping out of hot innards, filled it to capacity and beyond.

It has become too big to carry now. I instead have to drag it behind me and it makes a furrow between every step I take. My shoulder knots, my brow knits tight into new and unforgiving wrinkles. Skin thins, muscles slack. These last years since you've been gone have filled my bag of sorrows to bursting.

Around me, life has gone on and all the sorrows gathered into the bag are not my own—they include the ones that surround and shed their weight through proximity and relationship, but circumstances do not differentiate. The burden of these is just as heavy.

In the end, I am tired.

Age can bring good things—perspective for sure, a measure of wisdom and confidence—but I never expected this weight. I will not be able to shoulder it forever. It will weary me to death.

It was easy to know when to put on widow's weeds. At the death. For the funeral. And it used to be that one knew when to take them off—a year later, when the worst of the mourning, or at least the formal part, was completed. But these days, the year-long public display isn't done anymore, and when we take off the black dress after the funeral is over, mourning isn't yet complete. Not by a long shot, and we are left with trying to understand how to grieve, and how long, and how much to show to the outside world.

In the normal flow of life, we don't desire to suffer. Instead, we desire happiness—every day, every moment if we can manage it. That doesn't happen, of course, but no matter. I want it just the same. And so do the people around me. Whether my unhappiness reminds them of their own, or whether it gives them an uncomfortable prod of guilt for what they might be bound to do to ease it, or whether they simply feel a painful empathy, no one around us wants us to be unhappy either.

But mourning was different. Your death gave me permission to be publicly unhappy. The tears hurt. I had cramps, I either couldn't sleep or slept all the time, my heart convulsed and left me gasping with waves of frantic beating. Most of all that I kept to myself, until it seemed that those around me were beginning to forget. For a long time, I couldn't permit anyone to go on with their lives as though you hadn't died or worse, that you hadn't lived. So, just when it seemed my life might return to normal, I let down my guard—the one that protected my raw wounds from common sight—and reminded whoever I thought needed to hear it that I was still mourning your loss, was still hurting, was still suffering.

There is a kind of nobility in imposed suffering—a subtle lift of the chin, a level gaze that says 'No, you couldn't possibly understand.' I wasn't playing to a crowd as much as reminding them that this could be them, too, and probably one day will be. I held up life torn in two for them to look at full face. I wanted them to imagine how I felt, how they have or will, too. I didn't want sympathy. I wanted recognition. Acknowledgment.

I really don't think they knew any of this, of course. All they seemed to see was the grace of controlled grief and the (very real) strength that faith made possible. Just what I wanted them to see. I thought it kept you alive for us all, but that's not all I have been nurturing and part of me has known it for a long time. I've held so tightly to the glory of our love that I've turned it from a golden memory into a golden calf. My manufactured nobility isn't keeping anyone alive. All it does is prolong the fading fabric of what has well and truly died, what was meant to die.

Your memory is made to live. That's the healthy part. But holding on to the deep, convulsive damage that your death wreaked on my life for too long past its purpose is the part that decays regardless of how hard I hold on, and, over the years, it has become an enforced territory I will let no one breach.

Suffering can feel wonderful—its stark magnitude seems to prove how much I loved you, how important you loomed in my life. Because the suffering of grief is so consuming and even motivating, I have been afraid to stop the pain, to cut it off, to let sweet memory take its place until the pain is nearly gone and I have none to show anymore. I am afraid to be happy, because that new happiness, the one without you, might negate your wonder and our love. What happens if I let you go, really go?

I could wear the weeds forever, after all. I could refuse to rise from the ashes of our life together. But we all know what happens to dead things not properly disposed of. They rot. They stink and dissolve into rancid jelly. It's already happening. Every time I retreat into the now-familiar suffering, I feel a little queasy, just this side of unstable. Awkward. Off-stride. Out of place. My suffering doesn't fit anymore.

I do not have an everlasting right to the presumed nobility of grief-on-command. I have to, once and for all, take off my widow's weeds. Underneath, I may still wear from time to time the sackcloth of misery and loss, but prepare to lay down even that when the reminders melt from agony to bittersweet, when even that time is done.

I have to prepare for the time I've been promised and, now that it is clearly coming, take hold of it. The indulgence of grief overstayed must make way for healing to creep in. There will be a time, I think, when, as a father takes his daughter's hand from his own and places it tenderly into the hand of a new husband, there will be also a time when a widow finds that although she is no longer a wife, she can still be the bride of Christ.

I've thought often about Lazarus and the whole incident wherein he was brought back to life. His rise from the grave was all fine with his friends and his sisters—and it certainly served Jesus' purpose as a bonafide, undeniable miracle—but what about Lazarus himself? What about the man?

The story makes no mention of how he responds to it all and I can't help but think that he wasn't thrilled. He'd just gone through all the misery of prolonged sickness and the grisly act of dying. That done, he was finally given his promised rest when suddenly he is beckoned back to the same grossly confusing, broken world from which he had just been released and destined to go through the whole process again. I don't know about him, but I would not be thanking my friend Jesus for that.

The only way it makes any sense to me is to think that Jesus had something greater in mind than Lazarus' personal comfort, plans, or desires. It's the short-term thinking trap, I think, to which we are all predisposed. After all, it's the way we live—in a limited world and linear time. How are we supposed to see beyond what eyes permit or hands touch? By our very nature, we're confined to finite space and it's all we have available when we have to make sense of circumstances or decide what to do next. There's no way we can see the picture the way God does. And frankly, I don't always like that.

It took months—more than a year after you died—for me to begin to understand that you weren't coming home. I looked around every corner like a reflex, continually listening for your familiar step. Even now, years later, I would not be surprised to see you walk through the door. Something died in me, is still dying, with every day you're gone.

And part of the dying is knowing beyond doubt that

God ordained this pain for me, yet another instance of His sovereignty and His long-term plan in which I play only a small, often unwilling, part. On the days when I remember again that God may have raised Lazarus, but will not raise you, I feel the temptation to slide. I want to relax into grief and ease into the ground after you, yearning for the rest you've been given, but I've been denied.

I'm tired, you see. Tired sometimes beyond taking one more step, tired of propping myself up to live and to carry the burden of unwilling change and desolate aloneness one more day. Some days, it sounds so very good to lay down long and still, hoping it will be enough so that maybe God will steal away my breath as He did yours.

But it doesn't work. I still wake up every day, knowing that with the waking, there is still something for me to do, something that it is not my place to escape or avoid. I get up, pick up my proverbial mat, and walk.

Maybe I'm finally beginning to learn the dance of love and duty, of going where I do not want to go, of doing what I do not want to do for the sake of something bigger than I can see. People have told me that caring for you during your illness was self-sacrificial, but this—this living—is much harder. Maybe it's because its end is so much less clear; maybe because it has less discernible purpose. Either way, it is what I'm given and, if I reach out, even in pain, I have to trust I will be met there by the God who put me in this life in the first place.

You were not, after all, mine. You were, and are, God's. And if that is true, then I was not yours either, regardless of how I sometimes feel. I, too, am God's. My heart may protest, but my head knows that you are dead. God, however, is not. Or maybe He is dead in much the same way you are, body no longer physically available but the rest of Him still very much alive.

Yes, it's all very confusing but, if I let my head—what I know to be true—rule my heart and how I sometimes feel, I can take whatever steps life offers and, with them, endure the joy and survive the pain. Life is still happening, after all, and for the meantime, I am part of it. One eye will probably always be looking for you and one ear listening, but I don't have to live in the past. The best parts of the past will accompany me wherever I go. You followed where you were called to go and I have to do the same. If I reach out my hand when I am lonely or when I lose my balance, a hand will reach back. I may be by myself, but I am not alone.

Mourning, in the end, isn't a static thing. For a while, it lays down next to you, spoons, then wraps familiar arms all around. It isn't completely comfortable, but belongs, like a stuffed substitute for what once lived. Room temperature, but at least present.

Then even the mourning cools. When I saw you not only as I chose to, but as you genuinely were, that's when I understood that I didn't really want you back after all. Oh, I was still glad to have had you—your fervor, your intensity—but it was clearer now that your aim had not been as true as you'd liked to think and that, when you missed the mark, left a smouldering scar that never quite healed.

So did I, of course, toward you. That's the dark side of marriage. When one enters into the contract, there are only two principle options. You either get lifelong calm normalcy, polite and predictable, or learn to gasp for breath between ecstasy, insult, and disbelief. We had to have the latter and I don't think we would have ever wanted to choose otherwise.

So finally, a day came when I couldn't stand on the porch watching the hearse pull out of the driveway any longer. I couldn't keep peeking around the same corners, trying to catch your fleeting shadow. So I left. From our home to mine. From country to city. From familiar burden to unknown possibility.

Moving changed the mourning again. Moving to a place you never knew, among people you never met, both helped and hurt. It drove home to a new measure the degree to which I'd enjoyed in you the opinion of at least one other person I largely respected. You were that person. Smart enough. Studied enough. Strong enough. You feared very little, risked well, and stood straight in adversity. I lack that now. All of it.

I dreamed last night that I was in a place of uncomfortable exposure, alone without friend or witness. It was in a school of some sort where I'd been teaching. I'd been detained there by someone who bore some kind of authority and had stripped me of everything that symbolized my autonomy—purse, keys, phone, money. He questioned me about my activities as though I bore some kind of mysterious guilt. I started to resist. It was time to summon backup. I took my phone back and made a call. To you. When the time came to summon help, you were my first and only thought.

When I woke from that dream, right at the place of the phone call, I knew that was the point. This is where I've settled for now. You gone. Me here, without you. Still in awe, still trying to catch my breath after the memories of the madness of what we once had, but no longer newly outraged at being left behind.

I should have known before ever beginning to reach for the phone. It doesn't matter how difficult or desperate this life gets. It doesn't matter that there's no one I can even begin to depend on but you. You won't answer.

I'm tired of missing you. It's like an old song losing its charm because it's played on the radio too often and no longer brings productive emotion, just the wretched, wrenching kind that leaves one breathless, but no better off. I want to know the worth of these days, not those—to hold the gentleness of early breezes moving curtains and the mourning doves calling in the first sun and the rain dropping easily from grumbling skies. I want to plan a trip or even a day without looking over my shoulder for you. I want to look ahead and find something worthwhile waiting there.

I wonder whether it's good that you're not here. What would you have done in this plague, this virus? Would you hide silent in lockdown or disregard it as irrelevant and cast yourself into the hands of God? You often surprised me with your reaction to situations like these— at times cautious and at others rash. Now, though, you left me to make my own fate in it. You don't care anymore.

But I'm still writing about you. I don't even really want to, but nothing else comes out with any degree of passion. Almost everything falls flat in pale comparison. Almost.

There is Florence. Florence has never paled. It's been two years since I first rounded the corner of the Via de Neri and strode into Duomo square, gasping, two years since days began with cornetti and blood orange juice, two years since I watched the sculptors through the alley window, two years since the bookshop and the street violinists, two years since eating al dente spaghetti olio beside the medallion recording the death of Savanarola in the Piazza de la Signoria, two years since the Arno at sunrise, two years since holding the head of Christ in my hands at the Opera Museum. And there is the deciding to live, the demolition of my flesh to repair my heart, and the subsiding real physical pain as it heals. There is the moving to a place all my own, where you are not a tenant but an occasional guest, where I wake up every morning marveling that the sun still travels west through all my windows.

Maybe that's how I exorcise you. Maybe that's the way I regain my freedom, to allow today to step in front of yesterday. You are, after all, part of yesterday. I woke up this morning and you didn't. You are either always awake or not at all, but I still cycle through days in repeating rhythms of work, rest, and sleep.

I have to decide. I have to intentionally move from this place to that. I've been lying in bed waiting for you to come back for more than four years. I can't do it anymore. I have to swing my foot out, put my weight on it, and take a step. See—I'm doing it. And I'm not looking back. I can't imagine where you've gone, but I say this to you, wherever you are: Don't reach for me. I won't be here.

PRELUDE: WEIGHT

CARMELA MCINTIRE

> This matters, the remaking of an untenable world through the nib of a pen, it matters so much I can't stop doing it.
>
> — —CAROL SHIELDS, *UNLESS*

When I was six, I learned to read, sounding out letters in Mrs. Heineman's first grade class at PS #3. I had found another marvelous world in this one. In my small blue bedroom in our upstairs flat, my books were always near. Daily, I woke early to a silent household, gazing out my window at the row of poplars outside, their leaves fluttering silver and green. I read by the brightening light till it was time to rise for school. Or I'd tiptoe to the shadowed living room, illuminated by street lamps. Double front windows looked straight into the huge chestnut tree at the front of the house, through its branches and beyond, over streets and houses, to the red sandstone crenellations of the Armory two blocks away. The view thrilled and disturbed. I knew the branches were called "boughs," and boughs could break, and down would come baby, cradle and all. The street lights, the enormous tree, the bigness of the world. I held my books close.

In first grade, we read Dick and Jane, and Baby Sally, and Puff the cat, and Spot the dog, and most wondrously, Mother and Father, enthrallingly different from my mom and dad. Mother wore pastel shirtwaist dresses and smiled all the time. Father smoked a pipe and wore a suit and tie. The children actually called them "Mother," and "Father," words we used quite differently: "Mother," as in "*my* mother says," and "Father," only in the terrifying dark of the confessional. Mom cleaned the house all the time, smoked cigarettes while we ate breakfasts of toast laden with butter and cinnamon-sugar, eating none herself, sipping black coffee.

She was always in the house. Dad was gone a lot. He wore a baseball cap and a T-shirt and a zipped-up short jacket to work. When he came home, the smell of cigarette smoke and machine oil clung to his clothes, rich, familiar. He put my hand on his stubbly cheek. "It tickles." But it didn't tickle, not exactly, it was dry, papery, familiar, Dad, tender, warm. Mom got us up, my baby brother and me, she tucked us in, our parents kissed and hugged us at every coming and going. We had rules, we asked permission, sometimes we got into trouble. Dick and Jane and Baby Sally did what they liked, smiling parental presences hovering just out of the picture.

I loved Dick and Jane. Their world was so different from mine that I longed to read more of it, that bright, pretty place, small and explicable, which belonged entirely to the children. No shadows, no boughs, no Armory, no night shift for Dad, no frazzled Mom. The book-world beckoned so, with its alternative family, its shining artificiality. No aunts or cigar-smoking uncles or cousins living downstairs in the same house. No blue-haired old lady nearby, rumored to be a witch. No baby brother breaking my things. No phrases flying in Italian, a code I could sometimes break when adults spoke at the dinner table about us kids or who they did not want living in the neighborhood. My world was full of puzzling incidents. Complicated. Why did I have a baby brother? Why didn't we have a dog and a cat? Why did Dad go to work at night and sleep during the day? Why did Dad carry me into the hospital one day, and when I came home three days later, there were balloons to welcome me?

Mother, Father, Dick, Jane, then books at our library, the Niagara Street Branch: "Childhood of Famous Americans," and "We Were There" books and the All-of-A-Kind-Family, the Famous Five, the Melendy family, and later, Sue Barton and Betty Cavanna's teen-aged heroines—in none of these books did I find lives that much resembled my own. I sought out heroines, but they lived either in Rockwellian small towns or in New York City, nothing in between, no gritty mid-sized communities like my own, Buffalo, the "Queen City" buffeted by Great Lakes weather. Yet the book-girls were much like me, no matter the size of their families or their hometowns. Shy, introspective, on the edges of things. Neither they nor anyone else thought they were pretty. As good students, they excelled at their English classes especially, but were otherwise unremarkable to themselves and to others. Often they longed to change just one trait about themselves, knowing that then, for certain, life would be perfect. They were too shy, too tall, too thin, their hair mousey or too red or too straight, their skin too freckled. Could they change? How would that happen? What would they be when they grew up? How could they discover where they belonged, who they could be?

I checked my favorite books out of the library two, three, four times, reveling in the pleasure of reading, especially, when I already knew the ending. It was so easy then to see the patterns, the signs, leading to the resolution easily guessed at the first time through. Always a resolution, sensible, happy. Series books were the best. I could follow my favorites through their lives, each stage preparing for the next. So I read and reread about the All-of-A-Kind girls and the March sisters and Anne Shirley, entranced at their progress from childhood to happy adulthood, where they found work and love. I longed to join their ordered worlds, to forge a plot, a pattern, of my own.

Those childhood protagonists, the red-haired, too-tall, too-thin, too-mousey? My heroines reconciled themselves to their imperfections, in their world the source of previously undiscovered strengths. Along with their realization of their talents came physical transformations. They blossomed as they learned to believe in their own competence and attractiveness. The inner changes fueled the outer ones. I did not know how to make that happen to me. In my books I found no one who looked into the mirror at a round face with cheekbones obscured, wide hips, doughy thighs. A sedentary childhood under the care of my too-protective mother—I got sick a lot—had made me awkward and reluctant at sports, my chest tightening at exertion. Snapped up immediately in the classroom for spelling bees and academic contests, I was always last in gym, my spot on a team the result of some bargain between the captains: "I'll take her. But we bat first!" High school, an all-girl college preparatory school with mandatory uniforms, spared me the daily agony of wardrobe decisions and boys' appraisals. But shopping expeditions for special occasions were mortifying. Three-way mirrors, solicitous sales ladies eager to troubleshoot, bypassing the chic, petite junior clothing for the darker stuff available in larger sizes—I'd start out hopeful and end dismayed. I could talk to boys only in my head, sparkling, charming, writing scripts for myself never performed. When our sixteen year-old neighbor Eddie stopped his car one day to offer me a lift on my way home from school, I didn't know how to refuse. I got in, looked at my feet, and said not a word for the next twelve minutes, the longest of my life to date. Poor Eddie! I thanked him, exited the car, and fled into our house.

Easy enough to say that girls should not succumb to cultural mores emphasizing beauty along with competence. When I was in high school, with *Seventeen* telling me what I thought I needed to know, knowing that I had the wrong body, the wrong hair, the wrong face, with no idea what to do, I longed only to change, to join, to be like everyone else. "*Your day will come,*" my mother told me, when I knew our junior prom was out of the question.

I felt, dimly, that Mom understood my longings and did not know how to help beyond those quiet reassurances about "my day" in the future. Dad, wonderful Dad, said nothing outright, but he too knew exactly why I worried and pined. When I turned sixteen, he said, "How would you like to try contact lenses?" Would I! I hadn't dared ask. I thought they'd be wildly expensive, not so much out of reach for my parents' careful budget, but, like the horseback riding lessons that I'd saved for, I'd be told, "people like us don't do that." Would I! Mom feared the very idea, as many people did in the early days of lenses, so it was Dad who set up the appointments, who got me to the doctor, who cheered me on through the process of adjustment.

How I loved my lenses. How I loved my dad.

With beaming family encouragement, in my own way, I

marked the usual milestones of a senior year of high school—the school play, the prom, senior antics, the breathless anticipation of college and Going Away. My Going Away meant only 50 miles, the farthest my overprotective dad would allow. Still. Away. The freshman year of my dreadful roommate, my first boyfriend, my first breakup, my discovery of my own strength. I came home in May to the awful fact of Dad in the hospital, surgery the following morning. The lung cancer was discovered two months before, diagnosis and hospital and imminent surgery—all unmentioned in weekly phone calls, because "we wanted you to finish your exams and not to worry."

Not to worry. My brother Joe, 13, and I, paralyzed, fearful, Mom so brittle with dread she hardly knew how to talk to us. So she did not. I found out, post surgery, only by eavesdropping as she talked with her sister Mary in our kitchen, that the planned removal of the cancerous lung could not proceed. Cancer had spread everywhere. Over the six weeks of daily radiation that followed, Dad shrank, unable to eat, weakening by the day. My return to school loomed. While Jimmy, an older cousin, waited in his laden station wagon to take me back to school, I spoke to Dad, still himself, still there, but smaller than I had ever thought he could be. "Bye," he said. "Take care of yourself, Carm."

I nodded, hugged him, and ran from the room crying. Jimmy, three years older than I, the handsome, solid almost-brother who did everything first so the rest of us could follow, did not know what to say. He watched the road. I cried, for myself, for Dad, in astonished bitterness that no one, not even Mom, had words for what was happening. Not even Jimmy, who always, always knew what to do.

A week into September, a phone call summoned me

home. Dad was in the hospital. Arriving home late on Friday, a neighbor, an older and dear friend of the family, told me I could see Dad the next morning. "Best not to see him now, at night, he's hooked up to tubes and things." I did not know how to insist; Mr. Eccleston meant well. Dad died during the night, Mom at his side, Joe and I at home. The wake. Family, friends gathering. The briefest of funeral Masses conducted by a priest who didn't know him, or us, the church cavernous on a Monday morning. "You have to go back to school," Mom said to my offer to spend the semester at home. "You have to go back, or you won't go back."

Grieving, bewildered at the speed of it all, relieved to leave our sad, sad house, I went the next day. At the dorm, the girls tiptoed around me, leaving flowery Hallmark cards to mark my loss. Mom, Joe, and I—each of us grieved alone. I clung to my studies—straight As, always, except for math—holing up in library carrels, eating stashes of candy bars from vending machines, eating every bite of the dining hall food we'd made fun of all the previous year, Jell-O and bread and potatoes and pasta and starchy desserts. All of it. Trying to quiet an insistent inner clawing I'd not felt before Dad's illness. Ate and ate and ate, always hungry.

My college life, just starting, grew stunted. Studying, my dorm girlfriends, dear and supportive and funny. And that was all. Hours each night with my textbooks, heavy, dependable textbooks, reading, eating, my world diminishing as my body grew, hidden in jeans, oversize sweaters, my face smaller in its frame of my thick dark hair, curly, wilder by the day (in the restroom: "Wow, where do you get your hair permed?"). I didn't care. I had my friends, my studies, my food. I mourned alone, eating and weeping in corners all over campus.

That was how I got through college, through a teaching internship, graduation, through my first job, teaching grade 7 for two years in the big junior high school in the adjoining town. To all appearances cheerful, competent, managing my life and work by retreating whenever I could for solitary reading and eating; dismal cycles of eating, dieting, brief weight loss, succumbing again to that sad gnawing only temporarily stilled with lots of food. Was I mired, permanently, in grief for my dad? In then-unrecognized depression?

Graduate school, two states away. Transformation still eluded me. I wanted to be better, stronger. How would it feel to cast off the weight of fear, anxiety, sadness, self-doubt? Despite warm friendships and academic success, those internal weights persisted. Gradually I came to see my physical weight as mysteriously connected to this emotional freight. Still, I could lift none of it. I did not know how. I soldiered on, as I always had, food and solitude surefire stopgaps. But paralyzing self-doubt struck as I faced writing my doctoral dissertation. A table in a corner of my apartment held neat piles of library books and stacks of relevant notes. I looked at them, paged through the notes, and did nothing. I would have to leave school. I did not see how I could finish. I could confide in no one, least of all my director. How could I tell my mentor that I couldn't write? That for emotional sustenance I needed the literal sustenance of quantities of food I was far too embarrassed to eat in company?

In this bleak frame of mind, I saw a note in the local paper about a new meeting of an Overeaters' Anonymous group. I needed to try something, anything. In those days, 12-Step programs and their vocabulary had not permeated the culture as they have since. I knew, vaguely, that "Alcoholics Anonymous" had succeeded where other treatments

PRELUDE: WEIGHT

failed, and vaguely, that it focused on behavior somehow. I knew I didn't need a weight loss program; I knew, oh boy, how I knew how to lose weight. And oh boy, did I know how to regain it at the speed of lightning. Were there others who felt out of control? Were there others ashamed of the sheer quantity of what they ate, the lengths they'd go to for quieting the awful compulsion, even briefly? I needed help. I was afraid, too. For two weeks in a row, the meeting time came and went—I forgot. I fell asleep. I made it on the third try.

A church hall near a local mall housed my first OA meeting, a big square, beige room with metal folding chairs and, at one end, two long tables placed end to end, as though in a cafeteria. A few other people stood around, shy, uncertain, like me. Several women, one my age, the others middle-aged, fat, sagging, pale. No one knew what to do. A younger man walked in briskly and took charge. "I'm Jim. I started this meeting because I've just moved to the area. Take a seat, everyone." We arranged ourselves at that long table, relieved, still shy.

Jim began by reading the Twelve Steps, new to me. The first one cut deep: "We admitted we were powerless over food, that our lives had become unmanageable." But when the second mentioned "a power greater than ourselves," I wavered. Jim shared his story. "I"m Jim, and I'm a compulsive overeater…." and asked us all to take a turn. Ralph was an alcoholic, sober now, but eating like crazy. Florence could barely rise each day, leaving the bed unmade, eating, sad. Joanie, blonde, pretty, a nurse, admitted bingeing, hiding food, ashamed. Two women declined to speak. "You can pass," Jim said, "but it's your ass."

I belonged here. Didn't I? "Hi. I'm Carmela. I'm a compulsive overeater." The chorus of "Hello, Carmela, welcome!"cheered me on. Deep breath, "I don't need a diet. I know how to lose weight. But it's behavior. Behavior. I can't stop eating when I feel bad. And sometimes even when I feel OK." There. I said it. The meeting ended with the *Our Father*, said while we held hands—was it a little cultish, maybe? Religion on the sly? What was the big book (later I'd learn to capitalize it, to love it, to respect it)? Yet Jim looked so happy. Normal-sized. Calm. And the others, Florence and Joanie and Ralph...they did what I did. We told one another we'd meet again next week: we'd amended the *Our Father* with Jim's prompting, still holding hands, "Keep coming back! It works if you work it and you keep coming back!" I came back. We all came back, eager, less shy. I sorted out the rhetoric, falling in love with the common sense of the Big Book, with its focus on defeating fear and anger, its vignettes of change. Any group based on story-telling had my full attention. Stories—Jim, Joanie, Ralph, Florence. I shared my story and hung on the words of others. I wanted so very much to live—and write—my own trajectory of success.

Now through the Steps I had a guide for conducting my life, for overcoming anxiety and fear. The program seemed simple, but like so many truly wise directives ("Let go and let God"; "Keep it simple"; "One day at a time") it was toughest to follow when most needed. I learned to act ("use your tools: the Steps. The Big Book. Make phone calls!") rather than letting emotion wash over me, rendering me helpless, and worse, eating alone, frantically, to squelch pain or uncertainty. Even small changes in my reactions made enormous differences.

Hesitantly, slowly, I resumed writing, confiding my writer's block to a trusted member of my doctoral committee. Jay was six and a half feet tall, a warm, erudite, skinny, middle-aged chainsmoker, a specialist in Renaissance literature in charge of the department writing program. Over the years, I'd relay his kind, wise words to my own students as we finished discussing their work: "And remember, if you can't do any of this, if you're still stuck, if you forget what we talked about, come *right back*." That parting remark itself saved me from having to return—I could feel that Jay had said it out of his own struggles. I drafted a chapter. Reworked, redrafted. Built momentum. Accumulated pages. Prodded by my other mentor, I applied for teaching positions on the promise that I'd complete the degree. Four requests for interviews came as the December break was to start! I'd need to take copies of my chapter to those meetings at our post-Christmas professional convention, I'd need to have them ready the day after Christmas. How? Panic. How could I do this, in those pre-computer days? I called a dear friend. "That's great," Marty said, either not hearing or ignoring my panic. "Well, when you get home, rent an IBM electric [typewriter], type up the chapter, and get copies."

Keep it simple. I wasn't paralyzed or punished myself with a package of Hydrox cookies. I got it done.

Action: not evasion, not flight. I learned that transformation was actually self-discovery. I would not change as much as I would find within who I was, what I could do, who I could be, to the fullest extent possible. Pushing aside fear, pushing through anxiety and anger and grief, to see what I could be without those things. I'd always loved the Cinderella-arc of the stories of my childhood, the hidden talent and beauty finally recognized. Now, for the first time, I recognized my best self. With help, with persistence, with the program, I could lift all of that weight, emotional, spiritual, and physical changes happening in tandem.

It was at an OA meeting that I met Alex. I had volunteered to lead that night, opening the meeting, initiating discussion of the pre-arranged topic ("The second tradition"). Men were rare at OA in those days, but Alex stood out too because of his articulate comments, his poised manner—and his size. In a room full of large people, he was the largest. I took his phone number from the call list, thinking that I'd like to know him better, and not just to share program. Three days later as I was gearing up to call him, hoping to initiate I wasn't quite sure what, the phone rang. Alex asked me out. I was smitten.

Though I knew my own story was complicated in ways I was just beginning to understand, I did not think of these intricacies of inner life as they might have applied to Alex. With him there was relief at being completely myself, talking about our histories, the childhood hurt, the pain of adulthood, the shame and discomfort of oversized bodies. When I spoke about eating and weight and appearance and fear he understood. For the first time in my life, my body, with all its attendant emotional freight, became a bridge to intimacy, not an obstacle. Alex understood me. We met on that one vital point in a way impossible to me with anyone else. Hand in hand, we would offer each other experience, strength, hope, and love, writing our stories of joyful transformation, compulsions laid to rest, fears conquered. Our best selves. Ten months after we met, we planned to marry.

Alex's family embraced me; my mother counseled caution. She could hardly contain her reaction to his size: we hadn't known each other long, after all. What if he got *bigger*? I countered that at age 33, I knew my own mind; that Alex, immersed in OA and married to me, was definitely not going to get bigger. He did, though. Over the course of our marriage, he got bigger, he got smaller, he got bigger again. I realized afresh that our bodies tell our stories. Yet I did not know his, not really.

What did that body, waxing and waning, signify?

Alex's voice, his words, drew me to him. An even more voracious reader than I, he loved words, word play and cleverness and puns. He excelled at other languages too. He regained his deep fluency in Spanish over the course of our marriage. He read Russian, needed at one point for his graduate studies. He delighted in startling speakers of Hindi and Urdu with his conversational ease in both languages, hardly expected from a six-foot, two-inch bearded man of enormous girth, with russet hair and blue eyes. He'd learned both from long sojourns in New Delhi and Lahore years before we met, first as a language student, then as a teacher.

As a child, he too had craved what the world of books brought him. We talked about those old yearnings, how we'd both landed happily in academia to satisfy them. Predictably, our house was awash in books (the pile on his bedside table, spilling onto the floor, said Alex, was "intellectual compost"). Both of us had amassed sizable personal libraries. Now we delighted in the duplicates we found: I'm sure many academics bring to their marriages their Book-of-the-Month Club two-volume version of the *OED*. Of course. We now had two. Even on the tight budget of our early marriage, neither of us ever questioned a book purchase. Our only child learned to read early, just as we had. Like us, she was happiest with books in her hands.

With the books came talk about literature and film and philosophy and history and politics and religion. The range of Alex's readings, the scope of his book collection, dazzled me. Yes, I was a long time student and teacher of literature and composition. I read a lot. I still read as I did as a child—for the pleasure of losing myself in fiction, in poetry, drama, prose—living other lives, sharing insights with my students, exploring in my journal, talking with friends, now, talking with Alex. I read, always, to explore myself, to learn more about how to be in this world, to find a fellowship sometimes missing from my day-to-day life.

Alex, though, read differently. He did not read much fiction. Oh, police procedurals, the more intricate the better. Mostly he read to learn, to deepen his analyses of history, politics, and psychology. For an international relations professional that made sense. His personal book collection revealed that he also read as a means of self-help. Not self-exploration, but as a way to apply rules of conduct, perspectives, to his behavior. Outward change, not inward exploration. He read widely about religion and spirituality. His books included *The Journals of George Fox* and Quakerism and Zen and Buddhist practice. He read about early Christianity, about the Episcopal church, about Hinduism. He owned several translations of the Bible. He read the Koran, Thomas Merton on contemplation, Thomas Moore on the sacred in everyday life. Twelve-Step literature crowded the shelves: *The Big Book* (AA's foundational text); *Compulsive Overeater* (the Big Book of OA). *Twelve Steps and Twelve Traditions. The Twelve Steps for Adult Children. Resisting Recovery: The Food Obsession. A Guide to Step 3: Giving Up The Game.*

The library of someone seeking self-mastery, self-improvement, the library of someone who wanted a map, as I had, to living simply, without fear and anxiety, who wanted, above all, to stop eating compulsively, to be physically healthy. To do the things impossible at his current weight—fit easily into automobile and airplane and theatre seats, run up flights of stairs, ride a bicycle, hike and climb, buy off the rack clothing quickly and easily. To no longer be the largest person at any gathering. Not to have to eye the furniture in any home we visited, picking out the sturdiest seating. Not to have to stand, shifting from foot to foot, when no chair would accommodate him. Not to be dismissed by every doctor who saw him, with the faintly contemptuous injunction to lose weight as the remedy for any and all ailments. In years past, draconian diet regimens, a few supervised medically, others concocted by Alex himself, had gotten his weight to normal levels. Briefly. Then, bang, he was 400 pounds again. I don't know if, like me, he thought of OA as a last resort, the program that could, just maybe, address the compulsion.

What did ail him? I knew from my own experience and from every Twelve Step testimony and guide that lasting physical recovery could occur only through moment-to-moment willingness to go to any lengths for abstinence, the OA equivalent of AA sobriety. Looking within, pushing through somehow to find the causes, to heal on the inside. Working hard with a sponsor, working and reworking the Steps with the sponsor's guidance, going to meetings. Only then might emotional and spiritual recovery come. A trusted therapist told me after Alex's death that had she met him, she would have known that some internal scarring—pain now occluded by his flesh?—kept him where he was, that he could not, or would not, push through, that perhaps some deep trauma held him back, consciously or not.

Yet Alex approached recovery the way he approached everything. He would read, read, read, becoming an expert. He would look everywhere for answers. For *the* answers. If he could not or would not look within, he would turn his gaze outward, to Martin Seligman's *Learned Optimism: How to Change Your Mind and Your Life*, heeding George Fox's "Walk cheerfully through the world, answering that of God in every one." If he could not solve what ailed him, he would present to the world a determined helpfulness, his generosity leavened by good-natured humor. Twelve-Step literature and lore counsels that we can "act as if": we can act, we can practice recovery even before we have fully understood and experienced the spiritual underpinnings needed for it. Take action, says the advice; the inner disposition will follow. But might *acting as if* remain hollow, a repertoire of poses, nothing more? And might there be cracks in that facade of learned poses and attitudes?

Alex revealed himself in casual remarks, maybe more than he knew. "I may look like a grasshopper," he said to me once, "but inside beats the heart of an ant. He said he'd explained to our family doctor that "for some of us, anxiety relief is found only in eating sleeves of crackers." Worry, anxiety, fear—features of life for all of us. But the compulsion they sparked was never still.

We talked a few times about collaborating on a book about weight and compulsion. Happy at the suggestion— what a wonderful joint project! —I realized that this too was Alex doing what he did best—gathering and synthesizing information, presenting it to others. He could study and study and formulate ideas and present them. He'd be involved in a topic vital to both of us—but here too, as an outsider. One Sunday he leaned over to me as we sang a hymn, pointing out the phrase "robed in flesh." I knew instantly that he meant it as our book title.

So perhaps he did know: the robe was pulled tightly about him, shielding that tender, wounded core, with its pain and its secrets. He lived on the periphery, relentlessly directing the sight of others outward. He encouraged me steadily in everything I did, bolstering my self-confidence with gifts of clothing I would not have dreamed of buying for myself, so unsure was I of the new outlines of my body. He understood that I could not interpret what I saw in the mirror. More: he was an always-willing sounding board for professional questions, discussing and reading my work, urging me to formulate projects, to publish. I tried to offer support in turn, not knowing—because he never said, not even in answer to questions—exactly what he needed. Twice, in the year before his death, we talked intimately in a way new to us, Alex sharing childhood musings and memories that puzzled him, perhaps as the source of his deep anxiety. I loved those conversations, so rare, so essential, so delayed.

Day to day, nothing brought permanent weight loss, not our family practice of eating sensibly, always, without a scrap of snack or junk food in the house, not the repeated, conventional diets, not the liquid diet supervised by a bariatric clinic at the University of Miami Medical School, not the gastric bypass at East Carolina University Medical School, in the early days of that procedure. Periods of disciplined eating, exercise, weight loss, followed by compulsive eating that I never saw. Never knew where or when or how much, only the result, in rapid, nearly incapacitating weight gain. And the cycle would begin again, until one year, it didn't.

How fiercely I wished that we had talked again.

No matter the hushed tones or euphemisms or hesitations, no matter the means or the place, suicide is always public. After Alex killed himself, I had not only to cope with the loss of the man I loved, with the hideousness of his death, with our grievously wounded child, but also with the fact of his choice. I met questions everywhere, asked reluctantly sometimes, but asked nonetheless: was he depressed? Did he leave a note? Did you see any signs? What do you think happened? Do you think it could have been foul play? He must have been seriously disturbed. I was supposed to know. The wife should know. Moreover, I was supposed to share what I knew. No, there was no note.

I saw no changes in him. We had been planning a family summer vacation. No, I did not think it was foul play. Beyond that, I did not want to speak. His death was part of his life—our life—but by his inescapably public act, it had been torn from the deepest heart of our family, held up for public gawking.

Much as I longed for privacy, I wished I could control how Alex was remembered, I wished, hoped, that his death would not color everything that had gone before. Within limits, I fielded the questions. I tried to halt them. But the public nature of it all should not have surprised me. Alex, through his very appearance, had always drawn speculation and questions. Always. Despite his usual cheery demeanor, it seemed that his every demon was externalized, his struggle with weight so visible, so fraught. Those questions had come to me too: doesn't he try to lose weight? Has he tried...? You look fine, why can't he...? Again, the wife was supposed to know, to make it alright, to run the household so as to make normality possible, to insist on it (as others insisted, with their questions), not allowing this—this—aberration. This affront.

I had no control, none, not over the questions, not over our city newspaper of record, which included in its report a detailed account of the manner of his death ("He's a public figure, people have a right to know") despite the fiercest objection I could summon, not over the long piece on Alex's suicide in the local alternative weekly, a year later, devastating to his parents. There was that public story, accepted as an explanation. Oh, yes. That's what happened. It was *not* our story. It was not Alex's story. No one could really know our story.

Inevitably, though, the public version had to be folded into the private family narrative of Alex's life, our marriage, his death, the aftermath. Time passed; the

PRELUDE: WEIGHT

anguish became truly private. Eventually I found a hard-won peace, based less on resolution than on weariness, surrendering to living with questions forever unanswered.

Twelve years later, an email:

> "Carmella [*sic*], I'd like to send you a copy of the bound galley of my new novel, _____. Can you give me your hard-mail address? I want you to read it early, before publication, because one of the main characters will be thought to be based on Alex. . . .I know you, of all people, will understand the transformational process of fiction and will see that the character of the Professor is not a portrait of Alex, although there are certain aspects of his life and personality that will invite some literal-minded readers who happen to know bits and pieces of Alex's story to think otherwise. . . Anyhow, if you'd like to meet up for a drink or coffee then to talk about this, I'd love it. Fondly, Russell."

Alex cherished his friendship with Russell Banks, formed when both were undergraduates at Chapel Hill, and maintained over the years—when either of them found themselves in or near the other's current hometown, they'd make a point of meeting. So we'd seen Russell and his wife in Miami, where they had a place in South Beach, in New York City, at Chapel Hill. Once, we spent a weekend at their gorgeous summer place in the Adirondacks. Alex and Russell's mutual respect and affection and their shared undergraduate history fueled the connection, as did the fact that both, after bumpy histories, had married happily. A book Russell published just after Alex died mentioned him, citing his death date, in the dedication. Alex would have loved that gesture, as I did.

I was thrilled by the email, thrilled by the invitation to

talk, thrilled that Alex was remembered in print—for us book people, was there any better memorial? Though Alex had chosen to truncate his own story, casting doubt on the narrative of his entire life through his suicide, he would now have a fitting memorial, I thought, allowing of course for the "transformational process" that Russell mentioned. I didn't know what form that would take. What would Russell make of the man whose friendship he'd prized for so many years? Would fictional Alex be smart, kind, funny, generous? Normal size? A traveler, multi-lingual, who'd learned ease in other cultures? A loving and beloved husband and father and respected teacher?

The galleys arrived in a bulky brown envelope soon after I responded to Russell's email. The story compelled me from the opening pages. *Lost Memory of Skin*, set in a Miami renamed "Calusa," focuses on a shameful failure of the community—its treatment of men convicted of sexual offenses, major and minor. They'd completed prison terms; they might be on probation. The rules in place for where such men could live—not near schools or houses of worship or neighborhoods with families—meant exile. They'd lived for years in encampments under one of the causeways from the mainland to Miami Beach. The narrator of the novel, The Kid, is an uneducated twenty year-old with no sexual experience, ever. Arrested as he shows up at the home of a fourteen year-old girl he'd met online, the Kid never even gets a glimpse of her. He's stopped at the door by her father and then arrested. No "skin," no touching, for which he longs, his plans for their first meeting include watching TV, maybe popcorn, maybe snuggling, maybe, maybe, sex. But the condom he carries in his backpack damns him—he wanted sex with an underage girl.

Riveted by the premise of the novel, I read eagerly,

anticipating the appearance of "Alex." Entering the story on page 78, "the largest man the Kid had ever seen." He's The Professor, a bearded polymath conspicuous for his size and intellect. Smart, obese, academic, The Professor loved only himself, had severed ties with his aging parents. Married, with twin seven year-olds, but friendless, opaque even to his wife Gloria.

The transformational process of fiction, I reminded myself, my horror growing as I read. Anyone who knew Alex would recognize The Professor. Would they see what I saw, a grotesque, a caricature? Worse: The Professor committed suicide exactly as Alex had, the scene of his death described in such detail that at first I thought Russell had gotten hold of the police report—available to anyone who asked, I knew, for the cost of the xeroxing. $13.40. I had my own copy. Then I remembered. Details from the report had appeared in the local alternative weekly, *The Miami Times*. Russell had lifted them entirely, no doubt while reading his own contribution to the article in an interview with the reporter. He'd always known, he said, that "there was a deep well of darkness in [Alex]." He did not elaborate in his answer to the reporter. He was certainly doing so now, in the novel.

The portrayal sickened me. Alex was recognizable, though he'd been pulled apart and reassembled to make a heavy-handed point about narcissism, American culture, his physical monstrosity an objective correlative for some other kind of gluttony. Intellectual? Spiritual? Emotional? Did he batten on other people somehow? Or did he feed and overfeed to keep the world at bay, to maintain a fleshy barrier to intimacy?

Because I loved Alex, because I thought Russell loved him too, I was furious. Is this what you really think of him, Russell? That he's a deceiving monster whom no one can ever know fully? A man who manages his difficult past in part by inhabiting only the present, tending his own insatiability? Your valued friend of thirty years?

Yet I understood that The Professor was not Alex. Was not intended to be. But this fiction did not transform him, as Russell had promised: The Professor's past, hinted at, included lots of travel, language study in South Asia, in Latin America, perhaps even covert activity on behalf of unnamed government entities. Off the record, under the radar, deniability from all parties built in. A deep well of darkness. Parts of Alex's life matched those biographical snippets; the "covert activity," I didn't know, but given the extensive time overseas, a natural leap. How, really, had Alex paid for all that travel? Had Russell wondered too?

Magic realism? Hell, no.

Through my anger I could *feel* the reason for the book, the real reason. I could even sympathize: Russell had created The Professor to confront, explore, explain to himself, somehow, the awful question of how a prized friend from his youth, a friend of decades, could have ended his own life. What might make that happen? And so this Alex-like fiction ran away with the novel, snatching it from the Miami-pariahs-under-the-causeway and from The Kid, drawing us instead into the backstory The Professor invents to explain his own death. "I will be murdered," he tells The Kid in an interview recorded for his wife Gloria. "It will look like suicide, but it will be murder." He loves her and the children. His death is not his doing. As he intends, the tape reassures his wife. He was taken. He did not leave them. She is consoled, she tells The Kid, she can rest in the memory of The Professor's love.

But it's not only this death that Russell confronts; it's Alex's life, too, the eliding of past activities, the omissions, the voraciousness for information, for food, the pride in his outsize intellect, stolid coping with the outsize body he could not change, maybe that too, pride, a challenge to take him or leave him. And where that led him, how that led him, to his carefully planned death in a drainage canal miles from home.

I am not a writer of fiction. Nor do I want to explore the death of my husband through the scrim of someone else's fiction, though *Lost Memory of Skin* feels to me like a painful intimate glimpse of Russell's connection to Alex, alive and dead.

I want to meet it head on, to mine our sixteen years together, to replay that last morning at home when nothing happened, and later, when everything happened, to keep our daughter close, cherishing the best of her father, forgiving him if we can, and loving him still.

MAIDEN TO CRONE: A LIGHT BEARER'S JOURNEY

LISA LUCCA

Not long after my tenth birthday, I woke to find my dad's razor and toothbrush missing from the bathroom medicine cabinet. Mom said he went on a business trip, something he'd never done before. The truth was, she had asked him to leave.

The night before, my mother sat at the top of the basement steps eavesdropping while Dad cooed into the phone like a schoolgirl declaring the evening "a success." She suspected he was talking to the wife of his co-worker, Rex, since the couple had just been over for dinner. But it was Rex he was cooing to.

I would learn years later Dad's revelation that night of his "homosexual tendencies," and how they shocked my mother. Nothing in her Italian-Catholic upbringing prepared her for his admission that he was attracted to men. She asked him to go to a hotel; by the weekend he moved out.

"But why can't you come home, Daddy?" I cried, when he took my little sister, Dina, and I to his dingy studio apartment in the basement of an art deco building in Oak

Park. "You and Mom get along so good." Sitting beside him on a hand-me-down couch, where Dina and I slept like bookends during our visits, he said there were things I was too young to understand.

"Your mother and I still love each other. We just can't live together right now."

His answer was unsatisfying to my broken heart. I wanted to know *why*, to understand how two people who got along so well could suddenly be unable to live under the same roof with their daughters. Neither of my parents could give me a good reason for him to leave us.

My 1960s suburban childhood had been idyllic. We played in the shadow of airplanes departing and arriving at O'Hare airport, running through the sprinkler on hot summer days and building snow forts in the cold winters. My mother was a consistent figure at the kitchen sink washing the most recent meal's dishes, or she stood a foot to the left of it preparing what would be served on them next, usually something with a pound of ground meat. The rest of the time she did laundry, cleaned, and shopped for groceries. Dad worked in the brand-new world of computers, leaving our two-bedroom Georgian home each morning in a pressed shirt Mom had carefully ironed after sprinkling the starched cotton with water from a Coke bottle.

They were living the American Dream, except for the secret Dad kept to himself for years. But secrets can make a dream implode, splintering it like shattered glass.

My mother went to a priest with her story and her shame. At thirty years old, she had spent a decade as a homemaker and couldn't imagine life without my father. Reliable and steady, her husband had never given her a reason to doubt him. Their affection for each other was tender, if not romantic, a bond that went well beyond the family they created. Deep friendship, not lust, tethered them to one another.

The priest told her to pray, to preserve her family at all costs. When she went to a therapist, he said that her husband may just be going through a phase, and if she lost weight, perhaps he would come back to her. He referred her to a diet doctor who prescribed her amphetamines.

Dutifully obeying all these men, she lost sixty pounds in the next year while maintaining hope for our family to be reunited. Sure enough, Dad returned to us, though not for the right reasons.

With my parents' reconciliation came a fresh start. Dad moved us to Oak Park and into an 1895 frame house with huge rooms and gleaming wood floors. It was twice the size of my childhood home, and my joy of having my daddy back with us was only eclipsed by having my own bedroom. The dining room echoed the turn-of-the century charm of the surrounding Frank Lloyd Wright neighborhood, with a polished walnut table that gleamed from the meticulous attention my father expected of us when we cleaned. It stood regally atop an Oriental rug.

"Now comb the fringe, like this," he said, showing me how to separate each woolen strand in a straight line with a wide-tooth comb, grooming it like a head without a hair out of place. "And don't make me do a white glove test," he'd say, smiling, as he handed me the can of Pledge and a rag. He was most likely joking, but I never doubted a white glove could be produced to challenge my eleven-year-old diligence.

Fear of not living up to my dad's expectations took up residence deep in my bones during my parents' separation. The desperate prayers I offered up to God that Dad would come back to us often included a promise to be good, to not talk back. Thrilled to have him home, once we were all under one roof again, I vowed to please him.

As we all settled into our new life, I suspect Mom may have had a hard time trading their small first house, nestled in a factory town standing squat amidst the train yards, for the grandeur of an elegant one in Dad's world. She found joy in the backyards and basements of her family in the working-class suburbs that were home to them after migrating from Chicago in the 1950s. Her roots were in the small kitchens of Auntie and Gram, drinking coffee at Formica tables with those she loved.

The affluent suburb we moved into fit her like a too-large coat, bulky and uncomfortable. Yet, she never let it show. With their secrets swept under the carefully coiffed Oriental rug, Mom's life looked perfect and was exactly what I wanted when I grew up.

After living in Oak Park for nearly three years, I began seventh grade. My parents let me transform the attic bedroom into a hangout for me and my friends, tacking up posters that glowed with neon purple peace signs under the blacklight bulb I asked Dad to install in the ceiling fixture. My first kiss was in that room during an awkward game of Spin the Bottle in which my best friend, Phyllis, twirled a Fresca bottle just right so it landed on me and Guy Hockstein. From then on, I couldn't wait to see him every day at his locker across the hall from mine. My obsession with boys had begun.

As spring poked its head up in April, my father sat us down on the white brocade couch in the living room and told us he and my mother were getting divorced. Mom sat quietly as his words demolished my adolescent life.

"It's not fair!" I wailed, "Why? You guys never fight." It seemed impossible that these people who seemed happier than the parents of my friends could not keep our family together. When my mom said she would be moving us back to River Grove, I begged for her to change her mind. "Please, don't make me leave my friends, Mom."

"Lisa, that's enough!" Dad bellowed, "She can't afford this house, and she wants to live near your grandmother and Auntie."

Bereft, I knew I would be unable to change their decision. We moved into a townhouse when the school year ended.

"Dad, do you have a girlfriend?" I asked my father on a rare day when he picked me up from school. "I mean, Mom dates a little. I just wondered if you do." He looked at me and smiled. *He's so handsome*, I thought, *he could easily find a date*.

"Well, honey, no I don't have a girlfriend. That's not something that fits in my lifestyle."

Lifestyle? "But you seem like you could—"

"That's enough! Drop it."

I knew better than to push. My father's affection felt like a fragile thing that I risked breaking if I annoyed him, so I let it go, staying quiet until he dropped me off in the gravel parking lot of our run-down building. "Bye, Dad. I hope I see you this weekend."

"We'll see. Say hi to your mother and Dina for me."

As I walked up the steps, it hit me—*Terry*. For the past several Sunday outings with Dad, his young friend, Terry, had joined us. He was cute, and funny, and Dad was happy around him.

Is that why he doesn't date? The thought stole my breath as I considered whether my father didn't have a girlfriend because he liked men. *Is Dad queer?* This idea made my stomach hurt as I went in the house and called Mom, insisting she tell me the truth. A truth that would change everything.

∽

Learning my father was gay in 1975 Midwestern suburbia was devastating. Most of what I knew of being gay was what I heard on TV, much of it steeped in bigotry. *How can my dad lie to us about who he is all these years?* My mother's continued friendship with him was confusing, a dismissal of his betrayal that I had a hard time sharing. While Mom swore me to secrecy, Dad told me to go to the library to read about homosexuality, so I understood that he was normal. A horrifying thought.

Following my discovery, the awful secret took up residence inside me, too shameful to tell my friends. The demand that I shield my sister from the truth meant there was no one to talk to about this new information concerning our family. I carried it inside like a small, scared animal. At times it lay still and quiet, something I hardly knew was there. At other times it thrashed and gnawed at my insides, demanding it be fed and released, threatening to chew a hole through my soul. Sometimes it just ran around in circles until it fell in a heap, exhausted.

My high school rebellion led me to drop out to manage my boyfriend's band until he broke up with me. By the time I was twenty-one, I was headed to San Francisco, sight-unseen, to pursue my rock and roll dreams in a life far away from my family, called by the turbulent Pacific Ocean to come to the edge, to face who I was separate from those who brought me up in an illusion, a deceptive beginning that brought confusion and pain when the truth was revealed Because often, pain makes us run.

Two years later, my father moved to San Francisco to live with Robert, a guy he had met during a weekend visit with me. His move into Robert's studio apartment was an impulsive act that stripped away any remnants of the man I grew up with, the one who insisted I do my homework, to make prudent decisions based on informed choices. On my first visit to his new home, I uncorked my hurt like the bottle of White Zinfandel that disappeared in front of me, each glass strengthening my rage. I railed against him for compromising my mother's sexuality by marrying her.

"She was a nineteen-year-old virgin, for God's sake! And you just went ahead and pretended to love her?" As the red light of the sign on the Polk Street market outside the window began to blur, Dad told an even more startling part of the story.

"I did love her. You don't know everything. I was content to be with your mother and you girls. My needs were met in a relationship with Daniel that we kept to ourselves. And until he decided to end it, everyone was fine."

Daniel? He and his wife were my parents' best friends when I was a kid. "You mean you and Daniel had *a thing*?" The pieces of the puzzle started creating a picture of my father's sexual life I didn't want to see.

"Until he ended it. Then I began seeing a guy at work. Rex. That's when your mother and I separated. But being out was harder than I thought. It was expensive to keep up two households. So, we got back together and moved to Oak Park. After a while, I started going back to the bars, and you know the rest."

My head spun with the truth of my father's duplicity.

My heart squeezed with love for my mom who had been the victim of his betrayal. *How can she be less bothered by this than me?* I vowed to find a man so different from my father that I could not be duped like she was.

~

My search for Mr. Right was a long journey on a bumpy road. The men who paraded through my life, and my bed, filled my heart with hope and my head with bullshit. The dangerous allure of bad boys who promised to call after a weekend of sex and drinking permeated my young adulthood. It was the 1980s, when men called whenever they felt like it. This resulted in a few unintended one-night stands, and a couple of relationships lasting a few months in which I chased them and they used me.

They're a blur of disappointment in my memory, a matched collection of losers who were the opposite of my father, except for the familiarity of waiting by the phone. Rebelling against my gay dad's white-collar intelligence, I was drawn to vulgar, masculine men, or moody musicians, who were indifferent to me. As far from Dad as they were on the outside, they still left me with the same anxiety on the inside.

I poured myself into my career. The dreams that propelled me to San Francisco were manifested into jobs in the entertainment world. After working in video and film, and volunteering on music events, I landed my dream job touring the world with a major artist.

Once out on the road, I was taken by the Southern charm of the pop star's tour bus driver for the North American shows. Jimmy's swagger reminded me of Patrick Swayze with an accent like thick honey. He asked me out on a date in Salt Lake City, then picked me up from my hotel in a horse-drawn carriage.

"I thought I'd been in everything with wheels, but I was wrong!" he drawled, excited to ride me around in style. We rode through the quiet streets, holding hands, chatting about our lives. He regaled me with stories about growing up in Tennessee and told me about his kids.

"A girl and a boy, thirteen and nine-year-old. I miss, 'em," he said. "But they're okay with their mama. How 'bout you? Tell me about your life."

He stroked the top of my hand with his thumb while I talked about being raised outside Chicago and the life I had forged in California. He listened intently, kind of mesmerized. Sweet, and relaxed. When we asked the driver for the best place to have dinner on a Sunday night, he said my hotel was the only place open.

Our make-out session after a room service dinner normally would have ended in sex, but I knew we'd have plenty of time for that in the months ahead. Instead, we kissed slowly, letting the contours of our bodies pull close to one another in delicious anticipation. Knowing he would pursue me, I let myself hold back, savoring the romance of the moment as he murmured in my ear his delight in holding me, each word feeling like a promise. My heart fluttered like a bird imagining the possibilities.

I don't think Jimmy intended to deceive me in those early weeks when we were breathlessly intoxicated with each other. He let me assume he was divorced, never stating a marital status one way or the other. I chose to let the vague details of his life back home be enough information to forge ahead with our grand passion. But when his wife, kids, and mother-in-law planned to come down to Atlanta to visit him, he had to admit they were merely separated by the miles his work put between him and his family.

"I've done ask for a divorce every time I go home. She won't give me one. So, I stay on the road as much as I can." He lit a cigarette, stroking his beard as he exhaled. "I'm sorry, babe. I really am."

"How could you not tell me?" I cried, shaking. Jimmy had become my fairytale ending. In our month together, we had talked about my moving to Tennessee, and the house we could have there. Never had a man I was attracted to been so enamored with me. The safe bubble of love that had formed around us burst in an instant, leaving me gasping, as if it contained the only air I could breathe. "I can't believe you lied to me." *Like Dad*.

"Honey, I never lied to ya. I just didn't tell you the whole truth. I fell in love with you. For years, I've been asking for a divorce. We don't feel married no more. She's at the house and I'm out here most all the time. The money takes care of my kids. I'm sorry. I'll fix it, I promise."

Not knowing the truth had given me permission to open my heart to this man who was so exotic in his simplicity, the opposite of my complicated father. Knowing the truth didn't make me love Jimmy less, it just made me anxious and bewildered about a future with him when the tour ended after three months in Europe and Japan without him.

The day Jimmy arrived in San Francisco to move me to Nashville, I looked around my apartment, packed and ready to go to our new home, and felt wistful about leaving California. The call to come to the coast nearly a decade before had been a path to Jimmy, I convinced myself, and that's what I told my family when I shared the news.

"I'm moving to Nashville with him," I'd told my father, "I know he's the one." Telling him felt easier than telling Mom. His past impulsiveness gave me permission for my own.

"That feeling is all too familiar, honey," Dad said when we had our last breakfast together under the burlap ceiling at Higher Grounds. "I hope you're right that he's meant for you. As you know, I was wrong when I moved in with Robert." He motioned to the waitress to bring more coffee. "My biggest concern is this divorce business be finished before you start a life together."

"It will be," I said, "She wants it over now, too." The clatter of dishes being bussed filled the air between us while I doctored my coffee. Having shared the truth of Jim's marital status with my father early on, he knew I felt uncomfortable until the divorce was final. He didn't judge, most likely because of how he had left his own marriage to my mother to be with someone else.

"He loves me, Dad." The words echoed my father's certainty over Robert years before. Years that had softened my disdain for his choices.

His eyes held a dozen questions about what I would be leaving behind in the life I had crafted so diligently, in the beautiful place I loved so much. To say I hadn't pondered them myself would be a lie. Concerns over how I would continue my career, make new friends, and navigate a city I didn't know rang loudly through my head each night when I collapsed into bed after packing my life into cardboard boxes. I pushed aside the voice inside that whispered a warning about relinquishing too much of my independence—and too much of my money—to this relationship, like ignoring the flight attendants when they go over the emergency card. *Nothing bad will happen.*

Dad nodded. "Well, as long as you're happy." He asked how my mother was taking the news, though he likely knew.

"Mom is excited for me but thinks I'm jumping in a little fast. She likes that he stopped in to see her when he went through Chicago on the Alchemy tour, then he and Dina went out for a beer." Tears threatened as I felt the full weight of the coming changes. "Mom's glad I'm settling down with someone." I lit a cigarette, feeling the first calming drag of smoke push down tears. I skipped the part where I'd assured my mother that Jimmy's divorce was a "technicality," just simple paperwork to be filed.

"I look forward to meeting him on Sunday. I just hope he can handle you. You're a strong woman, not some quiet little country girl." We laughed easily at his joke, but underneath I could hear his concern.

The sun streamed onto our favorite window table as we finished our coffee. I felt the twinge of loss not living near him would bring. We had come such a long way since that night on Polk Street when he had just arrived in San Francisco.

As Jimmy strolled through the airport gate and into my arms, he had tears in his eyes. After longing to be loved without trying so hard, I barely knew how to receive his love, to allow it to wash over me without feeling like heartache was looming. This would take some practice, and faith still fragile from watching him leave his family.

The following night, all my dearest friends gathered to celebrate my thirtieth birthday and my departure from

California. Jimmy looked handsome as he met the people who meant so much to me, secretly telling them that he had an engagement ring stashed at my mom's in Chicago, to surprise me with on Christmas Eve. Free from the distraction of chasing men who let me down, I could relax knowing that being with Jimmy meant that this part of my life was finally settled.

Once we arrived in Nashville, trying to find a comfortable rhythm in our new life took some adjustment. So many of my daily routines had been put on hold for a year on the road, and now my life was upended again. Finding a balance between me and us was an unexpected challenge.

Our overwhelming love for each other was all-consuming, and we made love with fervor, sharing an intensity I had never known. Sex had been a portal to love for me, often not very satisfying. My wish that one day love and sex could intermingle with the right guy felt like it came true with Jimmy.

Still, money was a problem that led to arguments between us. There wasn't enough of it to go around, especially working in town with his brother. With the divorce final, his child support and alimony ate up more than half his pay. Unemployment took care of my share of the bills while I looked for a job.

Domesticity fit me like rubber gloves, loose and awkward. Dusting photos of myself in Holland or Tokyo astonished me now that I'd landed in a trailer in Tennessee. I missed my job, doing work that felt important when I had fifty people in my face all day in the production office. Now I had just one chirping bird—Jimmy. I realized how much time I'd spent chasing after men, scurrying around doing all I could to win their attention and love. They barely noticed and I rarely got it. Now that I had a man who wasn't going anywhere, I busied myself with the house, running errands, and making a good supper when he was home. While trying to be more accommodating to his needs, I forgot to express my own, if only I knew what they were. The hard part for me was the combining of lives, not flesh.

Within months, Jimmy went back on the road to make more money. I got a job as an event planner, not exactly the same gig as touring with rock stars. I was bored and prayed for a call to go back on tour, too, but it didn't come. When we got married a year later, in our living room with his kids, a few friends, and our mothers and sisters, it was on a Thursday when he had a four-day break. As a torrential rain fell around the house while we prepared for the ceremony, Jimmy's sister pointed a video camera at my face and asked, "What's the best thing about marryin' my brother?" Her smile was genuine and identical to his.

"The name!" I said, without missing a beat. Mom laughed out loud, still using my father's German surname none of us liked. "I'll finally have an easy last name."

The choices we make to marry and have children are colored by the people we choose to have them with. In my case, instead of the abundant Crayola 64-count I lusted for in my childhood, the one with teal blue and burnt sienna nestled in a box with a built-in sharpener, my life was filled in by the value pack of ten basic colors, a limited palette with which to paint my life. Choosing to marry Jimmy felt limiting, and less vibrant than I had imagined married life to be. But then, I hadn't imagined it that much; only the romance leading up to it.

I hadn't always imagined having a child either. For most of my life, the yearning to be a mother wasn't strong; the sacrifice scared me. So, when I got pregnant soon after we married, I finally felt like a member of the club my husband was in with his ex-wife and kids, but I was worried about my ability to surrender myself to motherhood. Especially after Zachary's birth, when Jimmy went back on the road and my mom's week-long visit ended. Being left home alone with my newborn son terrified me.

The love I felt for my child was tempered by frustration with the amount of care he needed that I had to provide by myself. Most nights I slept on the couch, the bassinet beside me while reruns of *Mary Tyler Moore* and *Cheers* played into the night. I was afraid that if I got in bed, I would sleep so hard even a screaming baby wouldn't wake me. Bone-deep exhaustion was combined with postpartum depression, though I didn't really know that was why I was sad. New mothers should not be left alone for weeks on end. Still, being mostly alone with Zac in those first months carried an almost holy quality. In the bubble of our endless hours together, I memorized every inch of him, all his expressions, and each cry. He became all mine.

Mom called Dad to let him know that his grandson had been born, and I had it in my mind that this news would prompt a call from him. It didn't. After an argument a few months earlier, in the throes of my emotional pregnancy, Dad wasn't speaking to me, still upset about a remark I made to him. Like all the other times we had judged one another, he was staunchly waiting for me to be the one to apologize. I'd refused, believing he was wrong.

It was devastating to not have my son acknowledged by his grandfather. As always, my dad put his own needs first.

By Christmas, I was heartbroken and called him to apologize for hurting his feelings. He accepted my apology by sending a silver Baby's 1st Christmas ornament from Tiffany & Co. We were so broke I considered returning it.

The unraveling of my marriage came slowly, mostly because my husband and I weren't together very much. I already felt like a single mom when it became clear our days were numbered.

"Who do you think you are to tell me what to do, Jimmy?" I screamed, desperate to be anywhere but married to a man who didn't really see me.

"I am your husband! And you are a wife and mama now, and you best well act like one!" His face was contorted with anger and disgust.

"Yeah, well, you don't own me, goddamn it!" Seething against his archaic view of marriage and motherhood, I knew in that moment the idea of divorcing him was not a matter of if, but when.

After Zac's third birthday and the leaves turned gold, my discontentment grew more ferocious. I started socking away a little nest egg of my part-time earnings in the pages of *Little Women*, planning my escape from the life I had wanted so badly.

At Christmas, our divorce was underway. Landing where I started, I moved with my son back to Illinois to be near my family. It was the last thing I had imagined in my grand adventure, yet here I was living near my mother to have free babysitting that wasn't free at all. Enduring her scrutiny was the price I paid.

To say my mother and I were opposites, especially as single mothers, would be an understatement. Where she was content to sacrifice for her children, work an office job, and have an occasional Saturday night date, I wanted to be a woman first, to retain a sliver of the identity I had before motherhood, to have a lover who became a partner. Of course, meeting my son's needs was my primary concern, but I could not surrender my entire being to him. I yearned for dreams of my own.

In the wake of my failed marriage, my desire for love and passion occupied my thoughts. A disastrous romance came soon after, the first of several men I loved and lost while raising a man without one around. After a job layoff post-9/11, I attended life coach training and found my way back to a career I loved.

Zachary's father wasn't in his life much. The distance Jimmy put between him and his son was a punishment levied against me for leaving him, creating a scar we all had to bear. For twelve years, finding a new partner who would also be a good father-figure for Zac felt like a job I kept interviewing for on each first date. Then I met Dave, who swept me off my feet like a tornado. Within four months we were engaged.

My second marriage was sweet— and short; a brush fire that burned out nearly as quickly as it began. By the time it ended I was miserable, with only myself to blame for believing he and I could blend our family into the frothy cocktail I imagined it would be while honeymooning in Mexico. I pulled the plug before our second anniversary, and watched it spiral down the drain.

"You will find love again, just like I will," my friend Kim promised over full glasses of Cabernet on her porch in the lush Wisconsin woods. Deep down I knew another man wasn't the answer.

Grateful for the five-hour drive by myself to Kim's bucolic cottage in Door County, the lushness of summer bloomed like the weekend I spent there with Dave that opened the bud of our future. It was hard to believe our future had bloomed, withered, and died already. I felt shallow, again abandoning my marriage just because I was unhappy; our love was divided by a wide chasm of resentment, mostly over money, the root of all that was difficult in my marriages. At least on the surface.

"I'm starting to remember who I was before husbands and children," I said, burrowing into a pile of thick pillows. "I don't think I've ever been as unhappy as when my marriages were ending. Or as hopeful when they started." I remembered myself as a young wife, full of romantic delusion as I made vows to Jimmy. By the time we were through, I thought only another man could fill the hole of loneliness I felt while he was on the road. Now I knew I needed to fill it myself.

"This time around I feel like I have much more control, more options. Dave didn't bring enough to our lives to have them change much with him gone. I think I'll move back to California when Zac goes to college."

Kim nodded, her honey blond hair hanging loose against an Indian print shawl. "I thought I would die when Hans and I broke up, but it's getting easier. Time. It takes time, love."

I was flooded with gratitude for her delicate grace, as thoughts of going home to a house without Dave felt like sinking into a very hot bath; you can barely take it until you slowly ease in, then suddenly, it's rapturous.

The tedium of my daily life, of helping Zac through his senior year, and planning my next move, fell away as the wheels touched down at San Francisco airport the following year. I drove straight to the Bistro to meet my dear friend, Mark.

We had met in those first days after my arrival in California at a club where he was playing drums. My crush on him got buried under friendship and insecurity over his many girlfriends. We'd stayed in touch since the advent of email, commiserating about life, love, and raising kids while seeking meaningful work in the world. My path had led me to become a life coach, and through a second divorce. His had kept him in an unhappy marriage he chose to stay in for his daughter. We got together for a drink when I was in town.

"Welcome home," he said, setting down two glasses of wine he had fetched from the bar. He folded himself into the chair in front of me, his limbs loose and comfortable. He took my hand across the table. Recently, our emails had become more flirtatious. An intoxicating blend of our ancient connection and midlife lust hung over us like an invisible vapor. We breathed it in, looking across at each other, grinning.

"Zac is visiting Jimmy in Tennessee, so when I leave California next week, I'll meet them to look at his school. It'll be the first thing we do as a family since he was little."

"Do you already feel things changing between you and Zac?" he asked.

"Yeah. It's bittersweet. But I feel so much more myself now that he's decided to go to college in Nashville and I can make plans to move back here. Tomorrow I'm going to Alameda Island to check it out. That feels like where I'll land."

Mark looked at me with a mix of pride and astonishment. "When you set out to do something, you do it. I know I need to make big changes to have the life I want, but I still can't see leaving my daughter behind with her mother. Which is why I'm still married." His eyes were earnest, as the precarious truth floated between us.

My heart lurched when he talked about his home life like he might stay indefinitely. "I know." *Stay in the moment*, I thought. *Just this moment.*

"Until you're ready to leave your daughter, you won't be free." I needed to say it out loud, too. *Don't say too much.* I took a slow breath, pushing down the temptation to offer my opinion that he needed to just leave his marriage already, that his teenage daughter would be fine.

"The way you're supporting your daughter is admirable, yet she probably senses her parents aren't happy. You are modeling security for her." He nodded slightly. "That's not a bad thing. When you want to model something different, you will."

"Thanks, coach." His eyes misted as he smiled at me like he had for decades.

Our lifelong friendship pierced through that moment like a soft white light, and something sacred beckoned, something bigger than us. "Sometimes it feels like maybe we're here to work together to help other people figure shit out, the way we do with each other," I said. Hope shot across his face; he nodded.

"What did you always want to be when you grew up?" I finally asked, borrowing the line from *Fight Club* that we had bantered about several times.

"Me!" he answered, looking me in the eye, fearless.

"Good answer."

"Honey, I'm home," I said six months later, as I walked through the open door of the short-term rental house I found on Craigslist. The sound of Frank Sinatra wafted through the air as Mark emerged from the kitchen, the late August sun creating a silhouette; a mirage to greet me.

"Welcome!" he said, scooping me into a hug.

"Wow, this is amazing." Dropping my bag on the worn wood floor, I took in the panoramic view of the Bay Bridge to the Golden Gate from my temporary home atop the Berkeley Hills. "I know the owner of this place is a yoga instructor, but it looks like a guru lives here. Thanks for getting the key for me."

Mark smiled and took me by the hand, drawing me into the kitchen where he was preparing fish tacos for lunch. "Wait till you see her book collection. You'll love it. This is the perfect place for you to land, juju girl." He went back to food prep, the thing he had been doing during all those email chats we'd had over the years. Now he was cooking for me.

"Good flight and everything?" Mahi Mahi sizzled in a cast iron pan.

"Yeah, uneventful. My favorite kind. I can't believe I'm here." I had said my goodbyes to everyone over the last few days, starting with Zac's departure the week before when he left for Tennessee. We were both ready for his next chapter, yet saying goodbye was hard, but made easier knowing I was leaving for my own new life. And here I was.

While we ate, Mark told me about the new job he had started that would allow him to make some choices, ones he had wanted for years but couldn't afford. I had been quietly praying for the money to show up for him, while being careful not to encourage him to leave. He had to make this happen on his own, and not for me.

It was as if while we embarked on our individual moves to new lives we walked on our own separate tightropes, supporting one another through each wrinkle and discovery. Sometimes we were close enough to reach out to the other's hand to steady us. At other times, the gap widened and we're unable to touch. It was then that we needed to rely only on ourselves to provide the needed balance to move another inch forward.

Now that I had reached my destination, he had quite a ways to go to reach the safety of his. Going out to bring him across was a dangerous temptation I resisted.

"Coming off the men's retreat and right into this new job feels auspicious," he said as we cleared the table. "I'm trusting I'll know when the time is right to leave." I agreed that riding the wave of positive opportunity would lead him to the right moment to make big change.

He came up behind me as I rinsed the dishes in the old farmhouse sink. "Mmm, you smell good." He nuzzled my neck, then slid my crocheted sweater off my shoulder. All my trepidation melted as his lips touched my skin. Clothes were wrestled off and tossed to the floor as the light of day poured over us. *Oh my God*, I thought, gripping the counter, surrendering to the kind of passion I only felt for him. By the time we had found our way to the bedroom, making love with an unbearably slow tenderness, I was overcome by emotion.

"I'm sorry," I whispered, "It's too much." I got up and pulled a sundress from my bag and over my head, then sat on the bed beside him.

"Are you okay?" he said, softly. "I thought you wanted—"

"I did. Oh, God. I do. I'm just overwhelmed by everything today. I'm fine." *And you're still married.* I thought but didn't say. *Slow down, girl.*

He got dressed, and we spent the rest of the day chatting on the couch, snuggling and laughing until he had to go. "I hate to leave. I'm sorry."

I hate it, too. As I closed the door behind him, I prayed he would reach the end of his tightrope soon.

It was clear my feelings about fidelity varied based on which side of the altar I was on. In both my marriages I felt secure that my husbands were faithful, even Jimmy on the road despite our beginning. I had been faithful, too. When it came to Mark, crossing that line had happened slowly over so many years that when we finally did, it was nearly a non-event. Our feelings for each other were so much deeper than sex could ever express.

Returning to my home by the Bay felt like stepping into slippers on a cold night. Comfy and warm. Within a month, Mark had rented a place near his daughter and soon-to-be ex-wife. I moved to a charming cottage in Alameda where we slept like spoons in my crooked bedroom every weekend. We cooked, we laughed, we shared secrets and bubble baths. He prepared beautiful food for my fiftieth birthday party, playing host to the same friends who celebrated my thirtieth. Like kids, we playfully romped on the beach with a connection and passion that had smoldered between us well into midlife. Finally, Mark had surrendered to his deep feelings for me, as long as I didn't label them.

"How does he introduce you then? Like you're his Aunt Bessie or what?" a friend quipped on the phone when I told her how adamant Mark was about not being 'boyfriend & girlfriend.'

"Not exactly. He says I've been his best friend forever, then launches into our whole story. It's actually kind of cute." It seemed Mark would tell anyone who wanted to listen how we had kept in touch for years after I moved back east, and how I had returned from Chicago just as he was getting divorced. If they were still listening, he'd share that we were weaving our emails to one another into a book. "It's one helluva love story," he would say, as if just realizing that for the first time.

∼

"So, Mark and I are publishing a book," I blurted out on the phone to my father while driving on a sunny morning. "It's our story told in the emails we wrote to each other for the past ten years."

"Well, that's interesting. What made you even think of publishing your emails? Epistolary, I think they call that; when a story is told through letters."

"Right. At first, I really wanted other people to read the beautiful words Mark had written to me. It seemed a waste to be the only one to read them. He's such a good writer." In moments, I still doubted my own writing talent up against his raw, eloquent rants about his crumbling marriage and devotion to his daughter. "So, we were initially going to weave the best ones into a story we wrote together, but after reading a bunch of them, we tried stringing them together and found they tell our whole story." It felt right to share this with my dad who had been a proofreader for my coaching website, making picky changes while giving positive feedback. Over the years, we had settled into a sweet relationship anchored in sharing my projects and listening about his health. Becoming a coach taught me a lot about the value of forgiveness and acceptance.

"Well, honey, you're a wonderful writer, too. Ever since you were a young girl you could write beautifully. I can't wait to read it." Hearing praise from my father was like swallowing the sun. I basked in the warmth of his approval.

"Thanks, Dad." I crossed the bridge onto Alameda,

almost home. "Hey, would you like to be a beta reader? We have to edit it way down and we need a couple people to give us notes as we go." My stomach clenched at the thought of him reading our personal words, but not much of it would likely offend my father, except anything negative about him. I had learned over the years that his self-centeredness was the root of our turbulent relationship. Not that he was gay.

"I would love to! Just send it along when you're ready." He paused. "I really look forward to reading it."

"Great. Let's keep this between us for now. I don't think I'll share it with Mom until it's finished. She's not a reader like we are." I pictured my father's current paperback beside him on an end table, tucked into the worn leather sleeve from Kroch's and Brentano's bookstore, a fixture since my childhood.

"Sure, I won't mention it." I pulled up to my place, and we hung up. As I walked up the stairs, it occurred to me this was the first secret I could remember having with my father.

Most days, living alone suited me. In the evening, I caught up with my dear girlfriends scattered across the country, catching up on our work and our relationships, our kids if we had them. These nights held a certain sensual magic as we shed light on our feminine lives.

While sipping wine, I curled up in a soft blanket on my down-filled couch and listened to these women I adored, their voices ringing like bells in my ear as we shared triumphs and heartache. They listened, too, offering wisdom and solace. I felt held by their love in the amber glow of candlelight, surrounded by the treasures I had collected along my journey. Each item belonged only to me, except for Mark's toothbrush and a pair of pajama bottoms he hung on the back of my bedroom door. I liked living among my own things, with my tastes.

Until Sunday night rolled around.

On Sunday nights, after Mark and I had spent a couple of days enchanted by the beauty of the island, after a couple of nights tangled up in my bed together, we would wind down with a movie and a delicious meal he had undoubtedly prepared.

By nightfall, I could feel Mark withdraw, subtly anxious for our movie to be over. Once it ended, I began clearing the dishes from the coffee table, cheerfully chattering about whatever we had done that day.

"I'm gonna get going," he'd say, starting to gather the belongings he scattered around since his arrival.

"Okay." I hated the familiar sense of loss that bloomed in my gut. After a few awkward moments of standing there watching him, I'd busy myself with folding the blanket that dangled off the edge of the couch, our body heat still clinging to it.

.His laptop went back into the worn leather satchel I had bought him for his birthday; books and his journal were stuffed in beside it. His black leather gym bag was packed with everything else, sometimes overflowing. He left nothing behind. It seemed silly, but each item felt like a tiny piece of my heart was being stowed away for later.

"See you, baby," he said when he had loaded up his gear, pulling me in for a kiss like he was going off to war.

I sighed when he reached the bottom of the stairs, then closed the wide heavy door behind him, noticing the temperature in the house seemed to lower by ten degrees. Pulling my sweater tighter around me, I turned to the television to keep me company.

By Tuesday morning I loved my solo life again, after a shaky Monday of waiting for Mark to call, knowing full well he was enjoying the solitude he craved after a weekend side by side. Even though taking his need for space personally was like a bad habit you barely realize is hurting you, when we finally did connect, something would settle inside me, like so many times in my life with men, starting with Dad.

"Here I am," he'd say, aware I was anticipating his call but determined to take care of his inner hermit. We'd drift into our usual easy conversation, and all tension would dissipate. In time, I realized seeing solitude as a mistress to be jealous of was a perspective that only hurt me. Our time apart recharged him and didn't need to feel like rejection. *Suffering over his choice to be alone instead of cuddled up next to me every night is my doing, not his,* I wrote in my journal. *Acceptance is the key that will free me from it. We're Apartners. Partners who live apart.*

"Zac and I will stop in to see you again before he takes me to the airport," I said to my dad during a spring visit to Chicago. He was in a rehabilitation facility to improve his failing mobility. As we took the elevator to Dad's room, I glanced at my son beside me. Life in Tennessee with his dad had not fared well. He missed his friends, so he dropped out of college and moved in with his aunt, registering for culinary classes in Illinois. Dina loved having him there, but he was already thinking of getting his own place with a buddy.

He seemed so robust in his youthfulness compared to my ailing father, a stark contrast in how life changes us. Dad's health made me keenly aware of how swift the slide into old age can be if you don't take care of yourself. He had been a virile man through his fifties. But once his back pain began, and chemistry ruled his life, he seemed to age two years for every one. At seventy-three, he seemed like a man well into his eighties.

Eventually, the drugs didn't even work for him, so his pain management doctor happily wrote scripts for more and stronger meds. Seeing my father several times during this trip had helped me understand my sister's desire to demand Dad stop abusing the prescription pain meds that ruled his life. I also knew on a soul level he was choosing his own path and none of us could change that for him. The systemic effects of opioid addiction were debilitating to every part of his being, robbing his genius mind of its luster. Now he could barely walk.

"Hey Grandfather, how's it going?" Zac said when we pulled a couple chairs into Dad's room. My father was in a wheelchair and his partner, Benny, was watching something on TV.

"Not bad. They're springing me soon. I'm looking forward to my computer. And *smoking*." He mouthed the last word. Benny had been wheeling him outside for a cigarette, but in late March it was pretty chilly to keep up his two pack a day habit.

"Good. I bet you'll be glad to have him home, Benny," I said. Their smiles hid some inside joke between them. *A couple of old queens*, I thought. What used to blow a gust of shame through me made me chuckle inside now.

Time had softened us. My father wasn't a gay man on the prowl in the Castro hitting the bathhouses anymore, and I wasn't the twenty-something disapproving daughter who found him selfish, wishing for a worthy role model for a husband. He was just my dad. A good man, unashamed of his life, happy to be talking with his family.

"I hear the job is going well, Zac. You've really stuck with the restaurant business." My son had pulled up next to him in the cramped room. I sat at the foot of the bed.

"Yeah, it's great. I'll get some bar shifts after I turn twenty-one in August. So, yeah, I'll be making some pretty good money. I'm excited." I watched the two of them talk, remembering when my father tried so hard to get him to care about school, and like the rest of us, Zac was living on his own terms. I saw the pride I felt in my son reflected in my father's eyes.

"As long as you love what you do, Zachary, you will enjoy your life. I loved my work, I really did. We started out together, computers and me, and I spent many happy years in my field. I've always wanted that for you." Zac nodded. "You're smart, and if you work hard in a business you're passionate about, you'll succeed. Look at what your mom did." Dad looked at me and smiled. "Neither of us went to college, but we still did great things." Tears welled up behind my eyes.

"Thanks, Grandfather. I really want to work my way up into management. Maybe own a restaurant someday." Like a fly on the wall, I silently took in the alchemy of my father and his grandson, watching burnished gold form between them.

Dad patted Zac's arm. "Good," he said, looking at his watch. "Don't you have a plane to catch?" he said to me. I nodded. "Sure am glad to see you again today," he continued. "And you, Zac. Such a nice visit." Zac stood up, gently patting my dad on the back.

"Say hi to Mark for me, honey." I moved between them and leaned over to hug my father. "I will. Bye, Dad." I kissed his crepe paper cheek. "I'll call you tomorrow."

Back at home, I checked in on Dad almost every day. Our calls averaged seven minutes long, but there was something about the routine we both enjoyed. He always seemed surprised to hear from me; I agreed with everything he said, being easy—and sweet. The way he always wanted me to be, which wasn't so bad after all.

"I have a simple procedure tomorrow," he said, on a Tuesday in late April. "Shouldn't take too long. I'll be in my room by noon if you want to call after that." He was finally home after bouncing back and forth from the rehab center for a month.

"Sounds good. I'll call you then. Love you."

"Love you, too, honey."

Aren't you prompt? I thought when the phone rang just after noon the next day.

"Hey Lis. Dad's in the ICU." My sister's voice was unexpected—and grim. "It's pretty bad. They said he's septic." I paused to remember what that meant. *A bad infection.*

"Oh my God. Wow. Should I come?" I said, knowing the answer was yes. "I should come." *Oh, Dad. Please, not yet. Hang in there.*

"Yeah, I think you should. I have miles on American if you need to use them."

"Yeah, thanks. Okay. What else, I mean, they're treating him, right? I thought it was just a simple procedure." I was opening the American Airlines website, looking for flights. My head was spinning. "I can try to get the 2:30. Wow, I don't think I can make that. There's a—"

"The procedure never happened. Dad called 911 during the night with stomach pains. He aspirated in the ER. They've got him on a respirator. He's not really conscious." *Holy Shit. A respirator?* Tears stung my eyes.

"There's a 4:50. I'll be there by midnight. Please text me your mileage number. Zac can come get me at the airport." I looked around, making a mental checklist. *Call*

Mark. Book ticket. Pack. Water plants. Pray. "You'll wait till I get there to, you know, to do anything, right? Maybe he'll wake up." *Please let him wake up.*

"Yeah, of course. See you later. Love ya."

"You, too. Hug Ma for me."

Throwing things into a bag, I optimistically chose not to take a black dress, believing if I packed for a funeral there might be one. Everything came from the freshly washed laundry basket I was carrying into the bedroom before the phone rang. *Before.* Before my day was irreversibly upended with the news that my father might die.

Mark arrived in what felt like moments, his calm presence helping me do the next right thing. *Don't forget a charger. Keep praying.* All this was happening in the numb fog of disbelief that comes when someone slips into a coma and they call you to come right away. An hour later, it didn't feel real as Mark drove me over the Bay Bridge into San Francisco, the sun shining as if this were a perfectly normal day.

"He's not gonna die, right?" I asked Mark because the word die had to be uttered out loud.

"No, I don't think so," he said, taking my hand. I didn't believe him but desperately wanted to. It felt safer to believe him if only till I got there.

The email confirmation from American didn't come, and I desperately kept calling to reach a real human. This repeatedly put me in a loop of recordings that had me freaking out that I wouldn't get on the flight.

"Why can't I reach a fucking human being!" My fear that Dad wasn't strong enough to survive this infection reached up from my gut through my chest, then grabbed me by the throat. I burst into tears.

"Take it easy, baby, it will be alright," Mark said. His words of encouragement didn't match the concern in his eyes, and I suddenly wished he were coming with me. As he dropped me off at the curb, I searched his face for proof that Dad would be okay. It wasn't there.

The cavernous airport terminal swallowed me. I headed straight to the American counter and frantically explained to the agent that I needed to get on the next flight out to Chicago and my email confirmation had not arrived. Her lack of urgency amped mine up as I watched each minute tick away on the clock above her head.

"I don't show a seat open in that class of service, Ma'am," she said, not really understanding that I was absolutely getting on that plane.

"There are seats available! You have five seats available! My Dad is dying, please, please let me speak to a supervisor." The words tumbled out of my mouth, bitter on my tongue. *Is he really dying?* It felt like I was just saying that to get on the plane. *Please, don't be true because I said it out loud again.* The next flight was in a few hours and wouldn't get in until the break of dawn. A man came up as the volume of my voice escalated. It was apparent that I needed more assistance than the ticket agent was offering me.

"How can I help you, Ma'am?" he said. He was tall, with an air of authority.

"Are you the supervisor, sir?" I took a deep breath, trying to contain my anxiety but unable to hold myself together.

"Yes, I am. How may I help?" He motioned for the agent to assist the next customer at an adjacent counter.

Suddenly I was a mess, repeating my story through gulping sobs, snot running from my nose. "My Dad is dying, and I need to get there to be with my family. If he doesn't make it, I want to be able to . . . say . . . goodbye. Please help me." I could barely breathe.

He looked at me with kind eyes and nodded. "I'm so

sorry. I lost my Dad last year," he said, "And I didn't make it there before he passed. I promise I will get you on that flight."

Something crumpled inside me at those words, as if the fact that he would go the extra mile to make sure I said goodbye meant that I would have to. I had long ago decided that it was my dad's life to live as he saw fit, and his desire to be completely pain-free would inevitably mean leaving his body behind completely.

I just wasn't prepared for that day to be today.

It was not yet 4AM when the flatline slid silently across the EKG monitor and my father passed away. We had all said our private goodbyes, and now we gathered around his bed, holding hands, saying a prayer over his peaceful body. A profoundly sad relief swept through me.

You're free, Dad. The relief may have just been mine, as I felt like the only one ready for him to check out of his broken body. As sorely as I would miss him, I'd come to terms with his determination to set himself free of the pain that plagued him, grateful that his exit wouldn't be from accidentally taking one too many pain pills. We were granted that small favor from the gods, and I was sad, so sad, yet with a sorrow I knew had a bottom to it. Being with Zac was a comfort.

But for Mom and Benny, who had been spinning steadily in Dad's daily orbit, the sorrow was palpable and bottomless, throbbing with their fear of the inevitability of this day. They both looked hollowed out by grief. In my sister, who had been somewhat at odds with Dad in recent weeks, something seemed to shut down right in front of us that night.

Mark flew in for Dad's memorial. I got through the eulogy I wrote with his support and a Xanax Benny gave me. "I'll take his brains and heart," I whispered to Dina as the funeral director handed us our father's ashes when it was over.

"Hey, then what do I get?" She cracked the first smile I had seen on her face since I'd arrived in Chicago a week earlier. The director had split the ashes for us, and we snickered over half of Dad being in a container with a golf club on it. "I don't think he ever golfed a day in his life," I said. "You take that one; I'll take the box."

She agreed, then we went back to our corners. Underneath our cordial exteriors we felt the others' ire, each of us judging the other for our reaction to losing Dad. I knew she found it appalling that I released my emotions like a faucet, letting my feelings splash all over everyone, making a mess. I couldn't help my inability to hold it all inside the way she did. I resented her retreat into a stone fortress of grief that felt like being shut out at a time when we needed each other most.

On the flight home, I leaned into Mark to look out the window as we descended over the inky black San Francisco Bay, preparing to land. The lights on Alameda Island sparkled like gems in the night welcoming me back to where I belong.

On my father's next birthday, I pulled a purple silk shawl from my closet to create an altar on the dock behind my apartment, then collected photos from many different times in my father's life. Along with his ashes, I arranged the photos, his baby shoe, and a couple of candles on a tile tray. I also brought down a bottle of tequila to toast the ancestors, one of which Dad had become.

Mark arrived as the sun sank low in the sky, and he softly played his djembe drum while I picked flowers. Once I had placed them on my make-shift altar, I lit the candles. "We honor you, Dad, on this day of your birth," I said, "Not just any day but on the full blue moon." The sound of my father's voice singing that song played in my mind as I scattered herbs--rosemary, lavender, rose, and sage--sending wisdom, remembrance, and love into the amber glow of the lagoon.

My heart swelled as I pulled the plastic bag from the box and opened one end. A flutter of excitement filled my chest while I felt the weight of my father's generous heart and brilliant brain in my hands. "I release you back to the earth with love and honor, Dad. Go in peace." I tilted the bag and watched my father's ashes flutter in the breeze and fall to the water. *Be free*, I thought, as the sun slid past the horizon, and the moon rose full in the eastern sky.

The voice from my family that said, "That's enough, Lisa!" has been quieted, like pulling a dandelion and blowing it into the wind, the stem a reminder of the thousands of its siblings waiting to raise their benign heads. My own voice has grown strong now, with sturdier roots not easily silenced. My parents helped shape who I've become, perhaps most by my desire to live separate because I felt different. Embracing who I am apart from my family has fortified my attraction to the mystical, to listening to the whispers of wise voices beyond the veil, and to act in ways that feel true to myself. Nowhere is this more evident than in New Mexico where Mark and I now share a home on the slopes of the Organ Mountains.

This past December, as darkness gathered to usher in the Winter Solstice, I crossed the threshold of my sixtieth birthday. It occurred to me that throughout my life my surname has informed my identity. For thirty years I bore the maiden name inherited from my father. For the past thirty years, as a mother, I have carried my son's father's name. As a crone, my name will be my own, chosen for the birthplace of my Italian maternal great-grandmother, a place I adore. It means Bringer of Light.

May thirty years more be mine to shine.

THE GODDESS DREAMS

SUSAN R. BROWN

Just before I turned thirty I fell in love with a goddess.

It was summer in Philadelphia, and everything was damp and limp in the thick, heavy air. I had an apartment in the funky, cool Philadelphia neighborhood of Germantown, where I was living by myself for the first time. Good friends from my women's group lived across the street, on a block where everyone knew each other.

I was twenty-nine years old, a skinny girl with wire-framed glasses and curly hair that became wild in the 90% humidity. My life seemed good that summer. I had a job as a counselor working with people coming out of state hospitals which I liked well enough, and had been accepted into an excellent graduate school nearby. My parents lived less than an hour away. I even had the perfect boyfriend, from my parents' point of view: Jeffrey was a brilliant, socially conscious Jewish lawyer. He wasn't dependable and he wasn't very nice to me, but he was better than nothing; at least that's what I thought at the time. So I couldn't figure out what was wrong with me. Why was I so restless, so unhappy? Why did there seem to be not enough air to breathe?

One day I went to a workshop that was required for my job. It was about "Death and Dying," a topic that sounded boring and depressing. I hated being stuck in a room sitting on a hard chair for six hours on a summer day, listening to someone drone on about the five stages of grief. No one close to me had ever died, and it didn't mean that much to me. I was impatient for it to be over so I could go home and get ready for my date with Jeffrey. The last exercise was the most absurd, I thought.

"Unfortunately," the woman who was leading it said, "after you leave this workshop you're hit by a bus and killed. Write your obituary."

I dashed off a few sarcastic lines, something like "Susan Brown grew up in Philadelphia, worked in the mental health field in Philadelphia for many years, and died in Philadelphia." I hurried away to meet Jeffrey.

He didn't want to go out that night, so I bought some takeout food and we had dinner in his apartment. I told him about the workshop, how boring it was and how tiring to spend all day in those uncomfortable chairs. He seemed restless, and got up from the couch, saying, "I want to show you something." He pulled out his video camera, and when he turned it on and showed me the screen I saw blurry images of Jeffrey walking through the woods, naked. Then suddenly he squatted down, and I realized he was taking a shit! The camera started to shake, then the film stopped; a moment later the camera was focusing on his blonde ex-girlfriend, also running naked in the woods!

"Why are you showing me this?" I asked, my voice small and thin.

"Don't you think it's funny?" he said. "The camera was shaking because she was laughing so hard."

I felt angry and humiliated, but I couldn't speak. My face was hot, my head felt fuzzy and my chest was tight. What was he saying? That I could never measure up to this woman who had broken up with him? That she was more beautiful, adventurous and funny than I was? As Jeffrey went to put away the video camera, I knew that the real problem was that who I was would never be enough for him. And seeing myself through his eyes, I thought he was probably right; I wasn't.

The next night I slept fitfully, and strange dreams came like waves in a slate-grey ocean. In the morning, after I'd squeezed out a little sleep, I woke up with aching muscles and a dry mouth, feeling like I'd been running all night. I pulled myself out of a dream which was so powerful it seemed hallucinatory, and which left me with a sense of great foreboding. This is how I recorded it in my journal:

I am on a flatbed truck, with a number of other people; we are soldiers heading for some kind of battle. With us is a woman, whose job it is to put people on and off the truck. We stop for a light, and a dirty, bedraggled, exhausted man tries to get on with us. He is very ill. The woman invites him onto the truck, though he is filthy and mud-covered. We ride for what seems like days. Suddenly we realize that he is dead, and that the woman is going to push him off the truck and into the mud. She does so, weeping; I am weeping, too, and so is one of the other soldiers, who says of her, "She has children; she knows what this means." The body falls off the truck with a thud and a splash.

I woke up shaken and horrified, but with a feeling of awe. Though I had been writing down my dreams for years, I had never recalled a dream in such vivid detail. I had the sense that the dream was not my dream, but was somehow given to me whole, as though it was a message. But from whom? The images were frightening and mysterious, but the dream felt important and I wanted to know what it meant. Who was this woman, and why was she there? She seemed ruthless as she threw the dead man off the truck; but then she wept. And the soldiers seemed to trust that she was doing something difficult and necessary.

The next day it was hard to shake the disturbing images from the dream. The woman on the truck at first seemed merciful, but why did she then become so cruel? During my lunch break I took out my journal and began to free-write about these questions. I decided to try talking to this woman directly in my imagination. "Why did you do this?" I wrote. Her answer came almost immediately: "I tried to save this man, but there was no saving him. He is dead, so I must get him off the truck to make room for others. I am so, so sorry, because each person is like a child to me."

What did she mean? Though it saddened her, she did what had to be done. The woman was not really being cruel. She was implacable, a bringer of justice, even when it seemed ruthless. That's what they used to say about the gods. Who was the man? As I wrote, I began to shiver. Was he a part of me, a part that had to die? What part was that? Suddenly it became clear. My love for Jeffrey had to die, so there could be more room for me, for something new. My need for his love and approval had crowded out everything else. Whatever that was; I didn't even know!

She came to me several times over the next few weeks. Her form changed from dream to dream, but I always knew when She had come. Her coming was accompanied by a sense of mystery, of awe. Sometimes I would awaken knowing she had been there, though I remembered just a fleeting image or a fragment of song. Often there was singing, chanting, or sometimes a kind of keening.

The days started to seem flat, just time I had to pass until I could go to sleep. But I was having trouble sleeping because I had much more energy than usual; my mind was extremely alert and clear and ideas were coming rapidly. Many nights I went to bed in a state of heightened perception and excitement, the way you feel when your lover visits. Because I had worked with bipolar patients, I worried I might be having a hypomanic episode, but I didn't care because *I* felt like something important was happening to me.

One night, after a tense weekend with Jeffrey, I woke up with my heart pounding from another dream:

I am with Jeffrey in a huge old empty house, which reverberates with ghosts. It is the home of Howard Hughes, and a woman, his housekeeper, is showing us his belongings. She is a tall thin woman with a severe countenance, her hair pulled back in a tight bun. We feel very small in this cavernous house, which is dark and filled with dust and echoes. There are many objects scattered around, one of which is a large black box. "Open the box," she says in a quiet voice. I open it, and inside is a large black snake, seemingly dead. I jump back, and the woman reassures me saying, "Don't worry. I won't let anything happen to you. You will be alright." Suddenly the snake rears up and begins to bite me painfully on my outstretched arms. The woman shrugs and turns away. Jeffrey stands there, just watching. The snake bites and bites and bites…

. . .

I awoke in a state of agitation. The dream stayed with me all that day. I went to work in a kind of daze, the images from the dream seeming more real than the tasks I mechanically performed.. How could Jeffrey let this happen to me? Why did the woman promise to protect me and then do nothing to stop the snake?

That day after work I went to the library and found a book about dream symbolism. There was the obvious Freudian explanation that the snake was phallic and that I felt in danger from men, but somehow that didn't seem right. Then I found something that made my breath stop. According to the book, the ancients believed that the snake, capable as it is of shedding its skin, was a powerful spirit whose appearance signified rebirth and transformation. There was a picture of a Snake Goddess, worshipped by the people of ancient Crete, with a snake wrapped around her outstretched arms!

My arms started to tingle and my breath quickened. I thought again about the dream. What was it trying to tell me? I realized that although while the snake was biting me it was frightening and painful, I was somehow withstanding it. The housekeeper was right. It didn't destroy me; I was in pain but I was "alright." I would survive whatever transformation was in store for me.

I suddenly felt afraid. A curtain had been raised, revealing mystery, and I wasn't at all sure I wanted to look behind it. How did this image come into my dream? I had never heard of this Snake Goddess, and yet somehow she was there, telling me to "open the box." What was the box I was supposed to open? What was happening to me? I started to believe that maybe I was being visited by a goddess. But I also started to wonder if I was losing my mind.

In the weeks that followed, I continued to have trouble

sleeping and became more and more obsessed with the need to find out about my dream goddess, if that's what she was. The rest of my life--work, school, even Jeffrey--faded into the background. I no longer waited by the phone for Jeffrey to call; in fact, I was relieved when he didn't, because he began to feel like a distraction from my real life.

About a week after this visit, She came again. I had just had my wisdom teeth removed and was in a great deal of pain; the next day there was to be a large family party. I woke up from another vivid and disturbing dream:

I am fourteen years old, in the house where I grew up. Suddenly people and cars piled high with flowers begin to move past the window and into the back yard. I go outside, and realize that it is a huge funeral procession, with flower-filled cars, strangely haunting music, and hundreds of people filing past our window and across the back yard. I follow behind; when we get to the grave, several people in long robes are lowering the body of a young girl into the grave, which is just bare earth with a pool of water at the bottom. As she touches the earth her body begins to move, and I realize she is struggling and alive. The others continue to lower her into the pool and are trying to drown her in it. The girl struggles and struggles--the others push and push. Suddenly with a surge of strength she lunges up and rises out of the grave, her face screaming and distorted, like a demon face. I turn and run back into the house and wake up in a state of terror.

"Who is this horrible demon-girl?" I wondered as I lay in bed trying to shake myself out of the dream. Memories flood into my mind: I'm fourteen years old, sitting at the dinner table, everyone silent as my enormous father sits at the head of the table radiating anger, his big pianist's hands clenching and unclenching. My mother's anxious eyes as she entertains us, telling stories with an actress' skill. My middle brother, defiant and provocative, my little brother silent. And me, frantically trying to connect with each of them. Staring at the closed door of my parents' bedroom, hearing my father's thunderclap voice and my mother's tears. Then after, the door still closed though now my mother is gone somewhere, feeling his pain radiate through the door and wondering what I had done and what I could do. My little brother's dream of my father picking up the house and smashing it down over and over. My middle brother, spitting contempt as a huge hand smashes him across the face, and me, yelling at my father when he did that, and the same hand across my face. Then later, when Jeffrey disrespects me, the verbal hand across my face as I stand there turned to stone.

The flood of memories left me terribly shaken. I lay there unable to move, as if pinned to the bed by the feelings of sadness and anger these memories evoked. And, as I lay there I suddenly remembered a similarly haunting and vivid dream I had had years before. In that dream there was a female figure, dark and fierce, who reminded me of the girl in the "sacrifice" dream and the woman on the truck. I wasn't ready to hear her message then, but I knew it was an important dream and I had recorded it in my journal. I took out my journals from the last several years and somehow found it pretty quickly, almost as though it was waiting for me.

There is a beautiful girl--she is of many races, many ages—who stands on a rock in a desert. She is unmistakably a leader of her people, driven by a relentless urgency. She stands on her toes, poised as if pressing against the air. Her hair is drawn back in a bun and parted in the middle, and she wears a long white dress. She is half speaking, half singing to a group of people whose father she has just killed because he has destroyed her family. These people are her enemies, but at the same time, they are her people, her family. She has gone beyond hate and speaks/sings to them with a love that is mystical, almost impersonal. The pain and anger of centuries are in her voice; as she chants, the people sway and weep. They do not hate her for what she's done; they are awed by her.

When I read this dream, the hair on the back of my neck stood up. This was the same figure from my other dreams, I knew, but when she first appeared I wasn't ready to know her. Again she seemed ruthless. Why did the father have to be killed? This fierce goddess was also doing something cruel but necessary.

As I thought about this dream, I realized that the destructive voice of my father was inside me and had to be "killed." Instead I had taken on the impossible task of trying to heal my father, in fact my whole family, and the burden of that was drowning me. I could no longer remember the dreams I had for myself.

The procession in the "funeral" dream was not, I realized, a funeral, but a sacrifice. The girl was not a demon but me, fighting for my life. She looked frightening to me because I was frightened by my own rage and by the struggle going on within me, one which I vaguely realized could lead to the shattering of my peaceful but stultifying life.

Over the next several months, while my life seemed to go on as usual, I was in greater turmoil. It became harder to deny that my life was both empty and suffocating. I could no longer ignore the painful ways Jeffrey made me feel humiliated and devalued. He was brilliant and funny, but his joking often had a sarcastic, mocking edge that threw me off balance. I was proud to be seen with him, but I was painfully aware that I was not the one he was looking for.

I had grown up in Philadelphia and, after being away at college for several years, I had come back. I had a community of good friends, was in a women's group that had been meeting for years, and my family was close by. Sometimes too close, I had to admit; it was too easy for me, the person everyone talked to, to become embroiled in their dramas.

My job was meaningful-- helping people make small steps towards health after being released from the psychiatric hospital-- but I wasn't being challenged, wasn't growing. I was bored. I wanted to become a psychotherapist, to learn to work more deeply with people, one-on-one, not just in groups. I had applied--and been accepted-- to Bryn Mawr School of Social Work, an excellent program outside of Philadelphia. So why did the prospect of going there make me anxious? Why did I feel trapped when I imagined it?

What did I really want? Was I planning to become a therapist merely to continue the role I had in my family? And if I did, did I want to stay where I was? I was haunted by the idea that my gravestone would read, "She Never Left Philadelphia." I knew that if I went to graduate school here, that's what would happen. I would make all my professional connections here and I would never leave. Like the young "demon girl" being buried in the sacrifice dream, was I sacrificing myself by staying in this familiar and comfortable but suffocating life?

I started to think that I might have to leave my life behind to save it. But where would I go? My good friend Marcia was living in San Francisco, a place I had always wanted to live; I could go out to spend some time with her. But as I thought about it, I realized that what I wanted, what I needed was not just a vacation but a sabbatical; a long break from the life I had been living. I wanted, not weeks but months to find what my own rhythm really was, to learn to listen to myself. I wanted to be able to let go of all my plans and see if something new would emerge. Of course, I was not in a job that gave sabbaticals; if I wanted that kind of time I would have to quit. If I went away for more than a few weeks I would miss the start of graduate school; I would have to defer my admission to the following year. I could sublet my apartment, or I could move out. And I would definitely have to break up with Jeffrey!

I started telling my family and friends what I was thinking about. Most became upset, angry, frightened that I was about to destroy my life. My father was furious and disbelieving: "You don't know what the hell you're doing!" he shouted; "You idiot, you're screwing up your life!" I was confused, anxious, and filled with doubt; my father's mocking anger fueled my self-doubt as it always did. Could I really do something that almost everyone I loved thought was wrong, stupid or self-destructive? What if they needed me? What if Jeffrey, disappointing as he was, was my last chance for a relationship?

It was hard for me to trust myself to make such a potentially life-altering decision in the face of almost universal opposition. One night, in desperation, I asked for Her help for the first time before I went to sleep. She answered this way:

I am at a magnificent concert with many musicians and singers performing. The last performer, a beautiful frail woman with a powerful presence, strengthened by another woman's love and encouragement, sits down at the piano and begins to sing gorgeous songs, one after another, and brings down the house. By the end, the audience is in tears, overwhelmed by the beauty of the music.

It seemed as though the "frail woman" in the dream was singing directly to me, to cheer me on. Or maybe she was me, finding my voice and hearing its beauty. The dream helped me make my decision. I was going to leave Philadelphia and go to stay with Marcia in San Francisco, if she would have me.

Marcia and I had lived together in a women's commune in an enormous stone house in an older section of Philadelphia. She was a lively doctor from the Midwest with a huge "Jewfro" hairdo and an ironic, cackling laugh. She lived with us while she was doing a Family Practice internship in Philadelphia. She was one of two women in her medical school class, and to survive all the contempt and harassment from her classmates she soon earned the nickname "Bard Parker" because of her sharp tongue. Bard Parker was the name of a company that manufactured scalpels.

Marcia knew my family well and she often sparred with my father when he baited us about our feminism. After her internship was over, she left for San Francisco to do her residency at San Francisco General Hospital. There was another commune, friends from Philadelphia that had

THE GODDESS DREAMS

moved to San Francisco the year before, buying three adjoining Victorians in the Noe Valley district and cutting doors in the walls between the houses. By the time Marcia arrived, all three couples in that commune had broken up so there was space for her in the middle house.

When I decided to leave Philadelphia, I called Marcia to ask if I could stay with her for a while. "Sure!" she said right away. "I just moved into one of the Philadelphia Victorians, right in between Gale and Arlene. There's plenty of room; it's a four-bedroom house, and the rent is only $250 a month for the whole house! It'll be a blast!"

A plan was forming for my new adventure. One or two friends--and my brothers-- seemed to understand and have faith in me. I talked with my mentor from college, an anthropological psychiatrist. He asked me when the last time was that I made such a radical change in my life; I said I wasn't sure, probably about 6 years before when I left Cleveland to return to school. He told me that the cells in our body are constantly renewing themselves, so that after about seven years we actually, in a sense, have completely new bodies! This, he said, is the real reason for "the seven-year itch." He told me that last time he experienced this need for change he arranged to be sent to Iran to study the mental health system there.

Because I was still feeling so confused, uncertain and guilty, I decided to see a therapist. I needed help to figure out if I really was destroying my life. Her name was Hannah, and she was older and a wise woman. I saw her only once. She told me that as far as she was concerned, if I wanted to move to California and live on the beach that would be perfectly fine, if it was what I truly wanted. But it was not her words, it was her warm clear acceptance that gave me permission to look inside for the answer. This seemed so simple and yet so difficult.

I knew what I had to do. I didn't know where it would lead or whether it would turn out to be the "right" decision; I only knew it was what I needed to do now. I would defer my admission to Bryn Mawr; I would quit my job; I would move out of my apartment; and I would break up with Jeffrey. Then I would get into my little Datsun B210 and drive across the country to San Francisco to stay with Marcia.

And that is what I did.

In June of 1978 I gave notice at my job and told my landlord I was moving in late July. I called the graduate school and arranged to defer my admission for a year; I would start the following September when I returned from California. I hadn't told Jeffrey about any of this and found myself putting off the conversation. I wasn't sure I could bear leaving him. I loved him, or at least I needed him, wanted him more than I had ever wanted any other man, and was proud to be with him even though I knew he didn't feel the same.

One night, we had dinner at our favorite Chinese restaurant, then went back to his apartment. I tried not to pay attention to the fact that he didn't seem to want to talk much that night. I asked him about his day, and he said in an offhand way, "I got an award from the National Lawyers' Guild for my prison work. They're going to present it at a dinner next week." "Oh Jeffrey, that's wonderful!" I exclaimed. "When is the dinner? I'd love to be there!"

He was silent for a moment, then said "Well actually I was planning to go alone."

"Really? Why?" I asked, not wanting to hear his answer.

"Well," he said, "We're not in a committed relationship, and this is a very public event."

I felt as though he had kicked me in the stomach. We had been together for over two years, and he didn't want me to meet his colleagues! Was he ashamed of me? Was he seeing someone else who was going to be there?

I said nothing. I froze, as though a cold fog was filling up all the spaces in my brain. My chest felt tight; it was hard to breathe and impossible to speak.

Suddenly I heard a voice, very quiet but very clear: "Enough." The fog started to lift and my voice found its way out of my chest.

"I can't do this anymore," I said.

Jeffrey was quiet. Then he looked at me and nodded; "Okay," was all he said. I couldn't look at him, and as I felt a wave of heat explode in my chest I realized I was terribly angry.

"You've been waiting for me to do this!" I shouted. "You have no respect for me. You like having sex with me, but you've never loved me!"

"Susan, I really care about you, I...."

"Fuck you, Jeffrey! I'm leaving you, and as a matter of fact I'm leaving Philadelphia!" I went into the other room, threw my few things in a bag, grabbed my toothbrush, and left.

That night I sobbed with grief, anger, and relief. I knew I should have done this long ago, but I never had the strength until now. I was too afraid of losing him, too afraid of being alone. But now I really knew that being alone was better than the constant feeling of rejection, of not being enough, that was my relationship with Jeffrey.

That night She came again. This time, I had a dream in which the goddess finally told me her name:

She came to me, talked to me softly and reassuringly, and sang a song---then disappeared, as if she had melted into the air. In the song, she told me that her name was Athena.

When I awoke I felt euphoric. Athena! She was my favorite of the Greek gods and goddesses from a book I had loved as a child--the Goddess of Wisdom. I loved her calm grey eyes, her compassionate wisdom, and her strength. I loved that she was a woman and a warrior. Now that I knew her name, I was hungry to learn more about this goddess.

In the days and weeks that followed, that's what I did. I scoured the library and bookstores for books about her, many of them written by followers of the great Swiss psychologist Carl Jung. Jung believed there were universal symbols and stories which he called "archetypes" that appear in different forms in the mythology of every culture, and also in the dreams of individuals who are in need of the messages they bring. He called this the "collective unconscious." Somehow this archetype, the goddess Athena, had come into my dreams to help me. But it wasn't until I had found the strength within myself to end the relationship with Jeffrey that she finally told me her name.

Athena was a "Virgin" goddess, meaning that she was alone, "one-in-herself", divine in her own right--in other words, she was just fine without a man. She embodied intuitive, practical, loving wisdom rather than the distant, abstract wisdom of her brother Apollo. She is the "ever-near", always ready to intervene; she guided Odysseus on his long journey, giving him the courage to face danger and battle monsters and, according to Homer, when she appears to him "she is barely seen and heard before she disappears"....just as she did in my dream.

With Athena at my side, I knew I would be all right---despite all the unknowns, all my fears and doubts, and the consternation and sadness of my family and friends. Though I was someone who usually preferred someone else to drive, I drove my little car all by myself from Philadelphia to San Francisco, strangely unafraid on that three-thousand- mile journey.

I had never driven by myself for more than two hours; how was I ever going to make it across the whole country? To my surprise, it was exhilarating to be on the road, on an adventure with no clear end. I drove until I felt tired, stopping for lunch at little diners along the road, or buying a sandwich and stopping at a beautiful overlook, thrilled by not having to worry about anyone but myself.

I had a few friends along the way, and names of some other people who I could stay with. In larger towns I sometimes looked for a park where the hippies hung out, and asked them where I could find a hostel or another cheap place to stay. A couple of times one of them invited me to crash at his place; these were more innocent times, where there were communities of counterculture people who looked out for one another, and I never had a bad experience. Was I being protected? Or was I moving through the world differently?

There were many nights, though, when I had no choice but to stop and check into a roadside motel. At first I was frightened to be a woman alone, in the middle of nowhere along an endless road in Oklahoma or Texas. Somehow, though I wasn't remembering any dreams, I felt sure I would be fine. It was as though there was, ever-near, a quiet confident presence beside me. I began to look forward to those cheap motel stays, when I would pick up dinner at the local diner, settle in to watch TV, and revel in being unencumbered and alone.

There were some bad moments. One night, in a small town in Texas, I was walking down the main street looking for a place to eat when I saw a man sitting in his car. I asked him where I could find a good cheap meal, and he gestured for me to come closer. I started to walk over to him, but when I looked into the car window I realized he was wearing nothing below his waist but a towel spread across his legs! I began to freeze, but then my jaw clenched and I started to feel more angry than afraid.

"Ugh, what a creep!" I exclaimed, and walked quickly away, silently thanking the Goddess for my escape.

There were other times when I lay under the not-very-clean covers in a cheap motel room feeling very alone and vulnerable, wondering what the hell I thought I was doing. But I almost always felt better the next morning, and I drove along the highway eager to see what lay around the next curve in the road. I stopped at almost every "Vista Point" sign, which Jeffrey never wanted to do when we traveled. I drank in the strange, hypnotic beauty of the Great Plains and the awesome spires of the Rocky Mountains.

Finally after about ten days I pulled into Boulder, Colorado where my old friend and housemate Erika was staying with her brother. She was going to drive with me the rest of the way to San Francisco for a little vacation from her job as a nurse practitioner working with HIV patients. We set out on the road, happy to be together and marveling at the vast, dry western landscape, so different from the familiar green East Coast forests. We travelled west on Interstate 70 across Colorado and into Utah, Erika driving and me looking at the map and trying to figure out how to get to Arches National Park near Moab, which we were eager to see.

"Oh look," I said. It looks like there's a road that cuts over from 70 to Arches!"

"Let's take it," Erika replied. "It would be great to get off this damn highway. I'm so sick of long, straight roads full of semis with nothing to look at!"

We turned off onto a small road, and on either side of us were small grey-green hills covered with scrub grass, and every once in a while twirling tumbleweeds skidded across the road like little tumbling cartoon people in a big hurry to get somewhere. The sun was starting to set, and the hills on either side of us started to rise towards the darkening salmon sky. As we gazed around us, we suddenly realized that we were no longer on an asphalt road; my little car shook as it stuttered over rocks and crevices. I started to feel afraid and very alone. What if the road never actually continued on to Arches? What if we got a flat tire out here in the middle of nowhere? I realized I had no idea how to change a tire because my father or boyfriend always did it.

It was dark now, and too late to turn around and return to the highway. We decided to keep going and Erika slowly drove on; we were hoping to see a sign to let us know we were headed in the right direction. It was now so dark that we couldn't even see the hills on either side of us, let alone what lay ahead. By now I was terrified. My mouth was dry, and a voice in my head mocked, "You idiot! Why would you take a road in the middle of the desert when you had no idea where it went?"

Erika said, "I think you should drive," so we switched places and I drove on very slowly. It was very dark and very late and we were both exhausted, with no idea where we would sleep. Then I thought I heard a faint sound, like a ghostly chuckle, and I began to chuckle myself as I inched along, trying to avoid the rocks that could destroy my tires.

"Let's look for a place to sleep," I said, figuring we'd just have to lay down our sleeping bags by the side of the road. But somehow I knew that we were going to be OK.

Then we saw what looked like a gift from the gods—or the goddess: a sign with an arrow that said "CAMP-GROUND." I turned the car into a little parking lot. We still couldn't see a thing, and I wasn't sure where our flashlight was. We seemed to be on some sort of beach; we could feel the sand shifting under our shoes as we walked carefully, feeling our way in the dark, and we could hear what sounded like moving water. Dark shapes dotted the landscape, which we hoped were other campers.

"Over here, I said, pointing to a little area between two small hills. Grateful and stumbling with exhaustion, we unrolled our sleeping bags and went to sleep.

We were awakened a few hours later by the caress of cool dawn sunlight on our faces. I opened my eyes and stared around in amazement. We were on a beach, and the sign by the parking lot said "Upper Colorado River Campground." The river flowed like a dark green moving road in front of us, and rising up on the other side were the soaring red sandstone cliffs of the Desolation Wilderness.

I was filled with wonder and gratitude; the fear and doubt of the night before were gone. I felt again that I was being protected, that no matter how lost I would get I would find my way. I realized, too, that I might not know what I was looking for until I found it.

∼

In the months after I arrived in San Francisco, though I was living in a beautiful Victorian house in a magical city with a good friend, I was very lonely and confused about what I was going to do and who I was now. For the first time in many years I had no plan, no goal, and felt unmoored. Marcia offered me friendship and a place to live, but when I left the house I felt disoriented, not sure which way to turn because the ocean was on the wrong side. I missed my family and my friends terribly. I even missed Jeffrey, missed his touch and his ironic smile

In time I began to feel less lonely. Marcia and I became close again, and with her as my guide, I discovered the dazzling new world of the San Francisco Bay Area, its golden beauty so different from the lush green of the East Coast. We laughed and played all through that foggy, magical summer.

When I wasn't roaming around with Marcia, all I wanted to do was lie on a plastic chaise lounge in the colorful, unkempt garden of the Noe Valley Victorian we shared and read novels. I read science fiction, historical novels, romances--anything that didn't demand too much effort. This was the first time since I left college nine years earlier that I didn't have a job; in fact, it was the first time in my life since early childhood that something outside myself wasn't structuring my time. For the first time, the rhythm of my days was determined solely by my own internal currents.

I was more tired than I had ever thought possible. I lay on that chaise lounge and could not imagine going to a job every day again. When I was in the mood for company, I wandered a few blocks over to 24th Street; I sat in the window of the Café Flore and drank espresso, falling in love with that bitter, syrupy brew. I combed the used bookstore for more trashy novels and tried on shoes at Rabat.

But mostly my days were spent in delicious, dreamy lethargy on that chaise lounge in the garden.

After a few weeks of this, I began to wonder if I would ever accomplish anything again. Would I ever pursue the siren call that led me to quit my job and drive 3000 miles to get here? Would I turn into a dull, apathetic loser in this magnificent city, one of those people who sat in cafes pretending to write?

I had been lying on the chaise lounge for about six weeks when, for the first time since leaving Philadelphia, I had another dream. The woman in the dream looked different, but as soon as I awoke I knew it was She. I wrote about it this way:

I am walking through a field of flowers, moving slowly in the summer sun. In the center of the field there is a woman sitting in a circular gazebo; she watches me with grey eyes. She wears a habit, hot and black; it coils around her body to the ground, hiding the pale flesh, its roundness. Her face is round and her glasses circular, smoothing sharpness. Her eyes are calm; she is still as sunrise. As I approach she stands; silently she takes my hand. We walk down into the field and she leads me, slowly, around the center; we walk together in a circle. She tells me I must find a way to complete the circle, and we talk at length about balance.

After this dream, I started to feel that sense of anticipation and excitement I associated with a visit from Athena. The virgin goddess had come back as a nun! I had finally had enough rest. It was time to come back to life.

I started to write in my journal again, drawing pictures of circles and musing on the dreams. Instead of trashy novels, I bought books about Greek mythology and

Jungian studies of goddess imagery. I learned more about Athena, and about the Jungian concepts of archetypes and the collective unconscious. I read books about dream work that helped me pay attention to my dreams even more closely.

I wasn't sure I would be able to do this on my own, so I found a class which was the perfect container for my incubating work--"Images of the Feminine In Mythology," taught by Judith Blanton at the Wright Institute in Berkeley. Judy Blanton was a peppy, attractive woman in her 40's who reminded me of a cheerleader. She had a formidable intellect and a passion for her subject and her students. She was excited about both my writing and the journey it described and, with her encouragement, I started writing, much less concerned about whether my subject--my goddess--was a legitimate topic of study.

I immersed myself in the mythological study of Athena, trying to understand why she had appeared to me at this particular time in my life. As I hungrily explored her mythology, I was astounded by the many images and stories that spoke powerfully to me.

In Erich Neumann's *The Great Mother* were many images of young girls who were sacrificed--to convention, to the father, for the good of the community. Karl Kerenyi, in his mythological study of Athena, tells several stories of virginal figures mythologically associated with Athena who fall victim to rape and death. Persephone was forced to marry Hades, God of the Underworld, to save the world from famine; she is symbolized by the pomegranate carried by Athena. In one myth, a virgin daughter is raped by her father and bears a child to him. In another, the giant Pallas is considered to be the father of Athena; he ambushes and rapes her, and in revenge she kills him, tears off his skin and wears it on her shield. There was actually a cult of Athena that involved human sacrifice, in which virgins were sacrificed to the Goddess as a re-enactment of this primordial drama.

According to Homer, Athena's own mother, Metis, was a victim. She was the "goddess of wise counsel," the lover of Zeus who, fearful that she would bear a child who would threaten his power, swallowed her whole while she was pregnant. From Zeus' belly Metis gave birth to the goddess Athena, giving him a terrible headache; Athena then sprang full-grown from his forehead. Metis stayed inside Zeus, whispering her wisdom to him: it is because of her that he was given the epithet "wise Zeus."

Athena is a fearsome warrior, a virgin goddess who has no need of a man, who uses her weapons only to defend her beloved city of Athens against invaders. She guides the hero Odysseus on his dangerous journey, protecting him by giving him the courage to face danger and the strength to act decisively. Jung names Athena, along with Sophia and Kuan Yin, as a "symbol of transcendence" who appears to "guide the hero on his lonely journey through darkness and danger, as he searches for release from a confining or threatening situation."

The Athena scholar Kerenyi says that "what she protects... is a core of womanhood as it finds itself beseiged by the archaic spirit of the father." She is a virgin goddess, a woman who is whole, one-in-herself, divine in her own right. As the Jungian analyst and writer Esther Harding says, such a woman "does what she does—not because of a desire to please, not to be liked, or to be approved, even by herself; not because of any desire to gain power over another, to catch his interest or love, but

THE GODDESS DREAMS

because what she does is true." In my studies I discovered that one of the mythological ancestors of Athena was none other that the Cretan Snake Goddess, the one from my dream!

Why was this fearsome and protective warrior-goddess appearing to me? I was a young, middle-class white woman with no real worry about my security, let alone my survival. I had a loving family, a good job, and a community of friends. How was I threatened, that I needed this warrior at my side?

As I muse on this question, I'm visited by the image of myself as a young girl—timid, insecure, longing for approval and terrified of rejection. I was the "good girl" who tried to do everything that was expected of her and more, who was helpful and supportive and who had very little sense of her own needs and desires. I longed for my father's approval, but he was an angry and unhappy man when I was young, and I never felt like I was enough because I could never make him happy. My Dad was a gifted pianist who decided not to pursue music, though it was his passion. He wanted to have a "normal" life—to play baseball, get married, have a family. It seems now that, though he loved us, he must have resented us for this choice. Instead of becoming a concert pianist, he followed his father into advertising, a job that allowed him to provide for us but for which he had contempt.

We were happiest together when we played music— Dad on the piano, my brother on the guitar, and all of us singing. When he played, he was lost and happy, and I loved him then. But, coming home from a job he hated, his anger could fill the house. Dinners became war zones, and when he retreated to his room, his pain still radiated through the closed door. I would fill with helpless rage myself and hated the way he was contemptuous of my mother and of us when he was in this mood. I wanted to protect my mother, who retreated into timid, resentful silence while he berated her or us. I was the one who saw her tears. I silently decided I would never have a marriage like theirs.

Then, of course, I grew up to love men who were very much like him---talented, sometimes brilliant men for whom I was never enough. Men whose love and approval I longed for, but who treated me with disrespect. Men who needed to be in control and to be admired from a distance. Jeffrey, who appears in the dream with the snake goddess, was brilliant, confident, and jokingly contemptuous of me. I loved and admired him, but never felt worthy of him. Around him I felt off balance, unsure. I thought this familiar, painful state was love.

It started to become clear. The dreams were showing me the danger I was in and offering me help to escape. I was the young girl being sacrificed in the dream. I was the woman who had to "kill" her father in order to save her family. I was the girl being bitten by the snake, which was forcing me towards a painful transformation. I was the one who needed a warrior goddess at my side, to let me know that though I would suffer I would be all right. And I needed a goddess to sing to me, and to help me find my own song.

I began to experience myself not as an insecure and timid girl-child, but as a young woman at the center of a web of support and wisdom from women over centuries. I had to find a way to wake up and listen to them; and in order to wake up I had to go to sleep, so I could turn off the noise of my life and pay attention to my dreams. Gradually, over that long, lazy time on the chaise lounge in my unruly San Francisco garden, my attention began to turn away from the outer world, from the voices of judgement that weakened my foundations. It began to turn inward, listening for the wisdom voice the goddess brought, thrilled by what I was hearing because it came from my own deepest place. I was on my own odyssey.

I was meeting new people, but had a series of relationships with men that were unsettlingly similar to my relationship with Jeffrey. I was tired of this romantic rat race. Where was Athena when I needed her? I wasn't having any dreams that I remembered and was starting to wonder if I had made any progress at all. I realized I would much rather stay home alone with a good book on a Saturday night than go on another date that ended up making me feel more lonely.

In the midst of this unsettled time my brother Adam invited me to visit him in Amsterdam, where he had been living with his boyfriend Albert. Adam knew I was unhappy, and he called one night to cheer me up. "Why don't you come over and visit me? I can show you Amsterdam, and then we can rent a car and drive through Italy!"

I had never been to Europe, and the idea of seeing it for the first time with my brother, who was not only someone I loved being with but someone who knew the area and the language and could be my tour guide, sounded wonderful. "I can only spend about two weeks," Adam told me, "I'm going to have to go back to work after Italy. But why don't you stay and go someplace else? It seems like a shame to come to Europe for only two weeks."

I planned to use a small inheritance I got from my grandmother for this trip and thought I could manage another week or two. But where would I go? I knew immediately that I wanted to go to Greece. The idea sent a thrill through me as I imagined visiting Athena's magnificent temple, the Parthenon, and exploring the islands. But the more I thought about it the more doubtful I became. I had never travelled to another country by myself, and the thought of being alone in a strange place where I didn't speak the language was very intimidating. Besides, I had always thought I'd go to Greece on my honeymoon, or at least with a man I loved.

I told Adam I had considered going to Greece, but that the idea of doing it by myself made me too nervous; I would return home after Italy. He looked at me in disbelief. "Really?? You've always wanted to go to Greece. It's not that far from Italy; you should go!"

Over the next few days I thought about it. I didn't know what to do. I tried asking for Her help before I fell asleep, but still no dreams came. But one morning I woke up and it was as though I was hearing a commanding voice; "You're not going to the one place on earth that makes your hair stand on end because you're afraid to be ALONE? That's ridiculous!" And I knew it was, and what I would do.

I made reservations to fly into Athens. Then I went to the library, found a list of inexpensive student tours, and signed up to go on a 5-day archeological tour of the Peloponnesian Peninsula site of all the great classical Greek ruins. I would start my solo adventure by spending it with a group of people who wanted to see the same things I did, with a guide who would make all the arrangements. I was going to find Athena.

In July of 1983 I flew to Amsterdam where I spent a few days in Albert's elegant 16th-century townhome on the Singel Canal, exploring that fascinating city. Then we took the overnight train through the Black Forest of Germany,

THE GODDESS DREAMS

and awoke the next morning in Florence. We spent a glorious week driving through Northern Italy.

Then it was time for Adam to return to Amsterdam, and I took a bumpy flight on a small airline from Rome to Athens. I was nervous as I found my way by taxi to the hotel where I was to meet the tour group, but when our guide, Georgia, a dark-eyed young woman with a sunny, slightly mischievous smile met me at the desk, I knew I was going to be fine.

The tour was to start the next day, so that evening I set out to explore the neighborhood around our small hotel in the old part of the city with narrow streets all leading to the Plaka, the cobblestoned town square lined with cafes and restaurants with tables spilling out into the square. Music drifted from doorways and people sat at tables eating and gesticulating as they talked. And soaring above it all, sitting in enduring grandeur atop the Acropolis, was the Parthenon, the temple of Athena--MY Athena--the goddess who was the guardian of the ancient city. As I stared at the temple with its perfectly proportioned columns, I shivered with a sense of awe, of mystery. But I also had a feeling of coming home.

The next day was a free day before the start of the tour. I decided to go by myself to look for Athena in her temple. I woke early and decided to go then, before the crowds and heat descended. Georgia had offered to take me but I wanted to go alone, with no intermediary between me and the experience. Following her directions, I made my way by foot through the Plaka, climbing the ancient path uphill until I reached a point where there were woods instead of buildings. Amazingly, there was hardly anyone else around; I walked in silence through the door of the Propylaea, the entrance to the sacred place. I stepped up over crumbling steps and at the top, turned to the west where I could see the port of Piraeus, the islands, and the mountains of the Peloponessos beyond. The air was hot but lifted by a little breeze from the Aegean Sea, and everything was very quiet except for the birdsong. I lifted my face to the east towards the massive grace of the Parthenon.

As I approached the soaring columns of the temple, time seemed to slow down: though there were other people nearby, the quiet around me seemed to deepen. I walked through into the central space and caught my breath as I gazed upward. Though it was actually not a place of worship, the Parthenon's builder created a space that feels very sacred. It is a building at once huge and intimate, because the tapering shape of the Doric columns surrounding the open space seem to lift towards the sky, while at the same time enveloping the visitor in a kind of light embrace.

When I entered the Parthenon, it was empty, but to me was full of Athena's energy and I felt like a worshipper. I sat and gazed up at the ceiling, imagining it bordered by the friezes, and leaned against the columns trying to absorb the ancient magic. I stayed for a couple of hours, unable to leave. Images of the dreams came into my mind and I silently thanked Athena for giving me the courage to go on this adventure. I didn't hear a response but felt like she was welcoming me to her home. Finally, when the crowds started to appear and the heat made the air vibrate, I reluctantly walked down the path and back to my hotel.

Over the next five days, as we traveled along the pitted roads of the Peloponnesian peninsula, I continued to have a sense of being at home, as though I had been here before. Though I spoke no Greek, I found its melodic sound oddly familiar and the people who spoke it were almost universally kind and warm. Because of my dark curly hair, people in the villages often mistook me for a Greek woman, and I got secret satisfaction from not correcting them. "Maybe I WAS a Greek woman in a former life," I thought.

The last stop on our tour was Delphi, home to the famous Delphic Oracle, the great temple of Apollo, and a beautiful, circular temple of Athena. Delphi is known as one of the places in the world with very strong sacred energy, and it is thought that this is why the ancient Greeks built their temples there. In the center of the complex is a large egg-shaped stone called the Omphalos, or "the navel of the world." It represents a stone placed by Zeus, and the ancient Greeks' belief that Delphi was the center of the world.

As I walked through the remains of the temples, Delphi seemed not a dead ruin but very alive with spirit. I sat by the Castilian Spring where the oracle, the priestess Pythia, heard her prophecies, and I secretly took a little stem and some seed pods from the spring-fed tree there; they sit in a small Greek pottery bowl in my office to this day. The light seemed different, brighter, casting a glow on the ancient stones. Again I had the feeling of being almost alone there, despite the crowds of tourists. I say "almost" because at Delphi, even more than at the Parthenon, the presence of the Goddess was everywhere.

At the end of the five-day tour, I said goodbye to Georgia and thanked her for welcoming me to her country. I had three more days before my flight home. Where would I go? I wanted to go to one of the famous islands— Mykonos, Santorini, or Crete—but it would have taken most of my remaining time to get there and back. Georgia suggested I go to the island closest to Athens, Aegina, which was only forty minutes on the little Flying Dolphin boat from the port of Piraeus. She told me many Athenians go there for the weekend, and that it would be easy to find a place to stay once I got there.

I boarded a boat the next day; and, taking out my guidebook, I read about Aegina as I sat between two chattering Greek families on a wooden bench, listening to the deep rumble of the engine and gazing at the piercing blue of the Aegean sea. Amazed, I read that Aegina is home to the best-preserved temple of Athena in the entire country. It was originally dedicated to the pre-Hellenic mother-goddess Aphaia, from a time when the Greek religion was matriarchal. In a cave beneath the main temple, little round-bellied female figurines from that time before history were still being found. Later, after the Greeks conquered the land and installed their own patriarchal religion, they built a graceful Doric temple on the site and dedicated it to the goddess Athena. As I read I had that now-familiar feeling of time slowing down and my skin prickling. Had Athena guided me here?

The boat deposited us in the center of a small fishing village. When I got off the boat I walked along the café-lined quay listening to the fishermen calling to each other as they tossed glistening fish and squirming squid into buckets. I was hungry, so I sat down at a table in a small café at the water's edge and ordered some spanakopita and some fried squid which tasted so fresh it could have been taken off a nearby boat an hour before. The waiter, a young man with dark curly hair and kind, warm eyes, asked in very good English where I was from and where I was staying. Feeling perfectly safe somehow, I told him I was from California and that I was looking for a place to stay.

"You should stay with my Aunt! She has a small pensione above her house—just two rooms—and you'd be comfortable there." Thanking him, I walked up the dusty hill to the little house he'd pointed out. A woman who looked old but probably wasn't, with the same warm eyes as the waiter, answered the door; I told her Yannis had sent me and she smiled and showed me to a clean, tiny room overlooking the water. Again, I had a feeling of coming home.

I fell asleep to the soothing sound of the sea, and after a deeply restful night I woke up early, ready to go looking for Athena. My hostess showed me where to get a bus that would take me to the temple of Aphaia on the other side of the island. After a lurching ride over the hills the bus, which was filled with squawking caged chickens and black-clothed women who stared at me, giggling, pulled into a dusty parking lot. Following the signs, I walked up a path toward the temple, again somehow finding myself alone.

As I turned a corner my pulse quickened as I saw the temple appear against the brilliant blue sky. It looked almost like a miniature Parthenon, no roof but lined with graceful well-preserved Doric columns and almost-intact pediments. Signs pointed to a cave below on the other side, where the Mother goddess was worshipped before any of this existed.

Feeling awed, I walked down the path to the cave. There was no one else there, and I bent down and carefully walked over what looked like stones or shards of pottery to the dark, peaceful center of the cave. I sat down, looking through the mouth of the cave to the scrub-covered hillside, and breathed the slightly musty air. I tried to imagine what it might have been like when women would come here to honor the fertility goddess.

After a while I felt ready to enter the main temple. I walked up the path into the sanctuary, sitting down at one end and leaning against a column. My hair, which was wild and curly in the humid air, blew away from my neck and I closed my eyes, savoring the cooling breeze. A young man came up to me and started talking, but he soon walked away when he realized I had no interest in him.

I don't know how long I stayed there. What I do know was that sitting on the floor of the goddess' temple, leaning against one of her columns, I felt completely at peace. My mind was quiet and my breath seemed to move in and out with the Aegean breeze. I felt both completely open and completely solid. I was by myself but not alone. I had no more questions.

Two weeks after I returned to San Francisco I met and fell in love with Steve, the kind, strong, open man who would become my husband; we have two wonderful adult daughters. I got a Ph.D. in Psychology and found work I loved. There is no doubt in my mind that Athena appeared to show me I had lost my way and to help me find my right path.

Athena came to me to teach me things: How to protect myself, how to turn my focus inward for true strength, and how to release into the world, no matter what others think, the things that are important for me to say. To no longer keep myself hidden, but to share what's inside me with the world. And to hope that others might be inspired to listen to their dreams and to the messages they bring.

NO ONE ELSE DOES

L.T. WARD

There was no time, there was no time, there was no time.

I was in my late thirties with four kids, a husband working two careers (civilian and military Reservist), a house with a never-ending list of projects, school volunteering, a part-time job, a hundred pounds to lose, dinners to cook, a dog to take to the groomer, aging parents with health issues to check in on, and I'd be remiss if I didn't remember the coffee dates with friends to give me a semblance of hope that I could cling to my sanity and they to theirs.

Who I was and where my life was going were defined by my roles as mother, wife, daughter, friend. The smaller positions—employee, PTO volunteer, neighbor—filled in the gaps so that on the outside, I was killing it.

On the inside, I suppressed Liz Ward. She was me, but I hadn't the time to worry about who she was or what she wanted from life. Her commitments to others meant that she came second, third, or maybe not at all.

Until my eldest child, through heated tears and a shaking sob, uttered the words, "No one else does," putting a halt to everything I thought was important, forcing me to recalculate the course and intent of my life.

Those four words ignited a spark in my belly, a long-thought dead ambition reignited, and the course of my life forever changed.

∽

At twenty-two years-old, I gave birth to my daughter Helen. Pampers commercials ruined my expectations of how parenting would go. Instead of a fat baby filled with giggles, Helen was scrawny and screechy. She was serious, introspective. When she wasn't happy, she let the world know with an ornery velociraptor's roar, earning her the nickname Velociraptor Baby.

Helen's toddler years were happy, but she was reluctant to smile. When she set herself to a task—her favorite activity, dismantling the DVD tower or removing every book from the bookshelves—Helen focused until she'd undone all of my organization, sitting proudly amongst the mess strewn all over the living room floor.

Then our family's life underwent several changes. Matt had been an Active Duty sailor in the U.S. Navy from 2000 until 2006. Post 9/11, he deployed more than 85% of the year and worked an additional 75% of the time when he was home. Doing the math, my husband was gone a lot, missing the first few years of Helen's life, so he opted to let his tour end to become a civilian.

The loneliness in my marriage and his exhaustion meant I ate my feelings. An overly filled stomach hurt, but it replaced the emptiness. By the time we moved back to our home state, I weighed over 240 pounds and felt far removed from being a woman in my twenties. My weight wasn't defining my beauty, but I felt the heaviness in all aspects of my life. I swapped out fitted shirts for baggy ones. My jeans were cheap and rarely cut well for my rounded body. Shortly after moving back to Illinois, we'd added another daughter to our family (one of the many changes we made to our family dynamic and lifestyle); food and baby puke stains were common accessories. I justified my slovenly yet clean clothes because I wasn't going anywhere. I wasn't seeing people. It wasn't worth the money to buy fun outfits.

I wasn't worth buying fun outfits for.

My kids were. They wore whatever cute graphic tees they requested, me spending hours between snack time and cleaning bathrooms and building block towers to find coupons and deals online for Dora the Explorer and sparkly puppy designs. My daughters gave me my joy and I was determined to keep them shining.

From the playground benches, monitoring my children at play, I discovered Helen's seriousness was not common amongst other children. While Vivian and Henry—my second and third children, Henry joining our family two years after Vivian—fit in perfectly with the other children at the parks, Helen tended to be an outsider, taking on the role of chaperone or referee. Their wild squeals and ability to ignore game rules displeased her. Sociable yet highly rule-oriented. That was my firstborn daughter.

Helen's whimsical yet parameter-craving personality was sated by dance classes. At the age of five, she fell in love with dance. Even more so, the audience during the recitals. But it lacked something which I hoped she could find once school and its plentiful extracurriculars were available options.

As a student, Helen had scatterbrained moments, forgetting homework assignments, but she always followed her teachers' instructions to the best of her ability. She considered it the utmost respect to adhere to their requirements, even when it caused her to feel overwhelmed.

However, fifth grade for Helen was a turning point. That year, I was pregnant with my second son and fourth child. I worked two part-time jobs—one data entry at-home job and one at Helen's middle school as a lunchroom dishwasher. I was onsite to learn of all the social activities the school offered, so I encouraged her to audition for the school play and the school Speech Team. She made both.

Backstage and on stage, my serious daughter was a crack-up. She played to her audience, earning applause and cheers. Although she was serious off-stage, worrying about scoring perfect grades, annoyed by her siblings causing trouble by being small children, or stressed over what her future would hold, Helen found her laughter in the creative community. She let go of everything but that moment. She lived in that moment. She worked for it through practicing scripts, reciting the lines in her bedroom until she nailed them without the paper, adding in movements to accentuate her points. Helen existed for opening nights and closing curtains.

Meanwhile, I schlepped the children to various sports, dance classes, art classes, cooking classes, playdates... Anywhere they might have happiness. We ate fast food in the minivan or casseroles on the go. For my active brood, the diet was easily burned off. For me, I ate my portion, their leftovers, and maybe seconds when I got home. Tasting my food was secondary to feeling full.

Adulthood was exhausting and I feared my children would lose out on their sole opportunity for happy memories if I didn't offer them everything I could. Instead of seeing how drained my family of six was, I pushed us to keep going. The end goal of a happy life was somewhere and we could find it. We would find it. We only had to keep trying for it.

When Helen was in seventh grade, her school put on Peter Pan. Due to the size of her school, the directing teacher decided to split the role of Wendy between two actresses, one for each half of the play. Against the odds, the teacher selected my seventh grader for the Act II Wendy instead of one of the graduating eighth graders.

On opening night, I learned why.

There is a scene in Peter Pan where Wendy stands outside her nursery window. She raps the glass and begs Peter to let her in. Wendy is done playing and wants to return to her life, to pet her dog Nana, to be in the loving arms of her parents, to grow up. Peter, the forever petulant child, refuses. In this heartbreaking scene, Wendy sobs softly, sweetly. She pleas for Peter to understand her request and to open the window.

For a twelve-year-old girl, this emotional scene would be daunting, possibly unachievable. She might get the lines right, but to provide emotional depth for a squirmy middle school audience—many of whom are reluctant younger siblings only there as an inexpensive means for families to kill off a Friday night and offer financial support to the school—this was a lot. A big ask.

Helen delivered.

The row of young children wept openly and loudly as Helen/Wendy cried for Peter to let her into the nursery. Small voices called out from the gym floor sunk beneath the stage, "Peter! Let her in! Peter!" The other actors on stage choked up at hearing these younger children so enchanted by the characters that they interrupted the production to advocate for poor Wendy.

Peter did allow Wendy entrance to the nursery and the audience cheered.

I couldn't. My breath was locked in a swell of emotions in my chest. My gaze moved between watching Helen and watching her audience. She was my daughter, but she was Wendy.

Afterwards, by the craft services table, I stood with my sons, waiting for Helen to be ready to come home. It took her a while as she made her way through the awaiting fans. Those young children brought their school play pamphlets to her, begging for her autograph, shoving their parents' phones in her face for selfies with her. One little boy about four-years-old grabbed her hand and whispered to her. Later, I asked Helen what he said.

"'Were you afraid Peter wouldn't let you into the nursery?' I told him I wasn't. He then said, 'Good. I was mad he was so mean to you.'"

Her performance lacked the fiction of a play, giving a small child a true connection to the story that unfolded on the stage. He wasn't happy until she'd reassured him that she and Peter were truly friends again.

Helen was a star, but not for fame. She'd fallen in love with the craft, worked hard to earn her place within it, and parted the clouds of a dark night to grace the world with her light.

My serious child had a light so bright, so brilliant. It was like none I've ever seen before, one that gave a warm glow, reminding me years later just how powerful her illumination was.

As often as Helen and my other children shined, I found myself feeling less and less like a woman, even a person. I'd become a thing defined by the label *Mom*.

A mother. Pregnancy, birth, nursing, nurturing. Why were these aspects of my being, despite them being directly connected to my female body parts, making me feel detached from my femininity?

Matt worked his civilian job and his Naval Reserve job. Meanwhile, I switched to a more flexible, better paying at-home, part-time job to accommodate our growing family's needs. From the time we woke up, we worked tirelessly to provide financially and emotionally for our kids.

We lived the lifestyle of those embedded in the suburban sprawl. We used our gym memberships to burn off stress, the workouts barely making a dent. I scheduled coffee dates with friends between the kids' activities. These sessions turned into sessions of pouring out the strains of everyday drudgery, caffeinating ourselves into a buzzing high, then returning to our homes to resume our lives.

"Us Time" with Matt was reserved for that special time where we recovered from the day after the homework was done and the kids were tucked into bed. However, our kids were terrible sleepers. It was rare to make it through the night without one child or another finding their way into our marital bed, curling themself between my husband and me.

No matter how much I tried, I never felt rested. Stress and exhaustion abounded. At social and school gatherings, people gave the ubiquitous follow-up of "You look tired," after they greeted me.

I watched as my children grew up. Beautiful in their innocence and mischievousness, their increasing ages reminded me that I was no longer in my twenties and my thirties were rounding the bend to late thirties.

Where the hell had my life gone?

It didn't matter. I hadn't the time to worry about frivolities like missed chances and deep regrets, not when I had carpool and group projects and high school registration for Helen coming up.

I would think about me later. Maybe when my youngest graduated and went off to college. Maybe when I was fifty-two.

∽

High school is rarely considered the best time of anyone's life. For Helen, it began fine enough. She made many acquaintances and enjoyed her classes. That is, until she was accused of planting bombs in the school.

Freshmen are required to take biology. Helen's class was assigned a long-term project where students were required to educate their peers about a concern in the world, advocating for a means to improve themselves for the betterment of society.

Helen decided she wanted to teach her classmates about endangered animals and the recycling or purchasing efforts they could make to protect those creatures. Buy and reuse metal straws instead of accepting plastic ones, saving the sea turtles from choking hazards. Recycle old cell phones so that their gold pieces could be reused for newer models, reducing the world's need for mining. Take your fast food wrappers and bags home to recycle, cutting back on paper products going to the landfills.

My daughter's artistic side took over. She collected toilet paper tubes, enough to set one out each school day for a month. She wrote on a scrap paper, which she decorated, pinched the tube's edges, glued them together, then painted the exterior with a note for the finder to open the tube for a surprise.

Helen, being Helen, sought permission from not only her Biology teacher, but several other staff members so that she could hide these tubes around the school. She worried the adults in charge would be upset at her littering so before she began, she got four teachers' approvals in writing.

But no one told the custodian.

He came across one tube resting on the back of a water fountain. Panicked, he contacted the school's police officer who quickly collected up the cardboard tube. Then, he called Helen to his office.

There, he sat her in the chair on the other side of his desk.

He asked her to watch a video. He turned his computer monitor towards her.

Helen watched herself on the school's surveillance video, setting her Biology project on the fountain, then more footage of her placing other tubes in the lunchroom and by the P.E. lockers. The officer asked her if she understood the terror she'd put upon her peers and the school's staff. Helen hadn't. She'd only been complimented for her creativity.

But an adult with authority told her she had terrorized people and that's how Helen then saw her project.

I got the call about an hour later. My daughter was interrogated, politely, by the local bomb squad representative. They verified that she had had permission and warned her against being so careless with the safety of her classmates in the future.

Explaining the fuckery of what she'd endured was awful. My well-behaved, well-intentioned child was accused by adults she was taught to respect. Told they assumed she was threatening violence to her school, to her teachers, to her classmates and friends. No matter what I said, I couldn't untwist the narrative the police officer had set into her mind.

This was an omen of how misfitted for high school Helen was.

From then on, the stress remained constant, pressurized by adults teaching my daughter their views of the world, contrary to the views she'd been taught at home. A smart child in all Honors courses, Helen struggled with the mounting homework, marching band, volunteering with the middle school's dramatic arts program, dance classes, the high school's dramatic arts program, being a big sister, being a daughter. The kid struggled.

She unraveled.

I stepped in and cut back on some of her extras. Her commitments at home were to focus on her physical health, then her mental health, then her academics. Chores were so low on that list that she need only to clean up after herself; I would take care of the rest.

None of this was enough.

By the middle of sophomore year, weekdays were tear-filled days followed by raging verbal attacks against me in the evenings. Helen was the embodiment of my own mental state. Only she was a fifteen-year-old whom I loved more than myself. My mirror's reflection wounded me, but nothing like witnessing Helen's downward spiral.

After winter break, Helen's brown eyes carried permanently etched bags. Her shoulders sagged even without carrying her forty-pound backpack (we weighed it and with the bare minimum books, it was forty pounds!). Her breathing remained on the constant edge of hyperventilation.

Something had to give before my child broke.

Sadly, I was too late.

I got the text from Helen to swing by the high school, to pick her up after she'd had Speech Team practice. Due to an erratic activities schedule, I was on call, always waiting for an updating text of where and when she next needed to be shuttled. Standing in the half-empty parking lot, snow flurrying around her, Helen stood a somber statue. I pulled up beside her. She whipped the door open, wedged her bag in the footwell, then climbed into her seat.

She wouldn't look at me. I heard the attempts to suppress the sobs. I saw her body curl into itself.

"Helen, what's wrong?"

"Nothing."

If that's not the most bullshit response a teenager could give...

I drove her home and allowed her to tuck herself away in her room. She needed space after whatever had happened. However, dinner came and went. Helen took hers in her bedroom, an allowance during school nights when the kids have too much homework. I went to check on her and clear her dishes, and to remind her that she had play practice soon.

"Okay," she said heavily.

"Helen, what's wrong?"

"Nothing. It doesn't matter."

"Baby, tell me."

Helen swiveled in her chair and looked up at me, her cheeks streaked by tears. "It doesn't matter."

"What doesn't matter?"

"I hate this. I hate school. I hate my classes. I feel stupid all the time."

"But baby, you're not stupid. You're far from stupid. And you don't hate your classes. You love Drama."

She glared at me with shimmering anger. "I don't know why you made me take that class."

I hadn't made her; I'd encouraged her. She loved Drama. It was the only course she never complained about, regaling her father and me with happy anecdotes about as she plated her dinner before retreating to her bedroom and insurmountable homework load. Yet, her anger cast doubt over whether she'd enjoyed Drama or had put on a show for Matt and I, attempting to placate us by claiming at least one of her courses was going along smoothly.

Then she said, "I can't become an actress."

The piercing anger in my daughter's eyes was as disarming as her words. Since fifth grade, Helen had declared she should become an actress. I'd been binge watching Gilmore Girls at that time. We laughed at how much I was the Lorelai to her Rory. When time came for Rory to choose a university, she chose Yale over Harvard. I, being relatively obsessed with rabbit hole research about my favorite shows, googled Yale. Their phenomenal theater program stood out and with their Ivy League status, Yale became the golden prize Helen yearned to achieve.

At twelve.

Now at fifteen, Helen sat before me, a sobbing mess. She had recanted a dream she'd held for years in one breath.

"Why? Of course you can become an actress."

"No, I can't. I'm not getting any lead roles in the school plays. I didn't get any roles in the community theater productions last summer. I suck at this."

"You don't suck! Getting roles is hard and it's not always about who has the best talent. Sometimes, you're just not a fit for that part. But if you keep working on acting, the opportunities will come. Like when you get to college. It's a whole other world."

"My teachers think I should focus on becoming something else. They said that it's wasting my time to become an actress, because it's almost impossible to earn a living."

What the fuck? I bit back my fury and quieted the profanities in my mind as I said, "Helen, if it's impossible, then television shows and movies would have no one in them. Clearly, someone, some people, become actors."

"Not in my life. In my life, no one else does."

I fumbled for a contradicting retort. She was right, her point valid. Of all the people in my daughter's life, I couldn't come up with one creative person who took a risk to live out their dream. For my logical daughter, she needed a tangible example to cling to.

I waited too long to respond and Helen filled the silence. "Mom, look at you. You always wanted to be something, and you're just a stay-at-home mom with a shitty job. You're always stressed. You're never happy. You don't like your life, but you're still doing what everyone else tells you to do.

"If you can't be more than what you were told to be, then how can I? My teachers say it's a bullshit idea to spend thousands of dollars for me to become an actress who will never be able to pay my bills. And they're right."

I was stunned. I don't remember what I said, my words insufficient, meant to retract her accusation. But they fell so short they would have had to have a shovel to dig their way out of that hole. I left Helen to her homework, carried her dishes to the kitchen, then went about cleaning up dinner before it was time to take her to her play practice.

Helen was right. I hadn't been killing it; I'd only been killing me.

My beautiful daughter was named for Helen of Troy,

not some ancestral family member. Named while in the womb because I knew there was an essence about her, that she was worthy of the launch of a thousand ships. My fierce daughter with her ability to drop a Shakespeare quote in casual conversation, with her ability to stand before audiences of hundreds without a single shaken nerve, who wore cosplay dresses to school each Halloween because it was who she was and damned anyone who disagreed. My indomitable daughter had been broken.

I was a role model, but in the worst possible way . I'd become a woman who repulsed her, a horror story forewarning her against her future. Instead of teaching Helen she could be anyone she wanted to become if she worked hard enough, I'd taught her to put others' expectations first and accept the hardships of a mundane, suburban life.

When the kids were all tucked in that night, I stood in my bathroom and stared at the woman in the mirror, disgusted. My hair was flat in a messy bun. My shirt, faded, a stain on the shoulder. My jeans pressed tightly into my waistline. The dark circles under my eyes were all for naught as I hadn't done the work I needed to.

Failing as a parent was only the start. My daughter needed me and as a role model, I represented everything she resented.

Depression draped itself over me. My energy was spent before I rose from my bed in the morning. I rarely laughed, rarely smiled. Worst of all, my four children were watching me deteriorate. Four people who relied on me to build them up, to showcase the possibilities their futures held.

No one else does.

It stung. I looked around at my role models. Laura

Dern. Ruth Bader Ginsburg. Carrie Fisher. Tammy Duckworth. Cloris Leachman. Strong, amazing women who reigned in their fields. Each had an air of don't-give-a-fuck, while giving all the fucks. Powerhouses.

Helen's *No one else does*, seething words muttered after a thoughtless teacher told her she shouldn't, rattled me. Shook me as a stone in a rock polisher. I had to shake off the dust and crust to find the gem beneath the surface, put that stone on a gold band, and flaunt it as proof of a life shining—before it was too late for my children.

I looked in the mirror again and was crushed. 284 pounds. My swollen face, hideous. At thirty-seven, almost thirty-eight, I still hadn't conquered the beast of my weight problem.

I downloaded the Lose It! app to my phone. Food journaling. It was a start. When those first hunger pains clawed at my stomach, I was pissed off. I threw on my athletic shoes and my headphones, then left the house for a long walk.

For two months, I stuck by this. My depression waned, but my children weren't happy. Especially Helen. My twenty pound weight loss wasn't enough to convince her that if she wasn't happy, we could make life changes.

No one else does.

These haunting words filled my daydreams and my nightmares. I'd lost enough weight to feel my clothes as baggy. The last time my clothes were baggy, I'd given birth to my fourth child, requiring pushing a human into existence from my womb to slim down. My energy also had a much-needed kick, but what to do with it?

Parenting involves hands on/hands off. Allowing my children to make mistakes while they figure out who *they* are meant to be, while my job was to stay on the sidelines, waiting to scoop them up when they needed me.

Me. My youngest was four, beyond the age of needing nursings and diaper changes and constant playdates with his mom. WIth my newfound free time, I could either work on house projects (the never-ending list unappealing), or I could figure out who I was.

Helen knew she wanted to become an actress, even though she didn't believe she could get there.

But me?

The scattered thoughts of what to do, what to do, what to do were unrelenting. I wanted to do something significant, to prove to Helen that *Someone does*. So, I gave myself permission to delve into those urges deemed selfish, because my children should come first.

I wanted to write a story. The one that scared me because it came from one of the most horrifying times of my life.

In 2013, an F-5 tornado struck my town. One Sunday morning, Matt was at Navy drill, he became a Naval Reservist about two years after he'd previously discharged, and I was home in my pajamas, dancing while cooking up a late breakfast for my three kids. Barefoot and braless, I was startled when my cell blared a screeching notification to seek shelter, interrupting me from my pancake flipping .

A tornado was nearby.

I turned off the burners and screamed for my kids. We barreled into the basement with my daughters crying, running before me, and my son in my arms. I then tucked them under the stairs as they pleaded for me to get our dog. Bolting back up the stairs, I grabbed the eighty-pound, trembling mutt and carried him to the shelter with my kids.

For an hour, we stayed huddled together in the dark. Survival tips had taught us to store our camping gear where our tornado shelter was, so I bundled the girls in sleeping bags to counteract their shivering. Meanwhile, I held Henry who babbled on at the excitement of an otherwise boring Sunday.

Then the F-5 rolled past.

I watched the small window at the top of the laundry room through the crack of the accordion door. The sky dropped into blackness, a darkness I'd only seen while vacationing and touring deep caves. I listened for the train whistle, but didn't hear anything over the air pressure. My ears filled with a pressing silence and the mumbled sounds of my children frantically asking me if we'd be all right.

Then the blue returned to the sky beyond the window.

I checked my phone. The warning had expired. I tried to send texts, make calls. Most failed. A few texts came in, asking if my family was safe. Of course. Were they?

Then the silence. I couldn't reach Matt. I couldn't reach my parents. My phone was nothing more than a handheld clock.

I assigned Helen to watch her siblings as I went outside to survey the damage. Our street was fine. A few tree limbs were strewn across the sidewalk, but otherwise, the world was fine.

My neighbor Bill returned from the street over.

"Did you see it?"

"What do you mean?"

"You gotta go look," he said, throwing a thumb over his shoulder in the direction he'd just come from.

Our clothes give us comfort, confidence. In my ratty pajamas saved for cooking bacon and going commando, I felt anything but confident. Exposed and vulnerable. But I was a mother with children to protect and Bill's words threw me. I mustered my bravery and marched down to the corner.

My heart sank and my blood chilled. The goosebumps

on my arms had little to do with the dropped temperatures.

My town was demolished. Gone. Cars were wrapped around trees. Houses were piles of splinters with colorful tufts of people's belongings spiked by the broken beams. Sirens screamed that emergency services were on their way while a hiss from snapped gas lines haunted the air.

I returned home. I brought the children and dog up from the basement. We'd lost power, but it was still warm enough in the house. I dressed myself and the kids. Helen proudly updated that while I'd gone to check the neighborhood, Henry had vomited and she'd cleaned it up. My son boasted that he hadn't been scared of the storm and that he learned that day he could vomit through his nose, which was gross but cool.

Matt came flying through the front door, a sweaty, panting, red-faced mess.

"You're all right, right?"

We were. I reassured him. "Where's the car?"

"I couldn't get it through. I had to park at the Wal-Mart and run home. When I heard about the tornado, they said it was an F-5 and the town was gone. My CO told me my family was probably dead."

What the fuck? Another person interjecting an opinion into my family's life, worsening our problems. As I buried my anger and ignored that he'd managed to drive twenty miles and run two more through the ruins of our town in under forty minutes, I calmed my husband with reassurances.

Our family was together and we were safe.

Seven people died from that storm. One thousand homes and buildings were destroyed. Act of God was filed on countless insurance forms over the next year. It took years for the town to recover, between the rebuilding of homes and businesses and the mental health toll of witnessing so much horror.

One friend told me she'd huddled over her children, shouting over the wind ripping her home to shreds from over their heads, "I love you both and will see you in Heaven."

One friend told me she'd come home from work to find her home gone. She searched for her children, finding her teenager covered in blood. Her daughter was not hurt; the storm's barometric pressure and the child's terror had induced a bloody nose, spraying her from face to feet in crimson. The traumatic image was permanently etched into her mind.

One woman I only knew as a librarian from the children's section of the public library hugged me when she saw me. "Are you all right?" "Yes. Are you?" "Yes." We held one another for several minutes, neither knowing the other's name, but remembering the shared smiles as I'd checked out books for my kids.

I later learned her name was Mary.

All of this impacted my family and four years later as I was searching for who I was in late 2018, the tornado and its aftermath swarmed my brain. As a coping technique, I'd created a speculative fictional story in my mind. It had played out over the years, developing into a comforting tale for me to find solace during the subsequent storms, a means to hide away from the howling winds that terrified me and my children.

I wanted a reason for the storm. I wanted purpose. But tornadoes don't offer purpose. It's not a greater plan to terrify the populace nor to destroy the tangible memories of an entire community. A tornado is a meeting of hot and cold fronts, clashing together, and slamming into the land below.

We had been in the way.

What does give it purpose is what is done with that experience. My family was lucky. The twister ground its way four houses down from mine, my small ranch home untarnished while destruction worse than that of any summer blockbuster movie splayed beyond the school bus stop.

But I wanted purpose for Helen and so in 2018 when I needed to prove something to her, I wrote. I wrote and I wrote and I wrote. For three months, I knocked out 155,000 words while losing more weight, working my part-time job, wrangling my kids.

When I wrote *The End*, I stared at the blinking cursor. My chest bloomed heat from a spark foreign to me for feeling, but one that I'd witnessed.

Helen's spark was acting. Mine was writing.

One thing *no one else does* is lose one hundred pounds. Not without crash diets or surgeries to modify internal organs.

Except that *someone does*. I did.

For more than a year, I journaled my food and exercise. I allowed myself to eat what I loved, but reined in the portions. There were rules. No food after 9 P.M. Workouts could not exceed an hour, unless they were long walks with friends. Aim for proteins at lunch and dinner.

I still consumed copious amounts of caffeine. I ate cookies. I devoured cheeseburgers. Just within reason.

Thanks to the running, hip hop classes, and utilizing my gym's equipment, I was toned. But I had a saggy ass and a stomach apron. Try as I might, I felt less feminine and more of a failure as a role model than I had at the start of my journey. Shame radiated through me that I'd had the excess poundage for so long that I had deformed my flesh.

My kids appreciated the new me. Yes, I'd cut back on the hours spent focusing on them, but I never stopped being there for them. When I did, my energy and drive spread to them.

Yet, I was still just some people's mom. I was someone's wife.

In my bathroom, stripped naked before showering, I stared into the bathroom mirror and cried over the disgusting body that was mine. The stretch marks from obesity and pregnancies streaked my belly, thighs, and arms. The thinning face bore my age, wrinkles at the corners of my eyes and mouth. What the hell was with the white hairs sprouting along my hairline?

Matt encouraged me to continue on with my writing and my weight loss. However, his passive support fell short of what I needed, so I approached him with a request.

Could we afford for me to get plastic surgery?

To my shock, he agreed. We moved money and I made a phone call.

In early December 2019, I had a tummy tuck. An intimidating surgery where my belly would be sliced from hip to hip. My belly button—evidence from my mother carrying me in her womb—would be pitched into a medical waste trash bin. There would be three months of recovery.

But I wanted that stomach apron gone. To not have to lift and adjust my lower stomach around my pants waistline.

The morning of the surgery, Matt drove me to the medical center. The staff ran the last-minute blood work and prepped me, burying me under heated blankets. The surgical nurse came out and introduced herself.

"Liz?"

Oh, shit. I knew her. Tara was a woman I'd worked with on political campaigns for more than a year.

"Hey, Tara."

"You look amazing!" She'd known me at my heaviest and was seeing me in a paper gown, one hundred pounds lighter.

I trailed behind Tara to the surgical suite. I laid upon the table as she and the other nurses prepped me for my surgeon. Just as the IV anesthetics kicked in and sleep seeped into my vision, a thought struck me. Tara was not only going to see me naked, lady bits and all, but she was about to see the inside of my body. For as openly vulnerable as I thought I had been, having someone you've shared coffee with there to slice you open and stitch you back up... Well, it's a whole other level.

The surgery was a success and when I got home, I was strapped into a full-body surgical girdle. Using the bathroom was to be done while I was fully dressed, the compression essential for my recovery. Oh, and there were two drains I had to pin to the hem of the girdle. Their tubes ran along internally behind the line of glued-together skin, sucking out the excess fluids so that I wouldn't develop cysts.

This was the most unglamorous, unsexy feeling ever.

But I was allowed to lower the girdle to sponge bathe myself. The first time, even through all the swelling, my belly was flat.

My belly was flat.

Forget celebrity perfect bodies. This was stretchmarked, stitched skin with a reconstructed belly button for aesthetic normalcy. It was my perfect.

Over the next month, pain ranged from extreme to moderate to phantom. Worst was my buttocks. The swelling from the tummy tuck forced my excess skin in the girdle to be pinched when I sat. Recovery required me to sit with short bursts of movement. My bottom developed sores and the excitement at my newly reformed belly was overshadowed by the upset that I had a hideous ass.

The surgeon had warned me there would be a second surgery. I discovered he spoke in vague timelines during my tummy tuck consultation appointments and even more so in the aftercare appointments. However, he conceded that my mental state had improved drastically after the first surgery. My body, too. He authorized the thighplasty.

The first week of March, exactly three months after my tummy tuck, I went under the knife again. This time, Tara wasn't there. Even my plastic surgeon's vagueness didn't affect me. I knew the area he'd work on and what to expect for the recovery.

What I didn't expect was a global pandemic to begin the week after my thighplasty, nor that I'd have a reaction to the different anesthetics, requiring me to live in my bed twenty-two hours a day for a month.

Matt tended to the chaos of kids as well as my physical needs while I was left to fend off my depression. Instead of optimistic goals of travel and cute outfits and feeling freedom in my last year in my thirties, I was locked in my home. I wanted to show Helen that her mother was brave and all of those things I'd put off out of fear, anxiety, were conquerable. The misery of being forced to hide away when I'd finally, finally, found my inner light to shine was breaking me.

I had to escape.

So I wrote. I lacked concentration for any of my novels, but I could dabble with short stories. They didn't have to be published, but I had to write them.

As the swelling from the thighplasty subsided, I had to

shop online. Before the tummy tuck, I was a solid L/XL shirt and size 16 pants. After the second surgery, I needed size M tops and size 10 bottoms.

Even though it was only fifteen pounds of skin, it was a lot of skin.

Instead of frumpy generic tees and blah jeans, I splurged. I sought sales items, as I had an entire wardrobe to replace—underwear and bras, too!—but I bought the skater skirts teenage me had always wanted and thought I was too hip-ish to wear. I bought sheer shirts to go over cute tank tops. Distressed jeans and flirty dresses. Fishnet tights and funky red Converse Chuck Taylors. Hoop earrings and makeup, too. Those were unnecessary, but I felt beautiful, saw myself as beautiful. I didn't want to blend in, living a life unseen.

By Spring, the weather turned lovely and I resumed my walking routines. I donned my outfits, knowing no one really saw me as isolation was necessary due to the pandemic.

But I saw me.

Helen saw me.

I'd love to say that my daughter's words were the quick fix I needed to right my life, but that would oversimplify all that I went through to find myself. To find my inner strength, my feminine power.

However, Helen's "No one else does" has been the mantra chanted in my mind, pushing me onward during moments of doubt. My daughter's need for a role model was the strike against the matchstick for my fire, while therapy has been the oxygen feeding it into engulfing flames.

Working backwards from now to then, my self-discovery revealed two major components. One, a relationship I'd had as a teenager wasn't a 'bad' relationship, as many of my then-friends had defined it. It was abusive.

Two, I have bipolar II.

In suburban living, my goals and expectations defined by those around me, I'd managed to back burner my entire mental state. I suffered bouts of depression, anxiety attacks, even negative medication reactions. I poorly coped by overeating and burying myself beneath the ever mounting expectations of others. My self-esteem was in the crapper and I thought that was how life was meant to be. But that day, when my daughter said with too much resolution I was letting her down, I had to put myself aside and focus on becoming who she needed.

I'd loved my child, my children, before I ever learned to love myself.

As I write this, Helen is a senior in high school. She was accepted by the university of her choice and will begin there in the fall. Her major is Undetermined, but she's leaning towards Sociology, Literature, or Dramatic Arts. She doesn't know who she wants to be. She doesn't need to know yet.

What she does know is that a few years ago, she made an offhand accusation that changed her mother's life. Instead of an unhappy mother, miserable with regrets and pessimism, she has me.

I've gained back a few pounds due to the stress of the pandemic, but nothing wildly out of control I can't fix once I get my gym and good weather back. My scale is stowed beneath my bathroom sink, but I rarely get on it. At this moment, I can only guess what my weight is. I'm also deep in therapy sessions, learning better coping mechanisms and releasing the buildup stress of a busy life.

And I'm a writer.

I have had several short stories accepted for publication, seen my words in print, and gotten paid for a few of them. I've even gotten celebratory tattoos of their titles, because I'm proud of them and me. My novels are still works in progress, but my dream to have it published will one day become a reality. January 2020, I ventured into querying my second novel. A few agents showed interest, but it's a dystopian novel about the world 150 years after a virus and climate change wiped out much of the populace in 2020 so... people lost interest pretty quickly.

Yet I know with intuitive certainty, I will one day have a published novel. My book will sit on a shelf in a bookstore, my name on the cover.

Because I am here to disprove "no one else does." I am someone and I am doing it.

AUTHOR BIOGRAPHIES

A.J. Van Belle is a 48-year-old PhD student researching microbial ecology, and they write genre-bending novels for adults and teens. When they're not writing stories or code, they explore the woods with their two dogs and make their husband and teenage daughter listen to the plot twists baking in their brain.

Micki Findlay likes to refer to herself as an 'artrepeneur', as she loves to be involved in a variety of creative ventures. One of her passions is writing; she is a published author, magazine columnist, songwriter, and poet. Her writing career began as a magazine columnist for EyesOnBC magazine. Editor and chief, Linda Tenney, not only gave her a start, but she recognized her potential and believed in her, more than she believed in herself. Sadly, Linda lost her third bout with cancer. The magazine folded shortly after her passing. Presently, she is a regular columnist for Oasis magazine, where she writes about local artists who are making a difference in their community through their own, unique talents. She is also a contributing author for the well-known Chicken Soup for the Soul series. She is presently in the midst of writing a candid, raw, memoir-based novel.

Cathy Warner's fiction, memoir, and essays have appeared in dozens of journals including Under the Sun, Water~Stone, and So To Speak, and blogs including

Relief, Ruminate, and Image's "Good Letters" among others. Cathy is editor of Viral Verse: Poetry of the Pandemic (2020) author of two volumes of poetry: Home By Another Road (2019), and Burnt Offerings (2014), and has been nominated for the Pushcart Prize and Best American Essays. A native Californian for 50 years, Cathy now lives in Western WA where she leads workshops, writes, edits, takes photographs, renovates homes, and sells real estate. Find her at cathywarner.com or on Facebook at: cathywarnerwriter, and Twitter @cathyjwarner.

Patti Lee grew up the often invisible third child in an unconventional family in a small town in Connecticut. She moved to Vermont in the '90s working as a preschool teacher, bookkeeper and office assistant before building a career in the field of child advocacy. Married over 30 years with three adult children, she began her writing journey. She brings women's fiction stories to life, tapping into the hopes and sometimes fears of readers. In 2019, her book, "Between February and November" placed in the Top 10 in Notebook Publishing's #IndieApril contest and later that year, she submitted the winning essay in The Writers' Workshop of N.C. 2019 Hard Times essay contest. Her short story "The Ward House" was included in Jazz House Publications "Of Cottages and Cauldrons" autumn anthology in 2020. She dabbles in acrylic painting, is a groupie of singer-songwriter Josh Ritter, but has also been known to play the soundtrack to Hamilton on repeat. And she has more cats than throw pillows. Read more about her and her writing at http://pattileewriter.com. Follow her on Twitter @pattiauthor and Instagram @authorpattilee.

Michelle Teems is a fantasy and horror author who dabbles in poetry, nonfiction, and screenplays. She voiced

Dracula with the writing project "Legends of the Fall" and is working on a mythical anthology called "Broken Legends." Her goal is to write fulltime and take a road trip across America to visit haunted places. Her Twitter handle is @MTeemsAuthor.

Rene Urbanovich is a voice and Creativity instructor, a Humanities professor and an award-winning writer. In 2020, her fourth book, "The Creativity Connection Conundrum," won an honor from Writer's Digest for Self-Published E-books. In 2019, Rene's column "Creativity Advocacy" ran in the local paper, The Signal. She dances on the pole and writes poetry for pleasure and can sometimes be seen writing alongside her life partner of 40 years at the corner cafe on Sunday nights. Their four children, raised near Los Angeles in the Santa Clarita Valley, are all scattered across the globe, contributing their gifts to others via music, documentaries, art, activism and comedy.

Rhoda Weber Mack writes long-form fiction, short stories, flash, essays, plays, and poetry as her way of understanding the nuances of a complicated world. She earned an off-label degree in ancient human history on road treks in Africa and Middle Europe. She has had short stories published in literary magazines including Epiphany and a Best of Carve anthology, has been a member and conference attendee at AWP, SCBWI, and other venues, and will participate in poetry slams to terrify herself. Currently, she has postponed a writing and research cross-country road trip to quarantine near an abandoned watercress farm and fly fishing stream in Pennsylvania. On her website www.webermack.com, the short story "Night Kitchen" is an open-source resource for workshops on climate change, library discussion or drama workshop groups. Follow her @wordward on Twitter.

D. Magada is an author, writer and journalist based in Rome. She published two books on art and culture in Rome, which are now in their third print run. She regularly writes articles, blogs, and op-eds and provides consultancy services to the United Nations and the Thomson Reuters Foundation. She is currently finishing a memoir on my years in Addis, from which this text is extracted. Prior to living in Rome and Addis Ababa, She was a staff correspondent for Reuters and Bloomberg news agencies in London.

Lucy James is a teacher, writer, reiki practitioner and transformational life coach. Her life's calling is to help people to find strength, courage and wisdom from their past experiences and to reconnect with their true and authentic self. She lives in Stratford-upon-Avon, England with a teenage goth, a lap cat called Cathy and a tearaway tabby called Keith. She is passionate about horses and provides board, lodgings and long country walks for trainee service dogs. In her spare time, she loves to create big, splashy paintings of beaches, horses and the female form, and takes commissions for animal portraits. Lucy spends as much time as possible in nature and is drawn in heart and soul to the wild coast of North Cornwall, where she one day hopes to settle down and stay.

http://www.soulfirecoaching.org

JoAnne Potter. Having published for more than forty years, JoAnne Potter retired from teaching in 2009 and now writes for Northgate Marketing, blogs, makes wine, and remembers her David from her upper room in south-eastern Wisconsin. Her poetry, articles, reviews, and creative nonfiction appear both online and in print, and she contributes regularly to a devotional blog, By This Still Hearth, at joannempotter.blogspot.com.

Carmela Pinto McIntire. After a fulfilling teaching career at Florida International University, Miami, Carmela Pinto McIntire turned to reading and writing creative nonfiction, focusing on a memoir about her family life in Miami. She and her family moved north, 1500 miles, so they are now exploring our new community of Grand Rapids, Michigan, including involvement with a local advocacy organization now beginning to coalesce—wonderfully educational and engaging, even on Zoom.

She admits to continuing to read the Miami Herald daily, however. At an eight-day writing conference, Writers in Paradise (2020) in St. Petersburg, Florida, she began to learn about submitting shorter creative work online, a world she hadn't discovered as a long-time academic. One of the joys of Writers in Paradise was becoming the third of a trio of women, Writing Buddies / friends who communicate daily, read and edit one another's work, and provide ongoing cheering, nudging, support, and yes, love.

Lisa Lucca's work has appeared in three anthologies, including Water Cooler Diaries. She and her partner independently published an epistolary memoir, You Are Loved, in 2012. Lisa was a #Blogher17 Voice of the Year Honoree and was awarded first prize for her essay, Ashes of a Purple Heart, at WOW-Women on Writing. She has been a blogger for The Gay Dad Project, with many of her essays and articles published online. Her memoir, Out of the Ordinary, is a Quarterfinalist in Roadmap Authors 2020 Write Start Manuscript Competition, and is the first book in a trilogy of memoirs she seeks to publish. Live True with Lisa Lucca, a weekly public radio show, has streamed globally since 2019. Her fifteen-year career in the entertainment industry included positions at LucasFilm and in production management on a world tour with Janet Jackson. She has been a life coach and motivational speaker since 2004, and has addressed audiences across the country.

Susan R. Brown is an almost-retired psychologist living in Davis, CA with her husband. She has been writing, mostly nonfiction (essays and family stories) and poetry, for most of her adult life. She tried to write about her encounter with Athena for over forty years, but self-doubt and the busy life of a working mother got in the way. During the enforced isolation of the pandemic, and with the support of her husband and a writing group, "The Goddess Dreams" was finally born. She hopes her story can serve as an inspiration to her daughters and to other young women searching for the truth of their own voices.- Susan R. Brown is an almost-retired psychologist living in Davis, CA with her husband. She has been writing, mostly nonfiction (essays and family stories) and poetry, for most of her adult life. She tried to write about her encounter with Athena for over forty years, but self-doubt and the busy life of a working mother got in the way. During the enforced isolation of the pandemic, and with the support of her husband and a writing group, "The Goddess Dreams" was finally born. She hopes her story can serve as an inspiration to her daughters and to other young women searching for the truth of their own voices.

LT Ward writes mostly speculative fiction shorts and novels while spending her days raising her children and satisfying her never-ending thirst for knowledge through reading, meeting people, and first-hand life experiences. She has several published short stories in the literary, historical, fantasy, and speculative fiction genres. She currently volunteers with WriteHive.